MW01610130

ANNALS *of* THE NEW YORK ACADEMY OF SCIENCES

EDITOR-IN-CHIEF
Douglas Braaten

ASSOCIATE EDITOR
Rebecca E. Cooney

PROJECT MANAGER
Steven E. Bohall

EDITORIAL ADMINISTRATOR
Daniel J. Becker

Artwork and design by Ash Ayman Shairzay

The New York Academy of Sciences
7 World Trade Center
250 Greenwich Street, 40th Floor
New York, NY 10007-2157

annals@nyas.org
www.nyas.org/annals

 **The New York
Academy of Sciences**

Published by Blackwell Publishing
On behalf of the New York Academy of Sciences

Boston, Massachusetts
2011

ANNALS *of* THE NEW YORK ACADEMY OF SCIENCES

VOLUME
1234

ISSUE

Perspectives on the Self

Conversations on Identity and Consciousness

In partnership with the Nour Foundation, the New York Academy of Sciences presented a six-part series examining the question "What is the Self?" from December 2010 through May 2011. A diverse roster of scholars, including philosophers, cognitive scientists, physicists, historians, evolutionary biologists, neurobiologists, psychologists, sociologists, and theologians from universities around the world, engaged in a series of interdisciplinary conversations to understand the experience of the self and the ways in which boundaries between self and non-self shape our common world.

TABLE OF CONTENTS

1   Introduction to *Perspectives on the Self: Conversations on Identity and Consciousness*
Richard Rass

To be or not to be

5   To be or not to be: The self as illusion
Krista Tippett, Thomas Metzinger, Evan Thompson, and Pim van Lommel

19   Near-death experiences: the experience of the self as real and not as an illusion
Pim van Lommel

Quid pro quo

29   Quid pro quo: the ecology of the self
Steve Paulson, Owen Flanagan, Paul Bloom, and Roy Baumeister

44   What do you think you are?
Christina Starmans and Paul Bloom

48   Self and identity: a brief overview of what they are, what they do, and how they work
Roy F. Baumeister

The pursuit of immortality

56   The pursuit of immortality: From the ego to the soul
Lisa Miller, Kenneth Miller, John Haught, and Nancey Murphy

70   Science, self, and immortality
John F. Haught

76   Immortality versus resurrection in the Christian tradition
Nancey Murphy

Become a Member Today of the New York Academy of Sciences

The New York Academy of Sciences is dedicated to identifying the next frontiers in science and catalyzing key breakthroughs. As has been the case for 200 years, many of the leading scientific minds of our time rely on the Academy for key meetings and publications that serve as the crucial forum for a global community dedicated to scientific innovation.

 **Select one FREE *Annals* volume and up to five volumes for only $40 each.**

 **Network and exchange ideas with the leaders of academia and industry.**

 **Broaden your knowledge across many disciplines.**

 **Gain access to exclusive online content.**

Join Online at **www.nyas.org**

Or by phone at **800.344.6902** (516.576.2270 if outside the U.S.).

A self-fulfilling prophecy

83　A self-fulfilling prophecy: linking belief to behavior
Esther Sternberg, Simon Critchley, Shaun Gallagher, and V.V. Raman

98　A self-fulfilling prophecy: linking belief to behavior
Esther Sternberg

100　The self in the Cartesian brain
Shaun Gallagher

104　A self-fulfilling prophecy: linking belief to behavior
Varadaraja V. Raman

Me, myself, and I

108　Me, myself, and I: the rise of the modern self
Robert Hanna, Gerald Izenberg, Raymond Martin, Norbert Wiley, and Jerrold Seigel

121　What is the self?
Robert Hanna

124　The modern notion of self has reached its ultimate conclusion
Gerald Izenberg

127　The American self and the long march to legal equality
Norbert Wiley

Who am I?

134　Who am I? Beyond "I think, therefore I am"
Alex Voorhoeve, Elie During, David Jopling, Timothy Wilson, and Frances Kamm

149　Self-knowledge and the practice of ethics: Ostad Elahi's concept of the "imperious self"
Elie During

158　"Much ado to know myself. . .": Insight in the talking cures
David A. Jopling

168　Understanding, justifying, and finding oneself
Frances M. Kamm

173　Corrigendum for Ann. N. Y. Acad. Sci. 642: 148–166

174　Corrigendum for Ann. N. Y. Acad. Sci. 1173 S1: E20–E30

175　Erratum for Ann. N. Y. Acad. Sci. 1229: 99–102

Ann. N.Y. Acad. Sci. ISSN 0077-8923

Introduction to *Perspectives on the Self: Conversations on Identity and Consciousness*

As a public charitable and nongovernmental organization in special consultative status to the United Nations Economic and Social Council, the Nour Foundation seeks to establish a universal platform upon which to draw human beings from all walks of life together in a greater spirit of unity, tolerance, and understanding.[a] The foundation strives to achieve this objective by exploring various expressions of meaning and commonality in human experience, for it is personal experience that serves as the ultimate touchstone of the human condition. This exploration of shared commonalities is based on a multidisciplinary and consilient approach that necessarily integrates the sciences and the humanities so as to encompass larger questions of meaning, purpose, and values that underlie all realms of human endeavor, including scientific and technological progress.

The foundation's conception some 25 years ago was inspired by the inclusive and experiential philosophy of the late Ostad Elahi, a contemporary thinker, jurist, and musician who dedicated the whole of his life to the investigation and pursuit of the classic existential questions of humankind: *Who are we, why are we here, and where does our ultimate destination lie?*[b] Indeed, according to Ostad Elahi, once we have dedicated ourselves to the pursuit of this knowledge and have understood it through practice, we have reached what he called the "truth."

One of the striking aspects of Ostad Elahi's life that distinguishes him from so many of his predecessors and contemporaries who shared similar metaphysical aspirations was the reversal of the means or method by which he undertook this personal quest. So while he spent the first third of his life steeped in the age-old mystical traditions of his remote native environment, he would eventually pursue a radically different approach to discover and understand the existential questions that confront all human beings. Rather than remain in ascetic seclusion and tranquil contemplation, Ostad Elahi set out to confront ordinary, modern-day life in the midst of society, assuming the responsibilities of a family and embracing the challenges and demands of an active and difficult judicial career.

His innovative findings and original conclusions were published in the form of several books after his retirement.[c] Juxtaposing his firsthand experiences as a full-fledged mystic with the pressures and demands of a distinguished professional career, these works indicate that the answers to these perennial questions are not beyond our grasp, provided that we are genuinely

---

[a] See www.nourfoundation.com.
[b] For more information on the life and work of Ostad Elahi (1895–1974), see Morris,[1] During,[2] and Elahi.[3]
[c] To date, only one of these works, *Knowing the Spirit*,[1] has been translated into English. However, much of Ostad Elahi's philosophy has also been expounded upon by his son Bahram Elahi, M.D., in various works that have been translated and published in several languages.

doi: 10.1111/j.1749-6632.2011.06204.x
Ann. N.Y. Acad. Sci. 1234 (2011) 1–4 © 2011 New York Academy of Sciences.

committed to their search and are willing to set aside any preconceptions and biases in their pursuit. Moreover, this existential quest—which Ostad Elahi believed must be undertaken independently and objectively on the basis of our own experience and the totality of the evidence available to us—need not be predicated on any particular creed, lifestyle, or environment, but rather should be initiated by delving within oneself and gradually acquiring "self-knowledge" through the ongoing work of active introspection and ethical practice alike.

Now it is somewhat self-evident that if we are to speak of acquiring self-knowledge, we must first understand what is meant by the *self*, which, after all, is the very object of this knowledge. What, in other words, is the substance or structure of the human self? What powers, faculties, and energies regulate and govern the self? What is the relationship between the conscious mind and its larger unconscious counterpart, inasmuch as cognitive science continues to accumulate evidence of the specific ways that our daily lives and conduct are more influenced by the unconscious part of our mind than the conscious?

It is in within this contextual framework that the Nour Foundation has partnered with the New York Academy of Sciences to present the *Perspectives on the Self* lecture series, as the foundation continues its tradition of introducing thought-provoking and informed discourse from an interdisciplinary perspective that is rooted both in sound scientific theories as well as the shared commonality and tangible reality of human experience. Indeed, the impetus behind much of the foundation's work is the underlying premise that just as all human beings across the globe share a common physical constitution that is addressed and treated through the *universal* science of medicine, so too must all human beings share a common psychological makeup. But unlike the atoms, molecules, and cells that constitute our physical bodies, what is the essential substance or nature of our psychological composition? What nutrients promote or hinder its growth and maturation? What mechanisms regulate or direct its evolution and development? What, in other words, does self-knowledge actually entail, and how does one go about acquiring it? If such questions point to the possibility of a *universal* science of the self that parallels that of the body, what might its fundamental principles and axioms look like, and where might we find them?

Although the subject of the self and the experience of selfhood have been with us since the appearance of the first human beings, it is quite telling to trace how the idea of "who we are" has changed and evolved over the centuries. Similarly, the persistent attempts and theories to answer this inevitable question in every era tell us something about the nature of this quest itself. How and why, for example, did we proceed from the Delphic injunction of "know thyself" to the concept of the autonomous individual endowed with rights and duties that emerged in the wake of the Enlightenment? How did we shift from this autonomous and rational agent to modern notions of the contemporary self as divided, multilayered, or fragmented, if not altogether an illusory or emergent "surface effect"?

In any event, the perdurable question, *Who am I?* appears to point to a deeply rooted metaphysical and moral urge within the human species. Notions and constructs of a self certainly constitute an integral part of the human condition. The experience of selfhood or the feeling of "being someone"—not to mention the desire to become someone or the common injunction to be true to what one is—seems so fundamental that it has somewhat obscured the more abstract question, *What is the Self?* Historically and canonically, concepts and theories of the self abound, and these have become so disparate that the term *self* has assumed radically different meanings, from early religious doctrines of the soul, to psychoanalytic interpretations, to definitions from current research in neuroscience and neuroethics.

So what does this bode for our current concept of the self and its ethical, moral, and social implications? Contemporary constructs of the self may point to a common, underlying theme beneath seemingly heterogeneous attempts to come to terms with the elusiveness of the *I* or first-person perspective. Despite the philosophical challenges by postmodern critiques regarding the "philosophy of the subject," and perhaps due to recent trends in neuroscience, the theme of the self has become more complex than ever. Yet, this merely compels us to synthesize results and perspectives from scientific, philosophical, and social domains of knowledge and to render them accessible to a wider audience.

One of the central aims of the *Perspectives on the Self* lecture series is to therefore provide an objective overview of the evolving notion, construct, and experience of the self, without losing sight of the subjective value that makes these matters so vital to us. By enabling an interdisciplinary discourse within and among experts from various fields of contemporary science and the humanities, the unifying fabric of this project is simple: the word *self* refers to a host of intersecting ideas, questions, concerns, and problems that are central to the human condition. As such, the series seeks to foster deeper analysis and reflection on the fundamental assumptions underlying various theories and models of the self. Toward this end, each of the lectures in the series features conversations among several experts addressing a particular facet of the self from different disciplinary perspectives.

In many ways, the concept of self is culturally embedded. It has a history of its own, which is important to remember when facing the challenges of contemporary science or coming to terms with the "disenchantment" of the self and the ethical questions that have arisen from recent explorations in psychology and neuroscience. Of course, the ongoing construction of new models of the self does not necessarily invalidate questions framed within different cultural and historical contexts. In fact, these may prove essential to both an understanding of, and regard for, the concepts of the self today, while recognizing the progress made in reaching a more comprehensive view of the anthropological, psychological, and physical mechanisms of the subjective experience of selfhood.

From this broader perspective, the self appears first as an umbrella term involving multidisciplinary approaches that generate a range of questions and problems, including consciousness (the question of the phenomenal self), agency (the self and moral agency), and individuality (the self as personal identity). Moreover, the self also appears as a relational concept, inseparable from embodied perception and agency, and the wider context that engages the environment and other selves. Finally, when considered in light of its most concrete implications, the self is a performative concept that brings its ethical dimensions to the fore.

Indeed, the self is manifest in our lives as the result of interrelational processes that involve the continuous production and performance of a particular person that we are, or seek to be. On a practical level, moral agency could be viewed as the construction of a self in ways that seek to maximize the good of life. But while virtue, care, and narrative ethics denote and call for an emphasis on the constructive dimensions of the self, insights from biology, anthropology, sociology, and linguistics might afford a better understanding of the ways in which boundaries between self and non-self are formed and shape our common world. Accordingly, this lecture series also attempts to raise such ethical and social questions in an informed and meaningful way.

One of the paradoxical characteristics of the concept of the self and the ongoing debate around it is that whether we ascribe to the notion that the self has a substantial existence, the very fact of entertaining beliefs about who we are or the nature of the self in general is bound to influence the way in which we behave, and thus our perception of who we are and what we can or ought to do. In other words, our notion of the self serves as a self-fulfilling idea or prophecy, in that whatever we may think of it, the very act of contemplating it in the first place lends it some level of weight and importance, which in turn contributes to some degree of its realization.

In the discussions and papers that follow, at least three primary facets or aspects of the self seem to repeatedly emerge, each of which is engaged with the others in a dynamic and symbiotic relationship: first, the physical, biological, and embodied self; second, the social, cultural, and relational self that interacts with and is shaped by its environment; and third, the reflective or spiritual self, as William James called it, which is intimate to each of us and expresses itself through an ongoing inner dialogue within us. The manner and extent to which each of these facets relates to and influences the others, however, varies considerably among the competing theories of the self.

But beyond the attempts to academically define and describe the self lies a more immediate, pressing question for our everyday lives—namely, why should we even concern ourselves with knowing the self? In other words, what is the utility or practical benefit of knowing the self in the first place? How and why does self-knowledge enhance the quality of our lives? Assuming that we can arrive at some consensus on the practical utility of self-knowledge, what then are the obstacles to its attainment? Or to put it in a slightly different way, how does the question, *Who am I?* relate to the more imminent question, *What should I do?*

Throughout this volume, the reader will encounter a rich and diverse array of perspectives and theories about the existence, nature, and functioning of the self. We invite and encourage you to keep an open mind as you read through these conversations, and in particular to consider how the perspectives that you read resonate with the reality of your own life experience and your own sense of self. Do the explanations and theories presented provide greater clarity, direction, and insight into your inner lives, or do they tend to induce the opposite effect?

Until such time as modern science can provide us with definitive answers, the question of existential meaning in general and the self in particular is ultimately a deeply personal matter, a subjective paradigm that each of us inevitably constructs and references time and again as we navigate and interpret the course of life's challenges and adversities. It is hoped that the cumulative outcome of this series will be to provide some of the essential elements that are needed to build or perhaps refine one's own paradigm of existential meaning, a customized lens through which to perceive and experience the world in a manner that addresses and fulfills all the various facets of the evolving self.

In closing, the Nour Foundation would like to express its deepest gratitude to the New York Academy of Sciences and its dedicated team of learned professionals, whose full collaboration and partnership on this series was instrumental in ensuring its resounding success. As well, we would like to acknowledge and thank the staff of *Annals* for their tireless efforts in meticulously compiling and producing this volume of intriguing discussions and papers. Finally, we are grateful to all of the gracious speakers who made the time to participate in this series and to share their personal and unique insights on the meaning and perpetual experience of the self.

References

1. Morris, J.W. 2007. *Knowing the Spirit*. State University of New York Press. Albany, New York.
2. During, J. 2003. *The Spirit of Sounds: The Unique Art of Ostad Elahi*. Cornwall Books. Cranbury, New Jersey.
3. Elahi, B. 1995. *Unicity*. Robert Laffont. Paris, France.

RICHARD RASS, J.D.

Program Director, the Nour Foundation
New York, New York

Ann. N.Y. Acad. Sci. ISSN 0077-8923

ANNALS OF THE NEW YORK ACADEMY OF SCIENCES
Issue: *Perspectives on the Self*

To be or not to be: The self as illusion

Krista Tippett, Thomas Metzinger, Evan Thompson, and Pim van Lommel

Moderated by Krista Tippett, creator and host of America Public Media's *On Being*, philosophers Thomas Metzinger (University of Mainz, Germany) and Evan Thompson (University of Toronto) join cardiologist and expert on near-death experiences Pim van Lommel (Hospital Rijnstate, the Netherlands) to examine recent developments in neuroscience and philosophy that shed light on whether our conscious experience of a unified self is reality or illusion. The following is an edited transcript of the discussion that occurred December 7, 2010, 6:00–7:30 PM, at the New York Academy of Sciences in New York City.

Tippett: Well, this was an irresistible invitation. And I think the fascination of the topic is manifest in the presence of all of you here tonight. It occurred to me, as I was preparing for this, that the question of whether the self is a fundamental reality—what we experience as our identity and inner life—may ultimately be in the same category as whether there's an afterlife, in the sense that what we can obtain by way of evidence may, by definition, remain a matter of subjectivity and metaphysical choice open to multiple interpretations and ultimately unprovable with the tools we have at hand. Though, as we are going to discuss tonight, science and philosophy are refining their tools for investigating this aspect of life, investigating what is subjective, what we have known as subjective. And the thinkers on this panel are contributing to that process from very different fields of experience and knowledge.

Pim van Lommel of the Netherlands came to this as a cardiologist, by way of discovering and then pursuing the meaning of near-death experiences. Evan Thompson and Thomas Metzinger (Evan is at the University of Toronto, Thomas at the Johannes Gutenberg Universit in Mainz) are working in the borderlands between philosophy and neuroscience, both Eastern and Western. An Australian journalist who was interviewing you, Thomas, wrote, "From out-of-body experiences to lucid dreaming, anarchic hand syndrome to phantom limbs, his investigations have taken him to places few dare to go. Be spooked, bewildered, amazed!" And as I was reading that and reading all of you, I was brought back to a conversation I once had with someone working in the field of cloning. She described her field as the realm of "fiction science." I think what we are about to start discussing here is another realm of "fiction science"—but these are inner frontiers, right? Inner frontiers of mind, consciousness, self, will—inner worlds that may amaze and, perhaps, even frighten us. Thomas, I'd like to start with you. I think that you, among the three of you, are the most resolute in insisting that the self is an illusion. And so I wonder if you would start by telling us what you mean by that and how you came to that.

Metzinger: Well, I wouldn't put it like that. People who like to intoxicate themselves in new age bookstores like concepts such as "self is an illusion;" but if one looks a little closer, the first question one would have is, who is *having* this illusion? So this illusion talk itself is conceptually problematic. If I had to stay with it I would rather say it's an illusion that is *no one's* illusion, or something like that. I think it is pretty obvious that there is no such thing as a self. As you know, philosophers all disagree all the time, but there's a pretty strong consensus in my discipline that

doi: 10.1111/j.1749-6632.2011.06181.x

the self is not a substance. This is not a provocative claim. It's actually something almost trivial. For philosophers, a substance is something that could hold itself in existence. It is "ontologically self-subsistent" as we say; it could maintain its own being in the absence of a living brain, or something like that. The self is not a thing in the brain or a thing outside of this world. That seems pretty obvious to most of my colleagues. What is very robust and very real is what we call the *phenomenal self*. Of course, there is a self that appears in conscious experience; for example, I feel like I'm someone, but that is not a thing but a process.

Tippett: Right.

Metzinger: That process is very different during the dream state: in dreamless deep sleep there is no phenomenal self, no self as experienced; we call it *phenomenal selfhood*. In its essence, this process is a representational process. So what we call "a" self or "the" self in folk psychological discourse is actually a time slice of an ongoing process in which your brain makes an image of you, your body, your emotional state, your memories, your plans, your social relationships, and so forth.

Tippett: So not an entity, but a process. You have used the metaphor that the ego is like that, that consciousness is like a tunnel. Explain what you mean by that.

Metzinger: Well, I think the knowledge we have about the world—and we do have knowledge about the external world—is a very real phenomenon. But if we just speak about consciousness in the sense of how it appears to us subjectively, it is a locally determined phenomenon. To cut a long story short, if all the properties of your brain are fixed, what you will consciously experience will also be fixed. So in that sense, it is an inward phenomenon. I've been in this consciousness community for many years working with neuroscientists and philosophers. Consciousness is not one problem, it's a whole bundle of problems.

But there is a core issue and that is the question: Who is all of these states and who or what is this self that lives through all these experiences? And that's how I come to this. That's why I'm interested in all of this. And as it turns out, I have a phenomenal self—a process that's very highly dependent and determined by information processing in the brain, for instance. It's the content of an image. The special thing about your self-model right now, about the self-model active in all of your brains right now, is that it is, as philosophers say, "transparent." That means you cannot experience it as an image. This is also true of everything you see, the colors and the objects, but also about the content of the self-model active in your brain right now. You *identify* with this image. It's like you're glued or attached to its content. And that's why you have this idea that you're someone right now.

Tippett: That you're someone.

Metzinger: Yes.

Tippett: You've said that the conscious self that navigates reality is a computational tool—really we were all living in virtual reality all along but have just now invented the concept of self.

Metzinger: And that creates this interesting sense of inwardness. It's not just that it is something in the brain or in a reality model of the brain. What I'm trying to get at is this subjective quality of *inwardness*. Because that seems to be the essence of the mystery to me.

Tippett: And it is a mystery.

Metzinger: Yes. But I think we have the conceptual tools at hand to understand how it could come about. How could any information-processing system, a natural system that has no self or no sharp identity, develop the *robust* experience that it is a self and has an identity through time? That's what I'm interested in.

Tippett: And absolutely biologically rooted and dependent. . .

Metzinger: Well, no, I think the human conscious self doesn't only have neural correlates, it also has social correlates. The human self-model is very special, in many respects different from those our animal ancestors have. There's a part that's not transparent. We're not fully caught in an illusion—it has strong social correlates; that's a very important aspect of it. But there's an inbuilt conflict in the human self-model. We have this emotional layer which has a very strong biological imperative, and that is, "You must not die!" You have to survive. Those who didn't have that weren't our ancestors. And we have this brand-new slow cognitive self-model. Our frontal lobe doesn't work so well, as we all know, but it makes us the first animal on this planet to have a clear, conscious, and explicit knowledge that we will die. So, there is an inbuilt chasm or schism or split in our self-model and that creates this constant intent in beings like us to become whole again, to heal ourselves. To somehow reconcile what we know with what we feel must not be true under any circumstance, namely that we are mortal beings.

Tippett: So mortality is as much a defining factor in our sense of selfhood and identity as anything else.

Metzinger: Absolutely. Apart from all the difficult philosophical and scientific questions in these exciting times right now, I think that is the core issue that is also relevant for everybody. Mortality. Can one come to terms with it without fooling oneself? Or is it something that, if you're really honest with yourself, one just cannot come to terms with?

Tippett: You've made a very interesting proposal and I want to move on now but come back to that later—that because of these very important questions you see being raised as we look closer at this, we need, as you said, a new "ethics of consciousness."

So, Evan, you were raised in a very unique environment that sought to bring together the arts and humanities, science, and technology, not just intellectually but as a way of life. I can imagine some kind of line between that and the fact that you are now navigating a territory between the Western mind–brain perspective of consciousness—viewing consciousness and studying it as a biological phenomenon—and the Indian–Tibetan perspective of consciousness—that has some kind of primary reality, perhaps transcendent of the body.

So, just tell us a little bit about that place you stand in and how you come to these issues.

Thompson: Well, since I'm in New York City, I will say just a little bit about my background. I was raised in the 1970s in a community alternative educational institute called the Lindisfarne Association, which was located in the Episcopal Church at Sixth Avenue and Twentieth Street, which is now the Limelight Marketplace, which I walked by today. It was an organization founded by my father, William Irwin Thompson, and he was trying to bring together scientists, artists, and spiritual teachers from a variety of different traditions. So I was raised in a community of ongoing discussion among Buddhist monks, Buddhist philosophers, neuroscientists, anthropologists, poets, and writers. And so what's very important to me, and what I learned from growing up in that context, is that there are multiple ways of knowing and multiple ways of seeing reality, and that it's very ethically important to respect this multiplicity.

I try to work with ways of knowing that are on the one hand rooted in neuroscience. I'm a philosopher by training and I work very closely with neuroscientists who are interested in mental functioning, the sense of self, and consciousness. But I also work with philosophers and scientists who are interested in the neuroscience of meditation and who have a background in Indian and Tibetan contemplative traditions, mainly.

So at the heart of my work is the idea that first-person mental training through, let's just call them *mindfulness methods* as a kind of umbrella term, can help us to understand how the sense of self is constructed, how attention functions, how attention is trainable, how there are different kinds of awareness that are also trainable, and how you can learn to differentiate in your own experience between the sense of self that you have now—as an embodied being sitting here in the room, listening to my remarks—and the sense of self that you have when your mind wanders— as when you get caught up in a train of thought about what you're going to do tomorrow or about something that happened to you at breakfast or something you remember from your personal past—where the sense of self depends on a consciousness of time and a mental image of yourself in the past or in the future.

These two different senses of self are intertwined and confounded from moment to moment, mixed together in our experience. And with mental training through mindfulness, one can actually see these in the first person from moment to moment, changing, oscillating, fluctuating.

Individuals who are highly trained in this kind of attentiveness to their own experience have been shown, in very concrete neuroscience settings, to be able to provide information that's valuable to neuroscientists who want to disentangle the different systems in the brain that construct our sense of self. For example, consider the difference between the sense of self that you have in your body in the present moment versus the sense of self that you have when you time travel mentally to the past or future. Individuals with mindfulness training can switch reliably between different modes of awareness in a way that gives neuroscientists new tools for interpreting the activity that they see in, say, the context of functional MRI or electroencephalography (EEG) studies.

Tippett: You've said that you advocate an embodied approach to the self, not a "neuro-centric" one. What's the importance of that distinction?

Thompson: I think it was the perceptual psychologist J.J. Gibson who said, we need to ask not just what's in the brain but what the brain is in. So, what is the brain in? It's in a living, breathing body caught up in multiple ways with the environment in perception and action, in a social context. Our human sense of self, as Thomas was mentioning earlier, is an intersubjective sense of self. That intersubjective relatedness means that the self can't be understood by simply going inside the brain and looking at neuro-patterns of activity. It's as if you were to try to understand Gothic architecture by just looking at the stones. It's the wrong level. It's one crucial level, yes, but it's not the relevant level for the intersubjective sense of self we have. What I mean by a non-neurocentric approach is taking account of this larger context of embodiment and embeddedness.

Tippett: And are you involved in the mind-life dialogue?

Thompson: Yes.

Tippett: The Dalai Lama has spearheaded and set in motion a lot of interesting dialogue among scholars studying neuroscience, philosophy, and religion. I recently had a conversation with the Dalai Lama's translator, Thupten Jinpa, who was part of those dialogues and is also a Buddhist scholar in his own right. We talked about the chasm that remains, and that may remain however fruitful and fascinating the dialogues and the research that flows from them, between a Western view of consciousness, as essentially biologically rooted and limited to biology, and the far reaches of, let's say, Tibetan or Indian philosophy, in which there is something that Jinpa describes mainly as a "stream of consciousness," not consciousness whole, not this entire thing we call the self, but something that, in Tibetan Buddhist teaching, in the person of the Dalai Lama, for example, has transcended particular bodies in time and space. So, where do you come out on that?

Thompson: The core of that question, as I understand it, is whether consciousness is fundamentally a biological process or whether there's some aspect of consciousness that transcends biology and that could be interpreted in different ways. I think that's an open question.

Tippett: It's also one of these things we can't prove.

Thompson: I think it's an open question and that intellectual rigor and honesty requires recognizing that from a scientific perspective, as it's presently articulated in our bodies of knowledge, there isn't compelling evidence that pushes us in the direction of a biologically transcendent view of consciousness.

We've had this discussion with the Dalai Lama and other Buddhists on a number of occasions and the point we usually come to is a mutual respect for different perspectives. What I see as the crucial thing that Buddhism brings home—but we can also see it in Western philosophy, in phenomenology, say—is not so much the metaphysics of whether consciousness transcends the brain or the body, but rather that from a Buddhist perspective the starting point is the primacy of consciousness in an experiential sense. So as a scientist, when you're examining the brain you're doing it within an experiential framework of your own observations—your perceptions—and the intersubjective agreement that you can establish with other observers, other conscious beings.

And so consciousness in that sense, as a mode of knowing, is fundamental. There's no way of stepping outside of consciousness to see it sideways and to see how it relates to something else. I think the Buddhists are very rigorous on this starting point: to stay with the primacy of experience.

Tippett: And I think they've also brought a very sophisticated and ancient tradition of thinking about consciousness in quite subtle ways, right? There's "gross consciousness," "subtle consciousness," "pure, luminous consciousness," yes? And these ways of describing consciousness have become useful for scientists.

Thompson: Well, to take a concrete example, Thomas said earlier that consciousness disappears in deep sleep and this is how we think about it in Western neuroscience and clinical science and in Western philosophy.

In Indian philosophy, however, there are long, detailed, fascinating debates about whether consciousness persists in deep sleep. Whether there's a kind of subliminal awareness and sense of self that's not a reflective or introspective sense of self but a kind of subtle awareness that enables there to be a memory-bridge from waking to sleep/dreaming. So, I think we could make some headway using neuroscience and other philosophical resources to tackle this question about subtler states of consciousness that are more difficult to understand in the spectrum and map of mind states.

Tippett: And that also will help us understand something about our ordinary, everyday selves. I think that's also the connection that is a bit harder to see on the outside.

Pim van Lommel, you come to this from an unusual vantage point of a physician, a cardiologist, becoming aware of the phenomenon of near-death experiences. You started thinking about consciousness as something that manifests itself in states of clinical death. I wonder what view of the self your study of near-death experience has given you. Is the self an entity? What is the relationship between the self and biology, and is a self something other than biology?

van Lommel: I was raised as a physician and on the idea that consciousness was just a product of the function of the brain. As a cardiologist I was involved in many, many resuscitations. The moment I started to ask patients who had survived a cardiac arrest—this was in 1986—if they had memories of the period of cardiac arrest, which is called clinical death, in which there is no circulation, no breathing, and if resuscitation isn't started within five to ten minutes the patient ultimately dies because of irreversible damage of the brain. To my big surprise 12 out of 50 patients who had survived a cardiac arrest told me about an enhanced consciousness during this period of a supposedly nonfunctioning brain. The inquiries started for me out of curiosity because these reports didn't fit with what I'd learned.

And so in 1988 we began a study of 344 patients who had survived cardiac arrest, 18% of whom had memories of the period of cardiac arrest. There was no scientific explanation for why 18% (62 patients) had near-death experience with enhanced consciousness during their period of clinical death while nearly 82% did not have any memories, even though there was no difference at all associated with the duration of cardiac arrest (two minutes or eight minutes) or in the duration of consciousness (five minutes of unconsciousness or three weeks of coma). There was no difference associated with whether they were given medication, had fear of death before the cardiac arrest or had foreknowledge of the event, religion, or gender.

So, we couldn't explain why people can have this experience of enhanced consciousness. Why they had cognition, self identity, and emotions; why they could experience a review of their own lives, with memories from early childhood, and feel connected with everything and everybody. It is described as an experience of *oneness, of unity*. Everything is connected; and when one has a life review—let's say in a cardiac arrest of two minutes—one can talk a day or more about it. Everything happens at the same time, instantaneous; one is where one concentrates on; everything and everybody seem interconnected or entangled.

Then we started to think about what happens in the brain during cardiac arrest. We know that the function of the brain stops; there's no blood flow in the brain. Within two seconds patients become unconscious, and the function of the cortex is gone, so there are no body reflexes, no pain reflexes; but also the abolition of brainstem activity is demonstrable, with the loss of the gag reflex and of the corneal reflex. Fixed and dilated pupils are found. The function of the respiratory center, located close to the brainstem, fails, resulting in apnoea (no breathing). The clinical findings are that there's no function of the brain. And in studies with induced cardiac arrest in both human and animal models the electrical activity in the cerebral cortex (but also in the deeper structures of the brain in animals) has been shown to be absent after 10–20 seconds (a flat-line EEG).

An interesting aspect of the near-death experience is the out-of-body experience where people can have veridical perceptions that can be corroborated later by doctors or nurses or family members who are present. They can tell in exact detail what happened during the resuscitation.

Tippett: Right. And these are the things that legitimize it in some sense.

van Lommel: Exactly.

Tippett: For example, you describe the story of a patient who had his dentures removed during his resuscitation, unconscious because of his cardiac arrest, with his eyes closed; he was in a coma for more than a week but later recognized the nurse who had taken his dentures out. Such reports take this out of the realm of "maybe these people are making up stories." There's a lot that people have done to make this be taken seriously scientifically.

van Lommel: You can corroborate these accounts of perception. In a recent review of about 100 cases of out-of-body experiences, 90% were 100% correct, which means it is not an illusion or hallucination. For me, I would like to call it the ego. It's our waking consciousness or ego—when we are awake—or daily consciousness. But the people who have an out-of-body experience when the brain doesn't function anymore still have self-identity, and on a higher dimension they feel that everything and everybody are connected. This is what people tell us in the moment that the brain doesn't function.

Tippett: So where does that take you?

van Lommel: In my opinion, the brain is not the producer of consciousness but the facilitator of consciousness. It makes it possible to experience waking consciousness in our body when we're awake. And the self, or the higher self or the enhanced consciousness, is a higher aspect of our consciousness. The ego is just an aspect that you can experience in your body.

I have spoken to hundreds of people who had near-death experiences, people who had been in a traffic accident or were in a coma, people who had a cardiac arrest, children who had been near drowning, or women who had been in shock due to severe loss of blood during childbirth. In these patients, enhanced consciousness was experienced during the loss of all functions of the brain. But even during meditation or depression, with presumably normal brain function, people can experience this kind of enhanced consciousness.

Tippett: So, the brain is not the producer of consciousness but the facilitator. Another way you come at this quite differently is you say consciousness actually pervades the body, right? Not just that the body doesn't merely produce consciousness.

van Lommel: You are right. In my view nonlocal or enhanced consciousness is received and not produced by the body.

Tippett: And this comes from stories of people who've had transplants, for example.

What are the questions that arise for you, Evan and Thomas, from this kind of experience and perspective? I'm curious how you react to each other's stories. Is there something in these stories that raises questions for you?

Metzinger: Well, as you may remember, in a book I wrote, *The Ego Tunnel*, I briefly reported that I had out-of-body experiences myself as a young man, and in the beginning, they were extremely realistic and very convincing. I'm just like Evan, a long-term meditator. They occurred in the context of very long ten-week meditation retreats. In the beginning I thought to myself, "Oh, boy, have you been so arrogant! All these stories about soul travel and astral bodies are literally true!" It was really shocking.

Now, I think they're all complex hallucinations, and I'm working in the lab with neuroscientists to produce them in healthy subjects. So I've had a long, long journey.

One thing one has to say is that there are no verifiable perceptions in the out-of-body experience state under controlled sleep lab conditions. I tried during my own out-of-body experiences three decades ago to make verifiable observations. I tried to experiment very systematically and I have not been able to make a single verifiable observation myself—for example, I tried to "fly" [out of body] to my girlfriend and observe things in her room; but it never worked. So, I have never been able to produce an intersubjectively verifiable perception.

However, I can understand how these experiences can be so realistic—how people just from that one experience come to unwaveringly believe in life after death for the rest of their lives. And that's just a very, very natural thing.

I think the only answer is to bring these experiences—and that's what we're doing—into controlled lab conditions. We must bring this question into a strictly scientific context. As I say, people are trying this and thus far there are no verifiable observations.

Also one must see that maybe the out-of-body experiences of cardiac arrest patients or epileptic patients are very different "things" from what a Christian monk or a Tibetan yogi might experience. Perhaps they are not all the same kind of experience.

What gave me doubt about out-of-body experiences was that a friend, a professor of psychology asked me, "In an out-of-body state how do you move, say, from one point to another; when you've left your body and then you go to try to flip a light switch and it doesn't work and then you go to the window and try to fly out." Initially, I was firmly against my friend's inquiries because she was trying to convince me that out-of-body experiences were hallucinations, and I just couldn't believe it.

And then I realized *I don't walk* during an out-of-body experience, instead I am in one place one moment and then in another place another moment, without any awareness of *moving* between the two places. So there are actually breaks or holes between memory points in terms of how movement is experienced in the out-of-body state. These breaks show us that out-of-body experiences are actually internal models the brain tries to create, and that these models have certain gaps because the brain creates them (i.e., they are not actual out-of-body experiences). It is like thinking of the next landmark in the cognitive map in your brain. When I closely inspected my motion pattern in the out-of-body state I realized, "Oh, out-of-body experiences are just constructions of my mind."

van Lommel: Can I comment on this? Until now it has never been possible to induce a real out-of-body experience with veridical perception from a position out and above the unconscious body. What has been written about in the medical literature on induced out-of-body experiences has been only about illusions.

I have mentioned that people who are blind from birth, who even dream without pictures, have had out-of-body experiences with veridical perception during cardiac arrest or coma. As I just said, in a review of about 100 cases of corroborated out-of-body experiences, 90% of these out-of-body perceptions were 100% veridical.

This proves that an out-of-body perception cannot be a hallucination, which is experiencing a perception that has no basis in "reality," like in psychosis; neither can it be a delusion, which is an incorrect assessment of a correct perception; nor an illusion, which means a misapprehensive or misleading image. What people perceived from a position out and above their lifeless body occurred in an operation room, in a resuscitation room, or in a car accident. It's not in an environment the people knew before. The patient with the dentures we described in our study, for example, was in a coma when he entered the hospital. And these out-of-body experiences with veridical perceptions seem to occur during unconsciousness, when the brain does not function anymore, for example, with a flat-line EEG.

Tippett: The out-of-body perception experiences you are talking about occur during catastrophic, cataclysmic events, not lab conditions.

van Lommel: Exactly. I think the main challenge is to find all those people and to corroborate the perceptions. That's what has been done and what we do. You cannot *induce* real out-of-body experiences.

Tippett: Evan?

Thompson: I'd like to say some things about this. The first is that at least based on my own reading of the literature, I'm not convinced that there are verifiable perceptions that meet the standards of evidence we would want in cognitive psychology and in neuroscience. Second, there are real difficult issues here about *time*. When you make a retrospective report about an experience that you had and you time it, you're subjectively representing time. But that's different from the objective timing of some event that's going on in the brain or in the body. We don't know that the time at which an *experience* is occurring is the time at which *biological events* are going on. It could be but we don't know this without some serious kinds of psychological and neuroscientific investigations, which haven't been done. So an important element here is the subjective consciousness of time.

A second point I want to make is that I think it's a mistake to treat the discussion about near-death experiences as *whether* these experiences are veridical or hallucinatory. I think what is fundamentally important in the near-death experience is that it's an experience that people have in the process of dying, and it says something very important about the phenomenology of the dying process. And this is something that the biomedical model of death has absolutely nothing to say; it treats death as the cessation of biological function and says nothing about the subjective experiential process of what it is to die. In the contemplative traditions of Asia, but also in Western contemplative traditions, there is a rich literature on the subjective process of the breakdown of your mind and body as you die. The out-of-body experiences have to be seen in this way. We have an ethical responsibility to face death as a subjective process and to think about what it means to train ourselves to deal with something that we're all going to face, and we don't know how each of us is going to face it.

So this is the real value in the near-death experience research: it brings out the fact that dying is something that has this experiential structure to it. And this is really very, very important.

Tippett: So we keep coming back to mortality, but I really don't want to stay there for the rest of our half hour. So let me bring this back to life a little bit.

Here's a really interesting echo that you all come back to and work with in different ways. There are distinctions that I think neuroscientists and philosophers are still making. There's brain, mind, consciousness, self. But there's also *awareness*, which may not be the same thing as consciousness.

Evan, it's interesting to me that "pure awareness," which has been much investigated, is actually what these near-death patients describe—their sense of oneness. Thomas, you've written about the "ego tunnel," the "tunnel of consciousness." And yet as human beings, we are capable of these moments of awareness, which might be this pure awareness—that, in fact, in the moment of becoming aware of the tunnel, we do rise above it or transcend it in some sense. It's an interesting thing about being human, and it's a question in this whole discussion.

Metzinger: I don't know if you're interested in this, but of course there is a wider context in which all this research is taking place. And that context is that we are undergoing a historical transition now, wanted or not. I call it "the naturalistic turn in the image of man." There's a lot of knowledge coming up that is emotionally unsettling. Neuroscience contributes to the philosophical project of self-knowledge but it hurts us. It is difficult.

Tippett: For example? This difficult knowledge?

Metzinger: Well, we are less rational than we think we are. We're much more vulnerable beings than we think we are. We're less moral than we like to think we are, and then there's mortality. . .

As societies, we have to create a new cultural context for this very difficult transition process or else we will just get swept away by the psychosocial consequences and the shift, the image of ourselves, and the new technologies and brain neurotechnologies that are emerging. And the core question for me is whether there can be a fresh and new, but fully secularized, spirituality. To put it differently, the question is whether intellectual honesty, like the core of the scientific attitude, can actually coexist with an absolutely clean form of spirituality, and I think that is also what you asked about. There are a number of things I think people are not fully aware of.

Let me make three bold statements here. I think the opposite of religion is not science. The opposite of religion is spirituality. And the scientific attitude, the strictly rational attitude, can be described as a special case of the spiritual attitude towards life and the world. Actually, the scientific, very sober, rigorous approach to reality and life and the spiritual approach to reality and life stem from the same values, from the same normative spring or core. It has something to do with truthfulness—I guess the English word is *veracity*—the will, the pure will, to absolute veracity, but also to accept the obligation of veracity toward one's self. That is where spirituality departs from religion and that is also where there's a bridge from spirituality to modern science. Because that is just what it is: ultimate veracity toward what you know and what you don't know.

I don't know if this is something you were trying to get at, but this is what I would describe as the wider context in the period we're now going through together, all of us, wanted or not.

van Lommel: Perhaps I can comment. This discussion is philosophy and science. And what is the definition of science? You have scientific methods, yes, but science, for me, is asking questions with an open mind. Forget the concepts. Look at what you see and try to understand. This is science.

For a lot of people, however, science is just a dogma. For me, science shouldn't be a dogma. Science should be: forget your concepts and be open. At least that's what happened to me. I have a quote: "He who never changed his mind has never learned something." If you always stay with your old concepts, you don't learn anything.

Tippett: So here's a question from the audience: Is there an afterlife?

I don't think anyone here could answer that question definitively. But I will ask you Pim, where does this fascination you have—what you know about near-death experiences—take you in your thinking about creative intelligence, God, or a higher power? Does it make you believe in an afterlife?

van Lommel: First of all, I never use the word *afterlife*. I talk about a "continuity of consciousness." I think consciousness is fundamental in the universe and everything originates from it. So, when you talk about continuity of consciousness, death, like birth, could just be a changing state of consciousness. And that's what I learned from all those hundreds and hundreds of people who wanted to share their near-death experiences with me.

Tippett: So, do you think about—and this is drawing on another question—there being a *source* of this enhanced consciousness? My experience of scientists thinking about spirituality is that they often don't have a need to tie it up [to explain it], I mean, they may say, "this is an open question, I don't know what it means but I don't need to call it God."

van Lommel: I think there are many levels of consciousness, and I think the higher the level of consciousness. . . it's an enhanced consciousness, the level of unity, the level of oneness, and above that will be a level we don't have any idea about but it will be the source of everything. The source of the universe, the source of consciousness, the source of life—and yet we will never understand these sources, I think.

Tippett: How do you think about this, Evan?

Thompson: Well, what's important to me is to turn our attention to consciousness as we experience it here and now, and as we live it through states—like waking and dreaming and memory and mind wandering and lucid dreaming and out-of-body experiences—so the full range of states is really important to attend to phenomenologically and scientifically. But to go beyond that is to speculate and I'm not a speculative philosopher. I'm a philosopher who likes to work phenomenologically and with what the phenomenological and scientific evidence presents us with.

Tippett: Question from the audience: "How do digital and social media impact our sense of self?" This may get back to what you were saying, Thomas, about how the world is changing and changing us. How do digital and social media impact stream of consciousness? How do you think about this?

Metzinger: Very important question. Totally underestimated in its relevance, I think. We have many means to change consciousness now. There are cognitive enhancers and neurotechnology brain implants; but I think many people still underestimate these new media environments in which we operate. Our brains just did not evolve for the internet. I guess the average British citizen now spends 46% of his waking time online, connected to media, a mobile phone or a computer, or in front of a TV set.

And I can see in my students how things have changed rapidly, only in the past five years, including how attention span is collapsing. Unlike my students, I can only multitask on three channels; they must multitask on five channels or they get nervous.

A new generation is growing up and we have no idea how the embedding of this natural virtual reality Mother Nature has created, which we now call conscious experience, into these larger technical systems of representing reality and processing information will change us.

I can only say that it changes me a lot. One can become hooked on these little novelty stimuli. Research has shown in Germany, for instance, that the average time one is interrupted in his/her work flow is every 11 minutes: the phone rings or a new e-mail message pops up or somebody knocks on your door. The frightening thing is that almost half of these interruptions of awareness, of the attempt to stay in a moment with one task, are *self-generated*. This shows that a brain learns, "I will be interrupted *anyway* after about 11 minutes," so if, finally, nobody calls, you end up checking your bank account or something similar.

It's dangerous to train ourselves to be inattentive and fragmented, I think.

Tippett: It's interesting to think about this emerging field of understanding consciousness and the brain, and this change in life, which, as you say, is happening in real time—almost too quickly for us to process or to understand what it means and how it's changing us.

Metzinger: One of the deepest cores of the sense of self is what I call *attentional* agency. In a nutshell, it's the sense that you control the focus of your attention. An infant doesn't have that. If you're seriously drunk, you lose it. In old age, dementia, you lose it. And if you think about it, if you lose the capacity to control your focus of attention, then you lose a core element of your conscious self-model. I call the entertainment and advertisement industries "the attention robbers," who attack us and our children from this information jungle. And there's actually an attack going on all the time of taking this capacity of attentional control away from us. There's an industry attacking us all the time, and in a sense that is an attack on the conscious self. It will change our experience of selfhood if we're not aware of it.

And I think the good news—I think something Evan and I share—is that there are old psychological techniques that are already available to stabilize and sustain attention. One thing I've been arguing for practically is to introduce meditation lessons in schools in an ideology-free setting.

Just like brushing your teeth, these techniques are things every child should know and have a right to learn in order to defend himself/herself against these attacks on the conscious self.

Tippett: Evan?

Thompson: I'm reminded of something William James said: that habit is the basic unit of mental life. And he meant that as both an ethical and a psychological statement. By habit, he meant specifically habits of attention. James' whole conception of free will had to do with being able to direct and sustain one's attention on what one chooses. That, for him, was the essence of free will.

This is something that animates my work a lot—that we have the means to train ourselves to be attentive and to do so in the face of the challenges to attention that are being presented to us by these new technologies.

Tippett: I think of meditation as a spiritual technology, the counterpart to these other kinds of technologies.

Here's a question I have to read to see if I understand it; maybe you will: "Thomas maintains that the self does not exist because its presence depends on the neurological functions of the brain. But doesn't the objective world essentially cease to exist without a subject to observe and interpret it? In this way, isn't the objective world 'philosophically non-self-sufficient and thus philosophically nonexistent?'"

Metzinger: Deep waters! We know about external and objective reality not through single brains and single streams of conscious experience but through scientific communities. Other people stay awake. So I think there's good evidence that the world doesn't disappear when I go to sleep or under anesthesia. The phenomenal world model disappears. Of course we have good reason to believe that an external language-independent, mind-independent reality exists, and simply through theories. Theories are constructed not by individual conscious selves but by whole communities of human beings. I don't know what the other speakers think. I'm a pretty old-fashioned guy.

Tippett: That's one of those conundrums, like the afterlife, that we might not be able to solve here...

I think these are good questions to spend our last few minutes on. "What are the implications of embodied consciousness for responsibility and decision making? What are the ethical implications of the questions we're raising here and how do we use this knowledge?"

Thompson: Well, this is another point I think I share with Thomas, which we've certainly talked about before, and that is the idea of an *ethics of consciousness*. What kinds of conscious states are wholesome? What kinds of conscious states do we want to encourage in our children? What habits of attention do we want to cultivate? How do we want to train our meta-awareness, our ability to be aware of the functioning of our own minds?

These are, of course, scientific questions, but they're also ethical questions. I see the scientific endeavor to understand consciousness—the sense of self, how the sense of self arises or is constructed—as having ethical roots as a product of self-knowledge, but also an ethical agenda. How do we want our minds to be? And there was never a time in world history when this was a more pressing and fundamental question.

Tippett: A question this raises for me—and maybe quantum physics would weigh into this interestingly—is: even if we assert that the self—this identity that each of us brings into the world or we feel like we bring into the world—dies with our bodies, isn't there some kind of imprint that our lives make on the cosmos? Thomas? You said that self and consciousness have a social aspect. It's bigger than our bodies and some of that impact remains when we are gone.

Metzinger: Even from a ruthlessly, very strictly materialist point of view, one has to admit that the evolution of life, nervous systems, and conscious experience, on this planet changed the nature of the physical universe itself: systems evolved for the first time that had an image of the world as a whole. One could talk about it in terms of self-similarity: the universe becomes slightly more self-similar by including beings that have conscious, integrated world-models. We have these individual first-person perspectives as a result of the evolutionary process on our planet. And this changes—in a modest, but interesting, way—our view of the physical universe, which has the potential to evolve conscious first-person perspectives.

Tippett: But we all also affect the consciousness of others.

Metzinger: Sure.

Tippett: Very directly, our own children, right? Hence the ethical question, How do we use this knowledge? We go around making an impact on other conscious beings all the time.

van Lommel: Perhaps I can add something about the ethical aspects.

Tippett: Yes.

van Lommel: One of the intriguing aspects of people with a near-death experience is the transformation they have after a near-death experience: they all experience a new life inside. One of the major things is that they still feel connected with other people; they still feel connected with nature; they still feel connected with the endangered planet.

Tippett: Do they feel more connected than they did before the experience?

van Lommel: Far more connected. As a result of their near-death experience they permanently experience this kind of connectedness, this experience of oneness, and they start to live differently. They start to help people, they are more compassionate, they have more empathy, and so on. The way we view the world depends on our state of consciousness. I would say when I'm in love, the world is beautiful. When I'm depressed, the world is awful. When I'm frightened—because of the press and the politicians—the world gets full of fear. So it depends on our own state of consciousness. Where we can change our state of consciousness, we can change the world as well. And this has an ethical implication, but in a negative way as well.

Tippett: Right. So we just have a few minutes left. I want to bring the larger question of the implications of this down to the ground as we conclude. How do each of you live differently? How do you work with the idea of the meaning of your life because of these ideas that you live and work with?

Metzinger: Well, for me it has sobering effects. I read neuropsychological literature a lot; case studies; what happens after certain forms of brain damage; how it changes the sense of self. And I become acutely aware of what could happen to me and everybody else every minute if, for example, just a little blood vessel explodes. So I've become very much aware that my psychological properties are something very delicate and vulnerable, and that somehow they emerged from a process—an evolutionary process—that had no goal and no direction, that was merciless and sacrificed many of my ancestors. Evolution is not something one can glorify.

In my work, I have really become more aware that we are suffering beings and that we had better take more care of ourselves, have more respect for each other and in our interpersonal relationships, and that we should maybe look to old-fashioned philosophical questions. Like, as Evan said, not only What is a good action?, but What is a valuable state of consciousness? Under these conditions we find ourselves.

Tippett: So evolution had no goal or direction but we as conscious beings can and should give direction to our lives.

Metzinger: Right. Our whole mind works like that. I think you cannot really, if you're honest, intuitively understand how there really was no goal and no direction to the process of the evolution of conscious minds. Is it really possible to understand that evolution had no goal or direction? These are the glasses we use to look onto reality: things must have a direction and a goal or else we don't understand. Yet we discover things scientifically that are very hard for us to digest. And I think we can be open about this. It's not easy to be intellectually honest in these times.

Tippett: Evan?

Thompson: What's important for me is to try to embody, as best I can, the kinds of things that I'm working with in the meditative contemplative traditions. So that means in my own life trying to maintain that familiarity with my own first-person workings of attention and so on, but also to show that that's something that students can do. I teach a lot of classes on the philosophy of mind, and I try to show students that philosophy of mind can be embodied in a personal way through these contemplative practices, and that in a way that's actually the true, deep, animating spirit of philosophy. Philosophy is the love of wisdom; it's tied in its history to what some philosophers today call spiritual exercises, and this needs to be brought back in to animate philosophy. So I try to live and embody as much of that as best I can.

Tippett: Pim?

van Lommel: Yes, I'm not talking about philosophy; I'm talking about what I have learned from people with a near-death experience. It's what life is all about: about compassion and about empathy. To accept one's own dark sides as well, and then to have empathy and compassion for others, for nature, and for the planet. We have to change our consciousness to change the world.

We forget about sustainability as we are now destroying and exhausting systematically our planet. We have to remember that our grandchildren will have to survive here on this planet. We are now living in a competitive and materialistic society, but we should stop thinking and acting as if we are better than others, because this will always be at the expense of children and other weak and delicate creatures around the world. We have to change our personal consciousness, not only to change the way we live, but also to change the way we want to treat, honor and respect other human beings on this planet. I'm very positive, and it's all about now. It's all about changing ourselves to change the world.

Tippett: Well, I hope this was a good beginning. It certainly was just a beginning. Thank you all for coming. This was fantastic.

Ann. N.Y. Acad. Sci. ISSN 0077-8923

ANNALS OF THE NEW YORK ACADEMY OF SCIENCES
Issue: *Perspectives on the Self*

Near-death experiences: the experience of the self as real and not as an illusion

Pim van Lommel

Department of Cardiology, Rijnstate Hospital, Arnhem, the Netherlands

Address for correspondence: P. van Lommel, Department of Cardiology, Rijnstate Hospital, Postbus 9555, 6800 AD Arnhem, the Netherlands. pimvanlommel@gmail.com

Because the publication of several prospective studies on near-death experience (NDE) in survivors of cardiac arrest have shown strikingly similar results and conclusions, the phenomenon of the NDE can no longer be scientifically ignored. The NDE is an authentic experience that cannot be simply reduced to imagination, fear of death, hallucination, psychosis, the use of drugs, or oxygen deficiency. Patients appear to be permanently changed by an NDE during a cardiac arrest of only some minutes' duration. It is a scientific challenge to discuss new hypotheses that could explain the possibility of a clear and enhanced consciousness—with memories, self-identity, cognition, and emotions—during a period of apparent coma. The current materialistic view of the relationship between consciousness and the brain, as held by most physicians, philosophers, and psychologists, seems to be too restricted for a proper understanding of this phenomenon. There are good reasons to assume that our consciousness, with the continuous experience of self, does not always coincide with the functioning of our brain: enhanced or nonlocal consciousness, with unaltered self-identity, apparently can be experienced independently from the lifeless body. People are convinced that the self they experienced during their NDE is a reality and not an illusion.

Keywords: near-death experience; cardiac arrest; consciousness; brain function; self-identity; illusion

To study the abnormal is the best way of understanding the normal.

WILLIAM JAMES

Introduction

A near-death experience (NDE) can be defined as the reported memory of a range of impressions during a special state of consciousness, including a number of special elements, such as an out-of-body experience (OBE), pleasant feelings, seeing a tunnel and/or light, seeing deceased relatives, a life review, or a conscious return into the body. Many circumstances are described during which NDEs are reported, such as cardiac arrest (clinical death), shock after loss of blood (childbirth), traumatic brain injury or stroke, near-drowning (children), or asphyxia, but also in serious diseases not immediately life threatening—during isolation, depression, or meditation, or without any obvious reason. The NDE is usually transformational, causing enhanced intuitive sensibility, profound changes of life insight, and the loss of the fear of death.[1] The content of an NDE and the effects on patients seem similar worldwide, across all cultures and all times. However, the subjective nature and absence of a single frame of reference for this near-ineffable experience lead to individual, cultural, and religious factors determining the vocabulary used to describe and interpret this experience.[1]

Near-death experiences occur with increasing frequency because of the improved survival rates resulting from modern techniques of resuscitation. According to a recent random poll in the United States and Germany, about 4% of the total population in the Western world have experienced NDEs.[2,3] Thus, about nine million people in the United States should have had this extraordinary conscious experience. NDEs seem to occur relatively regularly and to many physicians are inexplicable phenomena and hence often ignored results of survival in a critical medical situation. Physicians hardly ever hear a patient tell about his or her NDE, and patients are reluctant to share their experience with others

doi: 10.1111/j.1749-6632.2011.06080.x

because of the many negative responses they usually get.[1]

The phenomenon of the NDE raises a number of fundamental questions. An NDE is a special state of consciousness that occurs during an imminent or actual period of death, or sometimes without any obvious reason. But how and why does an NDE occur? How does the content of an NDE come about? Is there a biological basis of consciousness? Is it possible to speak of a beginning of our consciousness, and will our consciousness ever end? Why does a person's life change so radically after an NDE? Why is the experience of the self during an NDE so real? How is it possible to experience enhanced consciousness with the possibility of veridical perception independently of the lifeless body? In order to answer these questions, we need a better understanding of the relationship between brain function and consciousness. We shall have to start by examining whether there is any indication that consciousness with self-identity can be experienced during sleep, general anesthesia, coma, brain death, clinical death, the process of dying, and, finally, after confirmed death. If the answers to any of these questions are positive, we must look for scientific explanations and scrutinize the relationship between brain function and consciousness in these different situations.[1]

The Dutch prospective study on near-dealth experiences in survivors of cardiac arrest

In order to obtain more reliable data to corroborate or refute the existing theories on the cause and content of an NDE, we needed a properly designed scientific study. This was the reason why in 1988 we started a prospective study in the Netherlands.[4] At that point, no large-scale prospective studies into NDEs had been undertaken anywhere in the world. Our study aimed to include all consecutive patients who had survived a cardiac arrest in 1 of the 10 participating Dutch hospitals. In other words, this prospective study would only be carried out among patients with a proven life-threatening crisis. This kind of design also creates a control group of patients who have survived a cardiac arrest but who have no recollection of the period of unconsciousness. In a prospective study, such patients are asked, within a few days of their resuscitation, whether they have any recollection of the period of their cardiac arrest, that is, of the period of their unconsciousness.

All patients' medical and other data are carefully recorded before, during, and after their resuscitation. The advantage of this prospective study design was that all procedures were defined in advance and no selection bias could occur.[4]

Within four years, between 1988 and 1992, 344 successive patients who had undergone a total of 509 successful resuscitations were included in the study. In other words, all the patients in our study had been clinically dead. *Clinical death* is defined as the period of unconsciousness caused by total lack of oxygen in the brain (anoxia) because of the arrest of circulation, breathing, or both, as caused by cardiac arrest in patients with an acute myocardial infarction. If in this situation no resuscitation is initiated, the brain cells will be irreversibly damaged within 5–10 min, and the patient will always die.[4]

A longitudinal study into life changes was based on interviews after two and eight years with all patients who had reported an NDE and who were still alive, as well as with a control group of postresuscitation patients who were matched for age and gender, but who had not reported an NDE. The question was whether the customary changes in attitude to life after an NDE were the result of surviving a cardiac arrest or whether these changes were caused by the experience of an NDE. This question had never been subject to scientific and systematic research with a prospective design before. The Dutch study was published in *The Lancet* in December 2001.[4]

If patients reported memories from the period of unconsciousness, the experiences were scored according to a certain index, the WCEI, or Weighted Core Experience Index.[5] The higher the number of elements reported, the higher the score, and the deeper the NDE. Our study found that 282 patients (82%) had no recollection of the period of their unconsciousness, whereas 62 patients—18% of the 344 patients—reported an NDE. Of these 62 patients with memories, 21 patients (6%) had some recollection; having experienced only some elements, they had a superficial NDE with a low score. Forty-one patients (12%) reported a core experience: 18 patients had a moderately deep NDE, 17 patients reported a deep NDE, and 6 patients reported a very deep NDE. The following elements were reported: half of the patients with an NDE were aware of being dead and had positive emotions; 30% had a tunnel experience, observed a celestial landscape, or met with deceased persons; approximately a quarter had an out-of-body experience, communication with "the light" or perception of colors; 13% had a life review; and 8% experienced the presence of a border. In other words, all the familiar elements of an NDE were reported in our study, with the exception of a frightening or negative NDE.

Were there any reasons why some people did, but that most people did not, recollect the period of their unconsciousness? In order to answer this question, we compared the recorded data of the 62 patients with an NDE to the data of the 282 patients without an NDE. To our big surprise, we did not identify any significant differences in the duration of the cardiac arrest (2 or 8 min), no differences in the duration of unconsciousness (5 min or 3 weeks in coma), and no differences in whether intubation was necessary for artificial respiration in seriously ill patients who remained in a coma for days or weeks after a complicated resuscitation. Nor did we find statistical differences in 30 patients who had a cardiac arrest during electrophysiological stimulation in the catheterization laboratory and whose heart rhythms were always reestablished via defibrillation (an electric shock) within 15–30 seconds. So, we failed to identify any differences between the patients with a very long or a very brief cardiac arrest. The degree or gravity of the lack of oxygen in the brain (anoxia) appeared to be irrelevant. Similarly, it was established that medication played no role. Most patients suffering a myocardial infarction receive morphine-type painkillers, while people who are put on a respirator following complicated resuscitation are given extremely high doses of sedatives. A psychological cause, such as the infrequently noted fear of death, did not affect the occurrence of an NDE either, although it did affect the depth of the experience. Whether patients had heard or read anything about NDEs in the past made no difference either. Any kind of religious belief, or indeed its absence in nonreligious people or atheists, was irrelevant, and the same was true for the standard of education reached.[4]

We were particularly surprised to find no medical explanation for the occurrence of an NDE. All the patients in our study had been clinically dead, and only a small percentage reported an enhanced consciousness with lucid thoughts, emotions, memories, self-identity, and sometimes perception, from a position outside and above their lifeless body while doctors and nursing staff were carrying out resuscitation. If there were a physiological explanation, such as a lack of oxygen in the brain (anoxia), for the occurrence of this enhanced consciousness, one might have expected all patients in our study to have reported an NDE. They had all been unconscious as a result of their cardiac arrest, which caused the loss of blood pressure, the cessation of breathing, and the loss of all body and brainstem reflexes. In studies in patients with induced cardiac arrest, the electrical activity of the brain could be measured by the registration of the electroencephalogram (EEG), and in these patients the EEG became always totally flat between 10 and 20 seconds (a flatline EEG).[1] It is also well established that people without any lack of oxygen in the brain, like in depression or meditation, can experience an "NDE." Similarly, the gravity of the medical situation, such as long-term coma after a complicated resuscitation, failed to explain why patients did or did not report an NDE. The psychological explanation is doubtful because most patients did not experience any fear of death during their cardiac arrest, as it occurred so suddenly they failed to notice it. In most cases, they were left without any recollection of their resuscitation. A pharmacological explanation could be excluded as well, as the medication had no effect on whether patients reported an NDE.[4]

The later interviews in our Dutch longitudinal study were conducted using a standardized inventory featuring 34 life-change questions.[6] Among the 74 patients who consented to be interviewed after two years, 13 of the total of 34 factors listed in the questionnaire turned out to be significantly different for people with or without an NDE. The second interviews showed that, in people with an NDE, fear of death in particular had significantly decreased, while belief in an afterlife had significantly increased. We then compared these 13 factors, which had been so significantly different between the two groups with and without an NDE after two years, in the same patients after eight years. It struck us that after eight years the people without an NDE were also undergoing unmistakable processes of transformation. Nevertheless, clear differences remained between people with and without an NDE, although by now these differences had become a little less marked. We were also surprised to find that the processes of transformation that had begun in people with an NDE after two years had clearly intensified after eight years. The same was true for the people without an NDE. Nevertheless, the people who had experienced an NDE during their cardiac arrest continued to be clearly different.[1] An NDE is an unforgettable confrontation with unlimited dimensions in our consciousness. As long as one has not experienced an NDE, it seems that it would be impossible to really understand the impact and the life-changing aftereffects of this overwhelming experience. The existing worldview has radically changed. One person said, "It felt as if I had become another person but with the same identity." The integration and acceptance of an NDE is a process that may take many years, with feelings of depression, homesickness, and loneliness, because of its far-reaching impact on people's pre-NDE understanding of life and value system. Finally, it is quite remarkable to see that a cardiac arrest, which lasts just a few minutes, give rise to such a lifelong process of transformation.[1]

Other prospective studies on NDEs

Bruce Greyson, who published a prospective study of 116 survivors of cardiac arrest in the United States, found that 15.5% of the patients reported an NDE: 9.5% reported a core NDE and 6% reported a superficial NDE. He writes, "no one physiological or psychological model by itself could explain all the common features of an NDE. The paradoxical occurrence of a heightened, lucid awareness, and logical thought processes during a period of impaired cerebral perfusion raises particular perplexing questions for our current understanding of consciousness, and its relation to brain function. A clear sensorium and complex perceptual processes during a period of apparent clinical death challenge the concept that consciousness is localized exclusively in the brain."[7]

The British prospective study by Parnia et al. included 63 patients who survived their cardiac arrest. They found in their study that 11% reported an NDE: 6.3% reported a core NDE and 4.8% reported a superficial NDE. They write that the NDE reports suggest that the NDE occurs during the period of unconsciousness. This is a surprising conclusion, in their view, because "when the brain is so dysfunctional that the patient is deeply comatose, those cerebral structures, which underpin subjective experience and memory, must be severely impaired. Complex experiences as reported in the NDE should not arise or be retained in memory. Such patients

would be expected to have no subjective experience, as was the case in the vast majority of patients who survive cardiac arrest, since all centers in the brain that are responsible for generating conscious experiences have stopped functioning as a result of the lack of oxygen." Another, frequently cited explanation might be that the observed experiences occur during the early phases of the cessation or during the recovery of consciousness. Parnia et al., however, claim that, "the verifiable elements of an OBE during unconsciousness, such as patients' reports on their resuscitation, render this extremely unlikely."[8]

Over a period of four years, Sartori carried out an even smaller study into NDEs, in 39 survivors of cardiac arrest in the United Kingdom. She found that 23% reported an NDE: 18% reported a core NDE and 5% reported a superficial NDE. She concludes that, "according to mainstream science, it is quite impossible to find a scientific explanation for the NDE as long as we 'believe' that consciousness is only a side effect of a functioning brain." The fact that people report lucid experiences in their consciousness when brain activity has ceased is, in her view, "difficult to reconcile with current medical opinion."[9]

Some typical elements of an NDE

Out-of-body experience

During their OBE, people have the feeling that they have apparently taken off their body like an old coat, and to their surprise and confusion, they apparently have retained their own self-identity with the possibility of perception, emotions, and a very clear consciousness. Following a successful resuscitation, they can report veridical perceptions from a position outside and above their lifeless body. This OBE is scientifically important because doctors, nurses, and relatives can verify the reported perceptions, and they can also corroborate the precise moment the NDE with OBE occurred during the period of cardiopulmonary resuscitation (CPR). It is also important to mention that until now, it has been impossible to induce a real OBE with veridical perception from a position out and above the body by any method whatsoever,[10] despite incorrect suggestions about this possibility in the medical literature while just describing bodily illusions.[11–14] In a recent review of 93 corroborated reports of potentially verifiable out-of-body perceptions during an NDE, about 90% were found to be completely accurate,

8% contained some minor error, and only 2% were completely erroneous.[15] This proves that an OBE cannot be a hallucination, that is, the experiencing of a perception that has no basis in "reality," like in psychosis; neither can it be a delusion, which is an incorrect assessment of a correct perception, nor an illusion, which means a misapprehension or misleading image.

Most scientists are reluctant to accept the possibility of veridical perception from a position out and above the lifeless body, because this could be the decisive evidence that conscious perception by the self is possible outside the body, and so deliberately they call these perceptions just anecdotes. These scientists want to have more "objective" proof, and of course most NDE researchers will agree. This is why hidden signs or targets have been put close to the ceiling in resuscitation rooms, coronary care units, and intensive care units, with the purpose that these hidden signs, not visible from the bed, could be an objective proof for veridical perception if patients during cardiac arrest are able to perceive details of their resuscitation from a position out and above their lifeless body during their CPR, and that later these perceptions can be corroborated by doctors, nurses, and relatives. Until now, however, there has been no published case where a patient has perceived this hidden sign during CPR, despite perceiving veridical details of their resuscitation previously unknown to them. Could there be a plausible explanation for this impossibility to "proof" the reported perception during OBE by a hidden sign? This lack of objective proof could be caused by so-called inattentional blindness, also known as perceptual blindness.[16,17] This is the phenomenon of not being able to perceive things that are in plain sight. It can be a result of having no internal frame of reference to perceive the unseen object, or it can be caused by the lack of mental focus or attention caused by mental distractions. This inattentional blindness is the failure to notice a fully visible, but unexpected, object because attention was engaged on another task, event, or object, because humans have a limited capacity for attention and intention.[18,19] Only if we have the intention to decide where to place the attention will we perceive consciously the event or object we focus upon. Our conclusion, based on the many corroborated cases of veridical perception from a position out and above the body during an NDE, is that it seems obvious that perception can actually occur

during an OBE, and that missing a hidden target during an OBE must be the result of a lack of intention and attention for this unexpected hidden object, inasmuch as during the OBE, patients are too surprised to be able to "see" the resuscitation of their own lifeless body from above during their cardiac arrest or surgery.

Life review

During a holographic life review, the subject feels the presence and renewed experience of not only every act but also every thought from one's life, and one realizes that, in some way, we are connected to others and to ourselves, such that we influence ourselves as well as others. Because one is connected with the memories, emotions, and consciousness of another person, you experience the consequences of your own thoughts about, words to, and actions toward that other person at the very moment in the past that they occurred (interconnectedness or entanglement). All that has been done and thought seems to be significant and stored. Patients survey their whole life in one glance; time and space do not seem to exist during such an experience (nonlocality). Instantaneously, they are where they concentrate upon, and they can talk for hours about the content of the life review even though the resuscitation only took minutes. This panoramic review of one's life seems to contain all the conscious and unconscious aspects or the essence of one's self in constant and instantaneous connection with the consciousness of others.[1] Quotation:[20] "Not only did I perceive everything from my own viewpoint, but I also knew the thoughts of everyone involved in the event, as if I had their thoughts within me. This meant that I perceived not only what I had done or thought, but even in what way it had influenced others, as if I saw things with all-seeing eyes. And so, even your thoughts are apparently not wiped out. Time and distance seemed not to exist. I was in all places at the same time."

Meeting deceased relatives

If deceased acquaintances or relatives are encountered in an otherworldly dimension, they are usually recognized by their appearance, and communication is possible through what is experienced as thought transfer. Thus, it is also possible to come into contact with the consciousness or "self" of deceased persons (interconnectedness), even if it was not possible to know that these relatives had died.

Quotation:[20] "During my cardiac arrest I had an extensive experience . . . and later I saw, apart from my deceased grandmother, a man who had looked at me lovingly, but whom I did not know. More than 10 years later, at my mother's deathbed, she confessed to me that I had been born out of an extramarital relationship, my father being a Jewish man who had been deported and killed during the Second World War, and my mother showed me his picture. The unknown man that I had seen more than 10 years before during my NDE turned out to be my biological father."

Conscious return of the self in the body

Some patients can describe how they consciously returned into their body, mostly through the top of the head, after they had come to understand that "it wasn't their time yet" or that "they still had a task to fulfil." This conscious return of the self into the body is experienced as something very oppressive. They regain consciousness in their body and realize that they are "locked up" in their damaged body, meaning again all the pain and restriction of their disease.[1]

Theories about NDEs, consciousness, and the brain

In the last decades, many articles and books have been published about consciousness, but up to now, there are no uniform scientific views about the relationship between consciousness and the brain.[21] Most people who study consciousness, neuroscientists, psychologists, psychiatrists, and philosophers, are still of the opinion that there is a materialist and reductionist explanation for consciousness. The well-known philosopher Daniel Dennett still believes, and many with him, that consciousness is nothing other than matter, and that our subjective experience that our consciousness is something purely personal and differs from someone else's consciousness is merely an "illusion."[22] According to these scientists, consciousness originates entirely from the matter that constitutes our brain. So the prevailing paradigm holds that memories, consciousness, and the experience of self are produced by large groups of neurons or neural networks. For want of evidence for the aforementioned explanations of the cause and content of an NDE, this commonly accepted but never proven assumption that consciousness is localized in the brain should be

questioned. After all, how can an extremely lucid consciousness be experienced outside the body at a time when the brain has a transient loss of all functions during a period of clinical death, even with a flatline EEG? Furthermore, even people who are blind from birth have described veridical perceptions during OBEs at the time of their NDE.[23] Scientific studies into the phenomenon of NDEs highlight the limitations of our current medical and neurophysiological ideas about the various aspects of human consciousness or self, and the relationship between consciousness and memories on the one hand, and the brain on the other. A new theory about NDE holds that an NDE might be a changing state of consciousness (the theory of continuity), in which memories, self-identity, and cognition, with emotion, function independently from the unconscious body, and retain the possibility of "nonsensory" perception. Obviously, during an NDE, enhanced consciousness is experienced independently from the normal body-linked waking consciousness or ego, even during the period of cardiac arrest or during the period of apparent unconsciousness or coma.[1]

Consciousness and brain function

For decades, extensive research has been done to localize consciousness and memories inside the brain, so far without success. We should also ask ourselves how a nonmaterial activity, such as concentrated attention or thinking, can correspond to an observable (material) reaction in the form of measurable electrical, magnetic, and chemical activity at a certain place in the brain by EEGs, MEGs, and PET scans, and in the form of increased blood flow by shown by an fMRI. Neuroimaging studies have shown these aforesaid activities, with specific areas of the brain becoming metabolically active, in response to a thought or feeling. However, although providing evidence for the role of neuronal networks as an intermediary for the manifestations of thoughts (neural correlates), those studies do not necessary imply that those cells also produce the thoughts. A correlation does not elucidate anything about cause or result, and how should "unconscious" matter like our brain "produce" consciousness, while the brain is only composed of atoms and molecules in cells with an abundance of chemical and electrical processes? Direct evidence of how neurons or neuronal networks could possibly produce the subjective essence of the mind and thoughts is currently lacking. We cannot measure what we think or feel.[1] There are no known examples of neural–perceptual matches, and hence, reasons to doubt the truth of the "matching content" doctrine. The assumption in the matching content doctrine is that following activation of special neuronal networks, one will always have the same content of thoughts or feelings. This seems extremely unlikely, because neural activation is simply neural activation; it only reflects the use of structures. This could be compared with a radio: you can activate the radio by turning it on, and you can activate a certain wavelength by tuning in on a special channel, but you will not have any influence on the content of the program you are going to hear. Activating the radio does not influence the content of the program, and neural activation alone does not explain the content of emotions or sensations.[1]

Summary of conclusions from research on NDEs, consciousness, and brain function

In summarizing the aforementioned studies, one can conclude that, at present, more and more experiences are being reported by serious and reliable people who, to their own surprise and confusion, have experienced, independent of their physical body, an enhanced consciousness with a persistent experience of self. These experiences have been reported in all times, in all cultures, and in all religions.[1] In several prospective empirical studies, it has been proven that an enhanced and clear consciousness with self-identity can be experienced during the period of cardiac arrest (clinical death), when global cerebral function can at best be described as severely impaired and at worst nonfunctional.[4,9] One has to come to the conclusion that, based on these aforementioned well-documented prospective studies about NDEs in survivors of cardiac arrest, current scientific views fail to explain the cause and content of an NDE. Additionally, it seems indeed scientifically proven that during cardiac arrest no activity of the cortex and the brainstem can be measured, and also the clinical findings point out the transient loss of all functions of the brain.[24,25] In studying the function of the brain, it has been proven that under normal daily circumstances, during deep sleep, and during general anesthesia, a functioning network and a cooperation between many different centers of the brain is a prerequisite for the experience of our waking consciousness.[26,27] This is never

the case during a cardiac arrest. All scientists who performed the prospective studies on NDEs came to the same conclusion: lack of oxygen by itself cannot explain the cause and content of NDEs. This view is also supported by the fact that an NDE can be reported by people who did not have life-threatening illnesses but were in fear of death, in depression, or in meditation.[1]

Nonlocal consciousness

So, it is indeed a scientific challenge to discuss new hypotheses that could explain the reported interconnectedness with the consciousness or self of other persons and of deceased relatives; to explain the possibility to experience instantaneously and simultaneously (nonlocality) a review and a preview of someone's life in a dimension without our conventional body-linked concept of time and space, where all past, present, and future events exist and are available; and to discuss the possibility to have clear and enhanced consciousness with memories, with self-identity, with cognition, with emotion, with the possibility of perception out and above the lifeless body, and even with the experience of the conscious return of the self into the body.[1]

In my recent book, I describe a concept in which our endless consciousness with all the aspects or essence of self finds its origin in, and is stored in a nonlocal space as wave fields of information, and the brain only serves as a relay station for parts of these wave fields of consciousness to be received into or as our waking consciousness or ego in the shape of measurable and changing electromagnetic fields.[1] Could our brain be compared to the TV set, which receives electromagnetic waves and transforms them into image and sound? Could it as well be compared to the TV camera, which transforms image and sound into electromagnetic waves? These waves hold the essence of all information but are only perceivable by our senses through suitable instruments like the camera and TV set. The function of the brain should be compared with a transceiver, a transmitter/receiver, or interface, and the function of neuronal networks should be regarded as receivers and conveyors, not as retainers of consciousness and memories. This view is highly compatible with the concept of phenomalism or immaterial (or neutral) monism.[28] In this concept, consciousness is not rooted in the measurable domain of physics, our manifest world. This also means that the wave aspect of our indestructible consciousness in the nonlocal space is inherently not measurable by physical means. However, the physical aspect of consciousness, our waking consciousness or ego, which presumably originates from the wave aspect of our consciousness through collapse of the wave function, can be measured by means of neuroimaging techniques like EEGs, fMRIs, and PET scans. The impossibility to objectively measure or prove the nonlocal aspects of our consciousness, which also has been called "transpersonal," "enhanced," "higher," "divine," or "cosmic" consciousness, could be compared to gravitational fields, of which only the physical effects throughout the universe can be measured, but the fields themselves are not directly demonstrable.[1]

In trying to understand this concept of interaction between the invisible nonlocal space and our visible material body, it seems appropriate to compare it with modern worldwide communication. There is a continuous exchange of objective information by means of electromagnetic fields for radio, TV, mobile telephone, or laptop computer. We are not consciously aware of the vast number of electromagnetic fields that constantly, day and night, exist around us and even permeate us, as well as permeate structures like walls and buildings. At any moment, we are invaded by hundreds of thousands of telephone calls, by hundreds of radio and TV programs, and by innumerable websites. We only become aware of these electromagnetic informative fields at the moment we use our mobile telephone or by switching on our radio, TV, or laptop computer. What we receive is neither inside the instrument, nor in the components, but thanks to the receiver, the information from the electromagnetic fields becomes observable to our senses, and hence perception occurs in our consciousness. The voice we hear over our telephone is not inside the telephone. The concert we hear over our radio is transmitted to our radio. The images and music we hear and see on TV are transmitted to our TV set. The Internet, with more than a billion websites, can be received at about the same moment in the United States, in Europe, and in Australia, and is obviously not located in, nor produced by, our laptop.[1]

One cannot avoid the conclusion that endless or nonlocal consciousness has always existed and will always exist independently from the body, because there is no beginning, nor will there ever be, an end

to our consciousness. There is a kind of biological basis of our waking consciousness or ego, because, during life, our physical body functions as an interface or place of resonance. But there is no biological basis for our whole, endless, or enhanced consciousness because it is rooted in a nonlocal space. Our nonlocal consciousness with the experience of self resides not in our brain and is not limited to our brain. So our brain seems to have a facilitating, and not a producing, function to experience consciousness.[1]

Conclusion

Thousands and thousands of people have reported an enhanced consciousness with self-identity during cardiac arrest or during a period of clinical death, when the function of the cortex and the brainstem has temporarily ceased. These patients are able to have an OBE with veridical perceptions from a position out and above their lifeless body. Their consciousness or self can be experienced in another dimension, without the concept of time and space, where past and future events are available. They are convinced that in this nonlocal dimension, the reality they experience is much more real than they ever experienced in the physical world. Moreover, they experience an enhanced cognitive function, with emotions, with memories, and with an interconnectedness with the content of the consciousness of other people in the past. They can be in contact with the consciousness or self of deceased relatives, and communication is possible through thought transfer. Finally, they can experience the conscious return of self back into the physical body.[1]

They realize that the physical world, as well as their ego or waking consciousness, only seems to have a subjective reality. They are convinced that the self as they experienced independently of the nonfunctioning brain during the NDE is a reality and not an illusion. But what is a generally and well-accepted definition of an illusion? One could define an illusion as a false or misleading impression of reality. Others define it not only as an erroneous perception of reality but also as an erroneous concept or erroneous belief. Additionally, many philosophers demarcate illusion from truth and falsehood. And for a lot of Indian philosophers, illusion is not the opposite of truth, but it is something that is not true and not false. On the basis of this philosophy, the physical world as humans normally perceive is an illusion, but this does not mean that the world is not real. This could be said as well about the ego, or our body-linked waking consciousness, which can be regarded as a physical aspect of the self.

By studying people who have experienced an NDE, we found, to our surprise, that a persistent and unaltered self-identity can be experienced independently from the lifeless body at a moment the brain does not function during cardiac arrest, even with a flatline EEG, and so consciousness or self does not reside in our brain, nor is it limited to our brain, which proves that the self cannot be the product of brain function. Without a body, we still can have conscious experiences. Recently, someone with an NDE wrote me: "I can live without my body, but apparently my body cannot live without me." The conclusion seems compelling that endless or nonlocal consciousness with all the aspects of self has existed and will always exist independently from the body; people who have experienced an NDE tell us that the content of the consciousness they experienced during an NDE was far more real that they ever had experienced in their waking or daily consciousness.[1] For those people, the self is not something that is true or false, but it is real, even though it still can be called an illusion by some scientists, until, perhaps, they experience an NDE themselves.

It looks as if a single unusual finding that cannot be explained through widely accepted concepts and ideas is capable of bringing about a fundamental change in science. By making a scientific case for consciousness as a nonlocal and thus ubiquitous phenomenon, this view can contribute to new ideas about the relationship between consciousness and the brain. I am aware that this concept can be little more than a stimulus for further study and debate, because, at present, we lack definitive answers to the many important questions about our consciousness and its relationship to brain function. I have no doubt that in the future, too, many questions about consciousness and the mystery of life and death will remain unanswered. However, faced with extraordinary or anomalous findings, we must question a purely materialist paradigm in science. An NDE is one such extraordinary finding. Scientific studies of NDEs challenge our current concepts about consciousness and self and its relationship to brain function.[1]

Conflicts of interest

The author declares no conflicts of interest.

References

1. van Lommel, P. 2010. *Consciousness Beyond Life. The Science of the Near-Death Experience.* Harper Collins. New York. Translation from P. van Lommel, 2007. Eindeloos Bewustzijn. Een wetenschappelijke visie op de bijna-dood ervaring. Ten Have. Kampen.
2. Gallup, G. & W. Proctor. 1982. *Adventures in Immortality: A Look Beyond the Threshold of Death.* McGraw-Hill. New York.
3. Schmied, I., H. Knoblaub & B. Schnettler. 1999. Todesnäheerfahrungen in Ost- und Westdeutschland. Eine empirische Untersuchung. In *Todesnähe: Interdisziplinäre Zugänge zu Einem Außergewöhnlichen Phänomen.* H. Knoblaub & H.G. Soeffner, Eds.: 65–99. Universitätsverlag Konstanz. Konstanz.
4. van Lommel, P., R. Van Wees, V. Meyers, *et al.* 2001. Near-death experiences in survivors of cardiac arrest: a prospective study in the Netherlands. *Lancet* **358**: 2039–2045.
5. Ring, K. 1980. *Life at Death: A Scientific Investigation of the Near-Death Experience.* Coward, McCann & Geoghegan. New York.
6. Ring, K. 1984. *Heading Toward Omega: In Search of the Meaning of the Near-Death Experience.* William Morrow. New York.
7. Greyson, B. 2003. Incidence and correlates of near-death experiences in a cardiac care unit. *Gen. Hosp. Psychiatry* **25**: 269–276.
8. Parnia, S., D.G. Waller, R. Yeates, *et al.* 2001. A qualitative and quantitative study of the incidence, features and aetiology of near death experience in cardiac arrest survivors. *Resuscitation* **48**: 149–156.
9. Sartori, P. 2006. The incidence and phenomenology of near-death experiences. *Network Review (Scientific and Medical Network)* **90**: 23–25.
10. Penfield, W. 1975. *The Mystery of the Mind.* Princeton University Press. Princeton, NJ.
11. Blanke, O., S. Ortigue, T. Landis, *et al.* 2002. Stimulating illusory own-body perceptions. The part of the brain that can induce out-of-body experiences has been located. *Nature* **419**: 269–270.
12. Blanke, O., Th. Landis, L. Spinelli, *et al.* 2004. Out-of-body experience and autoscopy of neurological origin. *Brain* **127**: 243–258.
13. Blanke, O. & Th. Metzinger. 2008 Full-body illusions and minimal phenomenal selfhood. *Trends Cogn. Sci.* **13**: 7–13.
14. De Ridder, D., K. Van Laere, P. Dupont, *et al.* 2007. Visualizing out-of-body experience in the brain. *N. Engl. J. Med.* **357**: 1829–1933.
15. Holden, J.M., B. Greyson & B. James. 2009. Veridical perception in near-death experiences. In *The Handbook of Near-Death Experiences.* Praeger (ABC-CLIO). Santa Barbara, CA. pp. 185–211.
16. Mack, A. & I. Rock. 1998. *Inattentional Blindness.* MIT Press. Cambridge, MA.

17. Simons, D.J. & R.A. Rensink. 2005. Change blindness: past, present, and future. *Trends Cogn. Sci.* **9:** 16–20.

18. Most, S.B., B.J. Scholl, E. Clifford, *et al.* 2005. What you see is what you set: sustained inattentional blindness and the capture of awareness. *Psychol. Rev.* **112:** 217–242.

19. Chun, M.M. & R. Marois. 2002. The dark side of visual attention. *Curr. Opin. Neurobiol.* **12:** 184–189.

20. van Lommel, P. 2004. About the continuity of our consciousness. *Adv. Exp. Med. Biol.* **550:** 115–132. In *Brain Death and Disorders of Consciousness.* C. Machado & D.A. Shewmon, Eds. Kluwer Academic (Plenum) Publishers. New York, Boston, Dordrecht, London, Moscow.

21. Chalmers, D.J. 1996. *The Conscious Mind: In Search of a Fundamental Theory.* Oxford University Press. New York, Oxford.

22. Dennett, D. 1991. *Consciousness Explained.* Little, Brown and Co. Boston, London.

23. Ring, K. & S. Cooper. 1999. Mindsight. *Near-Death and Out-of-Body Experiences in the Blind.* William James Center for Consciousness Studies. Palo Alto, CA.

24. De Vries, J.W., P.F.A. Bakker, G.H. Visser, *et al.* 1998. Changes in cerebral oxygen uptake and cerebral electrical activity during defibrillation threshold testing. *Anesth. Analg.* **87:** 16–20.

25. Parnia, S. & P. Fenwick. 2002. Near-death experiences in cardiac arrest: visions of a dying brain or visions of a new science of consciousness. Review article. *Resuscitation* **52:** 5–11.

26. Massimini, M., F. Ferrarelli, R. Huber, *et al.* 2005. Breakdown of cortical effective connectivity during sleep. *Science* **309:** 2228–2232.

27. Ferrarelli, F., M. Massimini, S. Sarasso, *et al.* 2010. Breakdown in cortical effective connectivity during midazolam-induced loss of consciousness. *Proc. Natl. Acad. Sci. USA* **107:** 2681–2686.

28. Chalmers, D.J. 2002. Consciousness and its place in nature. In *Philosophy of Mind: Classical and Contemporary Readings.* Oxford University Press. New York, Oxford. Also at http:((consc.net(papers(nature.html.

Ann. N.Y. Acad. Sci. ISSN 0077-8923

ANNALS OF THE NEW YORK ACADEMY OF SCIENCES

Issue: *Perspectives on the Self*

Quid pro quo: the ecology of the self

Steve Paulson, Owen Flanagan, Paul Bloom, and Roy Baumeister

Moderated by Steve Paulson, producer and interviewer for public radio's *To the Best of Our Knowledge*, philosopher and neurobiologist Owen Flanagan (Duke University), and psychologists Paul Bloom (Yale University) and Roy Baumeister (Florida State University) examine current biological, psychological, and anthropological research on the complex interaction between the self and others, and consider the roots of empathy and morality. The following is an edited transcript of the discussion that occurred February 23, 2011, 7:00–8:15 PM, at the New York Academy of Sciences in New York City.

Paulson: Well, thank you. I am delighted to be here. Thanks to the New York Academy of Sciences and the Nour Foundation for sponsoring our event this evening, "Quid Pro Quo: The Ecology of the Self."

Can we ever really know ourselves? That's a profound question that philosophers have debated for centuries. Of course the self is a very elusive subject. And last week when I was talking with our panelists to try to figure out how we were going to focus this discussion, I suggested maybe we should start with a very basic question: Just what is the self? And Roy Baumeister very smartly suggested we not start with that question because we might all end up looking like idiots as we tried to come up with a succinct answer. And I'm guessing we'll sort of come around and get at that question, but maybe in a slightly roundabout way.

The very idea of the self, of what it means to be self-conscious, has a distinct history. On my flight out to New York I was reading Sarah Bakewell's wonderful new book about the great French essayist Montaigne. She makes the argument that the idea of writing about oneself, to create a mirror in which other people recognize their own history, had to be invented. It did not exist. And Bakewell believes it was invented in the sixteenth century by Montaigne; that is the subject of her book. Now, whether or not that's true—our panelists may want to weigh in with their own opinions—what Montaigne did was write a series of personal essays, 107 in all, in which he questioned himself, again and again. And he built up a picture of himself, as Bakewell says, "a self-portrait in constant motion, with various inconsistencies, which has since laid the foundation for the modern sense of self." And, I might add, for today's tell-all memoirs.

What's changed in recent decades, I think, is that scientists have also gotten into the act. Psychologists, biologists, and neuroscientists are now exploring a number of profound questions: When do children develop a sense of self? Do we need language for this? If so, does that mean chimps and elephants do not have an understanding of self? How does "myself" interact with "other selves" to shape *my* sense of morality? What does all of this have to do with our capacity for empathy? What would it take to create a robot with a sense of self and moral responsibility? Those are a few of the questions that I think we'll dig into tonight.

Let me explain our format. We'll talk for about 40 minutes or so then we'll open it up to questions from you, from the audience. These are written questions so you should be thinking about this as we're talking and writing down your suggested questions; then pass them to the ushers and they will hand them to me and we will respond to your questions.

doi: 10.1111/j.1749-6632.2011.06182.x

And now let me introduce our distinguished panelists. They've written lots of books and have named professorships and things like that but I'm going to cut to the chase: so just very quickly, Paul Boom, who is sitting in the center, is a psychologist at Yale University, Owen Flanagan, on the far end, is a philosopher at Duke University, and Roy Baumeister is a psychologist at Florida State University.

Owen, maybe because you're the philosopher here, let me start with you. Is there really such a thing as a unified self, or is that just a fiction?

Flanagan: Well, thanks. So it's interesting you mention Montaigne as the originator of the autobiographical self. Because in philosophy we usually talk about Socrates in about 400 BC. Socrates tells us that we should know ourselves, "know thyself." And then in my field we would talk about Saint Augustine in the second century as being the first autobiography. The way we philosophers think about this question—and this is where Augustine's is a really nice example and I think will connect up with the psychologists—philosophers usually say, "Is there a self?" Well, it depends on what you mean by the self. Just because there's a word *self* in the language doesn't mean there's a thing called self. The word is, as linguists say, polysemous—it means many different things. But we usually say something like this: for each and every one of us there's this question, What is it that makes me the same person over time, if anything does? The "if anything does" is included because there are people who think there is no such thing as a self.

But hearing Saint Augustine is kind of interesting because—and this goes along with the idea that autobiography had to be invented—he has one of those lives that is divided into two. Until he was 33 years old it was kind of like the movie *Animal House*: sex, drugs, rock and roll. And then there's a transformation—a complete transformation. Importantly he remembers both parts of his story. So the answer to the philosopher's question, What is it that makes someone like Augustine the same person over time? has something to do with the fact that he possesses autobiographical memory about his whole life.

Now then, what is it that grounds autobiographical memory? And there are two major views within the philosophical tradition. One is the view that's very common among world religions, east and west, that there's some kind of "diamond," a kind of a permanent, immutable, singular monadic thingamajig inside each and every one of us that goes with us through life and actually can go on after we die. Our bodies die, decay, and disperse, but perhaps, according to some traditional views, the part of us that is our essence goes on. And then of course there's a view that's more associated with naturalists like myself, which is that no, there can't be anything that permanent and immutable; instead there's something like a *conscious stream* and my ability to remember who I am over time and project myself forward—that is what we usually mean when we call the self a self. So in this view, the self is not a permanent thing but more like this: "I'm a series of self stages," maybe like Saint Augustine was.

Paulson: Paul Bloom, let me bring you into the discussion. Let me rephrase the question slightly. Do you think we have *one* self or do we have perhaps multiple selves?

Bloom: It's a good question and I honestly don't have a settled view on the self. I hope by the end of tonight to have resolved all these questions to my own satisfaction. But Owen nicely summarized, I think, the philosophical question: Does a self exist, or is the self an illusion?

Another option on the table, which might seem crazy but is getting more and more adherents, is that within each of our heads there are multiple selves: a community, a government. This is an old idea, actually; many philosophers have defended it, you can find it in Freud. And you find it a lot in work by behavioral economists and people who study addiction. The notion here would be, How do we make sense of something many of us experience with respect to dieting—we wish to eat less but still we eat more than we want to—or with smoking—we want to quit smoking, yet we smoke. Or we want to not check our e-mail every 30 seconds, yet we do. We have these "battles" inside our heads. And one way to construe this is in terms of multiple selves sharing a lot of memory and personality but each with different goals, and, interestingly, at war with one another. For example, the self that doesn't want to smoke can try to hide the cigarettes or tell its friends not to give it cigarettes. Or the self that doesn't want to drink can commit itself in various ways not to drink.

So there are internal battles that might suggest there's more than one self inside a single head.

Paulson: Well, Roy Baumeister, let me turn it to you. One self; multiple selves? Does the very concept of self have real meaning?

Baumeister: The idea of multiple selves surfaces from time to time in self theory but it seems always to fizzle out because the very essence of the self is sameness. Now, there's an important phenomenon here that Paul has called our attention to, which is inner conflict. And yet all these supposed inner selves are really different versions of the same self. Someone may be conflicted about smoking, but ultimately, there is one self who buys the cigarettes and smokes them or doesn't.

To get here I had to get on an airplane, and I had to show identification; and if the TSA person had asked me "Who are you?" and I had said, "Well, there are multiple selves [in me]," I don't think I would be here this evening (*participants laughing*).

I think the most recent version of the idea of multiple selves comes from brain work, because brain scientists can't seem to locate one spot in the brain and call it The Self. These scientists are beginning to say that maybe the self is not really there, maybe it's an illusion—something scattered all around in multiple pieces or something.

But in fact the brain doesn't *need* a self, i.e., it doesn't need unity, for its own operations. It has sort of evolved by adding on by bits and pieces and so on, and it could do lots of things at the same time.

To deal with the social environment, however, you need to have *one* self, because for things like ownership—is that your pair of shoes and your land and so on, or is that someone else's—continuity of self matters, as does unity.

In other words, relationships and other social interactions depend on selves that have unity and continuity over time.

Paulson: Let me follow up on that. To have a continuity of self, is this basically about memory? Is this based on the idea that we construct stories, we construct a narrative about who we are, and if you take away the memory, do you take away the self?

Baumeister: Owen brought up the important point that autobiography seems to create our sense of self as well. But there is also the argument that without self I can't remember that I did something, I can only remember that somebody did something. For example, I was born in Cleveland; I don't actually remember that, but so I'm told. Yet I could say, "Somebody was born in Cleveland," which is much less useful. So, there seems to be a presumption, or some underlying continuity, that has to be present to make memory possible.

Paulson: Well, let me follow up on that. Suppose someone comes down with Alzheimer's and obviously has severe memory problems. Is he/she no longer the same person?

Bloom: There's some notion of self—Roy is right—that we need. A notion of unitary self we need for moral and social obligation. Say Owen gets drunk afterwards, commits a terrible crime. Wakes up in the morning. . .

Flanagan. . . .that's an Irish slur. . . (*participants laughing*).

Bloom: . . .yes. . .Wakes up in the morning having no memory of his crime—still we would hold him responsible. So there's a notion of self that may or may not have a neurological or psychological reality but is *socially essential and transcends memory*. It follows around our bodies—baring some really extreme circumstances—and we need it from the standpoint of moral responsibility.

Baumeister: The person with Alzheimer's still has the same position in society. So again, the external demand one selfhood is still there: the person still has the same name, the same social security number, the same home. Even if the person doesn't realize it, other people do and thus can find the person suffering from Alzheimer's out wandering around and drive him/her home and then say, "this is your home."

So, again, the social environment requires the continuity of self.

Paulson: Owen?

Flanagan: John Locke in the 1800s talked exactly about these kinds of questions. Locke asked, What is it that makes a person the same person over time? And his answer is that what makes a person a person is autobiographical memory. So according to the Lockean view each and every one of us is the person we construct an autobiography for and hold in our head.

Locke distinguishes person from, say, man. So, a granny in late-stage Alzheimer's who no longer remembers her life, herself, her grandchildren and so on, she's lost the thread. According to the Lockean view we would say of her that she's the same *Homo sapiens* or the same human being but she's not the same person. And Locke is pretty clear that he thinks that terms like *self* and *personhood* are technical terms. He says *personhood* is a forensic narrative, a forensic concept. It's a legal concept.

Now, going back to this idea about the drunken Irishman or the granny with Alzheimer's. . .Locke has an answer given by his dominant theory: it's that on Judgment Day, God plays the role of correcting all your memories. So if you do what normal humans do, forget, engage in a lot of self-serving narrativity—none of us thinks that autobiographies are fully accurate reports; they are something the psychologists can talk about, but we spin them. On Judgment Day, Locke says, "God reveals the secrets of all souls."

Now, we don't have such a view among scientists, but I think the social community does play the role that my colleagues here were talking about. We do say to people, "even if you're amnesic about what you did, you did it."

Paulson: Well, let me ask the question then from the other end of life. We've been talking about people maybe with late-stage Alzheimer's. But what about the young child? When do children develop a sense of self? Can we actually pinpoint a particular age?

Paul, I know you've done work on this.

Bloom: I'm very interested in the development of babies and young children. But it's a very hard question you're asking because, like Owen says, a lot depends on what you mean by self.

Around the second year of life babies start to show self-conscious emotions like guilt and shame and embarrassment, which seem to be excellent indicators that there's some sort of self going on. But long before that, we and others find in babies' laboratory settings some degree of moral understanding, some degree of response to the pain of others, and judgment of certain acts as positive, others as negative. And one question I'd love to know the answer to, which would speak to your issue is, Can children at a very young age, say babies before their first birthday, judge their own acts as right or wrong?

We're trying to figure out a way to study it and so far we haven't made any progress, but that would speak to the very hard question of how the notion of self emerges.

Paulson: Do you need language to have a sense of self? Does a child start to develop some sense of self once he/she has some understanding of language?

Bloom: I would say no. And one reason I would say no is that there are people who grow up to be adolescents, to be adults, who are fully intact cognitively, yet they have no language. These are, for instance, deaf children raised in environments where nobody communicates with them. But later on, when they come to possess language and they tell you what they thought before they had language, it turns out that they had an extremely rich mental life. It would seem bizarre to deny them a sense of self in any sense of the term as we normally understand it. So based on these unusual people, I would argue that you don't need language to have a self.

Paulson: It sounds like you're making an equation between self and moral accountability. Do the two go hand in hand?

Bloom: I think so, in two ways. One would be to hold someone morally accountable for something in the past; I think this presupposes that he/she is the same person who performed the act. Otherwise, we would be holding that person accountable for something someone else did. That's ridiculous.

And second, which is, I think, more controversial, is that to some extent, our fundamental moral intuitions and moral judgments, particularly with regard to our own acts, presuppose a sense of self.

Paulson: Roy, do you want to weigh in on this?

Baumeister: Well, Paul knows much more than I do about development and so on. . . .

Almost certainly, it's going to be neither a continuum nor a single yes-or-no leap. It's going to be kind of a step function, such that understanding of self increases in pieces; so there will be steps and progresses. At which point does something qualify as a full-fledged self? Perhaps it's somewhat arbitrary. One could simply say at some advanced point "it's pretty much done" and there's a fully fledged sense of self, but getting there would be in pieces or stages. The same would go for talking about other animals that might have some bits and elements of selfhood, though to say they do or do not have a self is probably not entirely meaningful or satisfactory.

Paulson: That was going to be my next question, about animals. Do animals have selves? We know from research that certain species can recognize themselves in a mirror for instance. Is that a sign of some concept of self?

Flanagan: It's a very interesting discussion because there are people, of course, who think that a concept of self presupposes language. And if that's the case then it's problematic for most other of our fellow mammals to have selves.

I tend to agree with what Paul said about not only the human cases, but it's very hard to explain certain activities of other mammals without thinking that they have memory of episodes. The animal that knows where to go back for water or for food has something going on that looks pretty complex. It would seem to me we should presuppose that the animal has some kind of memory system that supports its recognition of its own life.

There's one thing I wanted to suggest about what Paul said about memory, about accountability—and I'll do so with an example. Take, say, a member of the 1960s protest groups the Weather Underground, who were involved in antiwar protests during which people were killed and bombs went off. A member of the group, a woman, is caught 30 years later and now is a mother of children in Oregon, or whatever. The courts do sometimes find it mitigating if such a person says, "I am no longer the same person I was then." That's an interesting way of using language and we seem to understand it. It's related to the Augustine situation: Augustine is no longer the same type of person he was earlier, yet for us he's the same historical being.

Take another example. If you think of the self as like a baseball team and ask, what makes, for example, the New York Yankees of today the same New York Yankees they were when Babe Ruth played for them. At one level you might say, that nothing does; none of the players are the same; the stadium's not the same; the blades of grass aren't the same; the owners aren't the same. But there's also this idea we have that there's a single historical thread.

So, the view I'm just now suggesting would be that the self doesn't have nearly as much unity as we ascribe to it, and we ascribe it a lot of unity because our moral practices require it. Another way to think about this is that while I, Owen, feel a lot like the guy I was ten years ago, I feel very remote from the guy I was when I was 13, although I remember a lot of stuff about that guy, I feel very, very remote to that guy. In fact I feel more similar to Paul, who I've known for a long time, than I do to who I was when I was 13 or 23.

Baumeister: May I say something here, though? If "self" is what you mean when you say "I," it's interesting that you're saying, "I am not the same person that I was when I was 13 or 30..."

Flanagan: We philosophers star that use of "I"... (*participants laughing*).

Paulson: Well, let me follow up on the question of animals and their sense of self and animal morality. Because there have been some remarkable stories, often more anecdotal than systematic, about chimpanzees that act empathetically. There's the story of a gorilla in the Brookfield Zoo: a child fell in, and the gorilla approached and picked up the child and basically carried it to the zookeeper for safekeeping. A remarkable story. There are stories of other species as well.

There seems to be some internal moral sense of good and bad. If some chimpanzees are very aggressive, others will come—and even if it's the dominant male—others will come and put themselves in between, say, the bullied chimp and the dominant male. Sounds like some sense of morality there, right?

Bloom: Frans de Waal would argue that there is. And other primatologists would argue that there is. But I think there's room for skepticism, or at least a distinction.

What you find in other primates and also in other animals are reactions we would reasonably call empathy or anger. Certainly toward kin and those they interact with. There's nobody who doubts that a mother chimp will protect her young or will strike out at someone who attacks her young. A lot of us do doubt, though, whether there's anything approximating a moral notion that would coincide with what we view as *fairness* or *justice*. And one way to ask this question is to ask, What extent do chimps and orangutans, and other creatures, respond to injustices committed by others where they are third-party observers? For these cases the evidence is very weak.

So, for instance, there are some lovely findings that I can summarize with an example: if Roy and I were chimpanzees and you, our trainer, gave him a delicious grape and gave me a Cheerio, I'm going to get very annoyed and I may throw the Cheerio down in disgust. On the other hand, there's no evidence at all that Roy's going to get annoyed and say, "Well, it's kind of unfair that we didn't get the same thing—that I got the grape and he got the Cheerio." In fact if this experiment is done with seven-year-old humans, they don't care much either.

But, if a similar experiment—in which there are clear inequities—is done with adults, they do respond. For example, Roy as a human adult may say, "That's not fair; you're not treating us properly." There's no evidence such a response comes naturally [for animals].

Paulson: Okay. You've said that there is evidence that certain animals, chimpanzees for instance, may show empathy. So you're distinguishing between empathy and a sense of morality?

Bloom: I am. Or you could call it two types of morality if you want. But empathy is this gut reaction to the pain of others, and it gets transformed into compassion. That's separate from a notion that some things are right and some things are wrong—an abstract, generalizable notion that is deeply fundamental to humans; it's the foundation for our laws, for large societies, for the objective treatment of those who are not our kin. I'm perfectly comfortable if you want to call them "morality$_1$" and "morality$_2$." But they're very different.

Paulson: So you're saying morality is mostly a product of reason rather than of emotional response?

Bloom: I'm saying that the morality that's most interesting, that we most want to explain, surprisingly turns out to be the product of reason and rationality, and surprisingly it isn't present in other species and in the young of our species.

Flanagan: It's an interesting idea. There's real division among moral philosophers and psychologists, and they're on both sides of this. There's a second century philosopher, Mencius, who plays the same role in relation to Confucius as Aristotle does in relation to Plato. Mencius, in a passage, says that any man, if he were to see a child falling in a well, would immediately feel alarm and compassion. So his idea is that we're *seated*—he calls these sprouts of morality. This might work on the view that Paul has.

The idea would be that there are some native dispositions, which might be easy to explain by evolutionary psychology: It's just going to be good (beneficial) if we're designed to have immediate reactions to children because usually the ones who will be near to us are our close kin.

So the question is, can you bootstrap a morality up from a system where mothers and fathers are trying to watch out for their own kin, and then build the kind of morality that I think is true? Although concepts of justice are really very, very far from the innate equipment, it might be that things like virtues of empathy or sympathy are quite natural. And so you might want to divide different virtues and consider that some are closer to the nature of the beast and others require a lot of social construction.

Paulson: Roy, let me ask you, do you think morality is ultimately more a product of emotion or of reason?

Baumeister: Well, that's a question I wasn't expecting ... (*participants laughing*). I think the essence of morality has to be on the reason side. It's something we can discuss and resolve; that we can argue about, which is not to say that Jon Haidt and others aren't correct in saying that moral reactions are often guided by emotion. But we use reason, perhaps, to *educate* our emotional reactions.

Paulson: Part of the reason I ask this is, Paul, I know you wrote the lead story in the *New York Times Magazine* on the moral lives of babies, and that babies as young as a year old seem to have some burgeoning sense of morality. Is there reason going on there?

Bloom: I think I'm happy to call them *sprouts* of morality.

I think that the story of human morality is first what babies start off with, which is extraordinary. But then there's another step. Thomas Jefferson said it was a self-evident truth that all men are created equal, which is ridiculous! Because if this was self-evident, why did it take us so long to come up with it? It's reason that brings us to such realizations. And the idea of a large community of people sitting together, many of whom are not related, who have never met before, sitting quietly and listening and respecting rules, is an accomplishment of reason. You won't find it in the crib.

Paulson: Let me introduce another idea here. Robots. What would it take to create a robot with a sense of self and with some sense of moral accountability?

Flanagan: My students are debating this question actually tomorrow. I didn't know we'd have this question here tonight. . .

Think about the IBM computer named Watson that was in the news in the last few weeks for beating the two *Jeopardy!* champions, or think back to the IBM computer Deep Blue, that beat the chess champion Kasparov. One of the things that almost everyone will want to say about those computer systems is that *there is nothing it is like to be them*. That is, for these computers there is no thrill of victory or agony of defeat; there's no depression; there's no angst; there's no excitement; in fact there's nobody home. You might want to think that this is maybe getting close to what it's like to be a very small infant or what it's like to be at late-stage Alzheimer's—who could judge that? I think it's interesting that in such systems, we're really not prepared to talk about selfhood even though they do have memory. It's easy to program computer systems that have complete autobiographical memory, but there's something about these systems not being conscious that keeps us from saying that there's any real self and that can be held accountable.

Baumeister: Can I add to this? It would be easier, I think, to get a robot for which you might say it has a self than to say it *knows* that it has a self. You could get it to be an autonomous, functioning entity in a system where it can distinguish between what belongs to it and what belongs to others, and has obligations that it fulfills. But how to make consciousness out of inanimate material? Nobody's been able to figure that. So *self-awareness* would be a much harder problem than merely saying a robot has a self based on all the other qualifications.

Bloom: I think part of the solution would have to involve emotions. I've come forth as a big fan of reason, but I think that without a spark of emotion, of feeling, morality doesn't get off the ground. It's an insight from Adam Smith and many others. You have to have some degree of caring for it all to matter. And I don't think you get a notion of self in any interesting sense that we're talking about without some response to pain or pleasure, some goals, some emotions. And that's bad news, because nobody has the foggiest idea how to put that into a machine.

Paulson: Okay. Let me put you all on the spot. Will scientists of the future create this robot with some emotional life, a sense of self, and, by extension, perhaps the ability for moral reasoning?

Flanagan: On the one hand, because I am a naturalist I believe that what there is and all there is natural stuff. Therefore, we are conscious beings that are made of natural stuff. So you might say, then, in principle it may be that robot beings are possible but that we're just not smart enough yet or haven't figured it out how to make it happen. But making it happen might require so much of the right stuff that it would be really making *biological beings* out of something else. I often use this analogy. Think about things that are sticky, like scotch tape is sticky, and superglue is sticky, and velcro is sticky. But you can't make water sticky. You just can't make sticky water; I don't believe that it's possible. Likewise, when people talk about eventually producing a conscious being out of silicon and plastic, it could just be like water not being able to be sticky: there's just no way to weave the water together to make it happen! It's not that any old thing can be made into any old other thing, and it may just be that it requires biological nature.

Bloom: I agree with Owen on both counts. Can physical things have consciousness and selves and emotions? Absolutely: *we* are such things. So, it's at least in principle possible to create a conscious robot if only by creating another human. Can you make this sort of thing out of metal or silicon? I have no idea and I don't think anyone else does.

All I'll add is, here's what I do think we will get very soon if we don't have it already: we will get people who cleverly create machines, robots, or computers that behave in such a way that it is *irresistible* for other people *not* to see them as having emotions and selves. Think of creating a robot dog that is so good at being similar to a dog that if you were to try to dismantle it by pulling off its head, people would scream, "Stop!" This doesn't mean a robot dog is any smarter or more feeling than my toaster. But one might be created that will give us the irresistible impression that it is conscious. And that discovery will change the world in interesting, and possibly disturbing, ways.

Paulson: But it sounds like that robot dog wouldn't have a sense of self, right? I mean, everyone else might *see* that robot sort of as a being, but that's not what we're talking about, right?

Bloom: That's right.

Baumeister: We'll be able to fake it much, much, longer before doing the real thing. It's an interesting exercise when you think about free will and what it would take for us to say that a robot has free will in a legal sense. A robot is a creation of humans, it's a tool made by us, it's an extension of our intellect; whereas to have free will, a robot would have to at least be self-programming. It would have to be able to reevaluate its own programming on an ad hoc basis, to size up the situation. And once a robot can do that we might say it's three quarters of the way to free will.

Paulson: So, I would assume that you think we humans have free will, right?

Baumeister: Well, there is *something* that we have, and certainly we make legal judgments and social judgments. Did the person act of his or her own free will—that is a meaningful question. So, yes, in that sense. Now, *free will* has a lot of different meanings, some of them you might find outlandish and some of them very plausible and likely. If free will means just *making choices*, well, yes, I certainly think we make choices.

Paulson: Owen, you're the philosopher here, do we have free will?

Flanagan: We make choices and decisions but we don't have free will. The basic idea is this—and there is pretty much agreement among philosophers about this: when I act, I act as if I'm a prime mover, myself unmoved—I'm sort of quoting a philosopher named Roger Chism. So what I do is caused by me and no one or nothing causes me to do what I do. Psychologists, neuroscientists, and neurobiologists are always looking at the causes. Just because we don't know the causes that make our preferences or desires what they are doesn't mean that those don't have antecedent causes. So, this would start to make it look as if—

Paulson: But free will is not the absence of antecedent causes.

Flanagan: This is the question about the way free will is defined. Historically, there's a concept of free will that has to do with what I just said. Namely, that I start causal chains and no one or nothing starts them for me. This is called the libertarian conception of free will—which is distinguished from political libertarianism. Many people think it's the dominant view in the culture: that there's room for a something that acts—leverages our lives—that itself isn't part of the causal fabric of the universe. This view is tied up with the traditional view that part of the self is a supernatural thing.

Bloom: There's a tension that this conversation is exhibiting, and it's a tension many of us struggle with, which is, it seems as if we're stuck with two options, neither one of them being very good.

One is to accept a traditional free will: it's separate from causation—and for this you've just got to believe in magic; it's not the brain that does it, it's a magic soul that has weird powers that no one understands. It's just magic and forget about it, which doesn't seem very satisfying.

Another alternative is simply to deny bluntly that we make decisions, choices, and so on. We're just robots in a very unpleasant way. That doesn't seem very good either.

So, it seems what we really want to be are happy compatibilists, accepting the reality of the brain and physics but also believing that we make free choices. This is the view everybody wants to have. The problem is that there may be genuine incompatibility between the sort of free will we wish to have and what we know about how the world actually works.

Paulson: Let me circle back to the questions of morality that we were talking about earlier because I think this relates to free will and how we act in the world. Do you see compassion and altruism as things that can be learned?

Bloom: Clearly they can be shaped. I think if a creature had none of those, it's not clear they could somehow be instilled. Imagine the world's worst psychopath, who simply has no feeling at all in the pain of others. You could train the psychopath to say, "Oh, that bothers me" and act appropriately. But I'm not sure you could train him to *feel* it.

Take the real-world case where we all feel compassion for the child in the well. Society and culture extend and enhance this compassion. Hundreds of years ago many people did not care at all about the fates of minorities and their cultures. Men didn't care at all about women; nobody cared about nonhuman animals; nobody cared about people in faraway lands. Now our compassion extends in all sorts of ways, and we have to credit culture and reason for this change.

Flanagan: Some traditions think that all you need for proper morality is to grow compassion or a sprout of empathy, and I think that is implausible. For example, think of a tradition such as Buddhism, which suggests empathy for others. Yet, there's never been a successful Buddhist state, never. And it looks to me like the real issue lies with the sense of *justice*, as if the sense of political justice is something that people can learn even if they don't have this sense of fairness to start with. What it gets built on exactly, I'm not sure. But it may be a highly cognitive virtue that we come to realize—that there's something right about living in a just society. It may not come naturally to us, though.

Paulson: We are starting to get some questions from the audience here. And one relates exactly to what we were just talking about. The question is, If morality and empathy are so fundamentally tied to self, do sociopaths lack a self?

Bloom: I would think that under any notion of self, sociopaths have a self. They have continued feelings; they can hold a grudge; they can feel pride about something they did. They are not robots. They have some sense of self.

The question suggests that to be moral requires a self. But I'm not sure it's the other way around. I'm not sure that a self gives you morality.

Paulson: So what is it that sociopaths are missing? What's the piece of it there that's lacking?

Bloom: There's no consensus on this. But one view is they're lacking certain fundamental emotional responses. As a result they don't bootstrap their way up into the full moral code we have. They may learn to fake it, to try to get around in society, to pretend to be upset by the pain of others; but they just don't care. They care about other things. They might care about having sex; they might care about having fun. But they don't care about moral things.

Paulson: So is that—getting back to the question of whether morality is ultimately rooted in emotion or in reason—is that an emotional deficit you're talking about?

Bloom: Yes, although again I'll champion reason. But I think emotion is a necessary part of becoming a moral being.

Flanagan: There's a ton of research on psychopaths now, and some people think they have structurally compromised paralimbic systems, so that the relationship between the emotion and reason centers is off. An interesting question concerns the relationship between a sense of one's own self and a sense of other selves. I don't know what the psychological research on it will show, but it looks as if, from the kind of things that psychopaths say—like the Johns Hopkins professor, I think, who was arrested and responds to the accusation, "You killed the flutist in the Baltimore Symphony," by saying, "Doesn't it sound better?"...or think of Anthony Hopkins in *The Silence of the Lambs*—that there's an inability for the psychopaths to in any way feel his/her way into the other person. I think psychologists find that psychopaths don't understand the difference between moral and conventional rules. Consider this example of the difference between certain rules: if the second grade teacher says, "You can wear pajamas to class," and you ask the kids, "Is it okay to wear pajamas in class?" they'll say, "Sure, that's okay." But if you say to the same kids, "Tomorrow you can give noogies [a hard poke or grind with the knuckles] to someone you like," and you ask the kids, "Is it okay to give someone noogies [cause pain]?" Most kids say, "No, you can't do that"—even if the teacher says it's okay. The difference is an understanding of the difference between moral and conventional rules.

Normal kids start to get this distinction, but psychopathic kids only understand that they shouldn't do certain things because the punitive consequences are really great, not because they have any understanding of other selves. That's one of the deficits in a psychopath: a lack of understanding that another self is a human being with a set of emotions, feelings preferences, and desires, and that these things are, in some important sense, worthy of respect.

Bloom: I'll just jump in to say one short thing supporting Owen's argument. There was a heart-wrenching interview with a 15-year-old psychopath who had mugged blind people because it would was easier and he couldn't get identified. He was asked, "Don't you care about the pain and suffering you've caused this woman?" He said, mystified, "Why should I? I'm not her." It is hard to reason with such a person. You can't respond by saying "you *should* care"; he simply doesn't.

Baumeister: But in terms of having a self, Paul is absolutely right. Sociopaths have selves. And I think one thing we haven't gotten to yet is that the self starts with the body. Each body is a unit. The beginnings of self-awareness are recognition of your body. Every living thing draws a line about itself to separate itself from the environment. You asked, "How does the self learn to relate to the world?" But actually the self starts by dividing itself off from the world. Some parts, some sources, of stimulation are always here, others are not. That difference is one basis or beginning of selfhood. Then we elaborate it more, adding a social identity and relationships, and other things. But dividing itself off would be the foundation.

Paulson: Let me go to another question from the audience. "Aren't the parameters by which we bound our moral behavior also imposed by our culture, and therefore do different cultures have different senses of self?"

Bloom: It's been argued cross-culturally by Nisbett and others that cultures differ in the extent to which they are collective, versus individualistic, and this corresponds to some extent with our moral views. Jon Haidt also makes a similar argument. We live right now in New York City at this time in a very individualistic society, which gives rise to an autonomous notion of morality, where people talk a lot about rights and "what you have a right to do," and "don't harm other people." Other societies are more collective.

There are moral notions concerning issue such as tradition and respect. And this corresponds to, for instance, the importance of moral values like patriotism. In an autonomous society you might say, "No, we should just all watch ourselves and focus on our own rights and privileges." In a more collective society you say, "No, the group matters above and beyond the individual."

Baumeister: More and more I think the distinctive purpose of the human brain and mind is to tap in and participate in this new kind of social group that we've created. Culture is a matter of a group with systems of doing things and shared information. This is humankind's biological strategy: this is how we solve the problems of survival and reproduction. We have basic capacities to relate and situate ourselves within whatever group we find ourselves. Each child learns the language that is spoken in its environment; it would have been a lot easier if nature could have programmed a language in, so that we were all born knowing a language, so we would all know the words and meanings and wouldn't have to go through the process of learning. But instead we learn the language the same way we learn the morals and the customs and the systems of where we are. So, individual selves will take different forms, but the basic capacity to learn to function as a self within a group of this sort is what made us human.

Flanagan: This question about natural foundations versus social construction of morality is a very interesting one, and I've been teaching and doing some research on this the last few years. If one goes back ~2,500 years ago and looks at the ancient Greek list of virtues, the Confucian list of virtues, and the Buddhist list of virtues—psychologists write about the magic number of vitues being seven plus or minus two—these ancient lists of virtues have about four or five that are the top virtues. It's interesting, each list is different. On the Western list, let's say due to Aristotle, is *justice*. On the Confucian list is the virtue of *filial piety*. I'm always struck when I'm in Asia and see people light candles for ancestors and place them on a shelf in the home; this leads to a visual representation, an embodied representation, of the way one is connected and has come from those people; and what is sometimes disparagingly call "ancestor worship" is not such a peculiar queer notion at all but a demonstration that someone is part of a lineage of persons he/she values and respects, and this leads to elder respect in their culture. On the Buddhist list you find virtues such as *loving-kindness* and *compassion*, which are not on Aristotle's or the Confucian list. On the Buddhist list you also have what I think is called *mudita*, or *sympathetic joy*. Which is actually happiness for others in zero sum games. That is *not* a virtue in this part of Manhattan (*participants laughing*).

And so you might wonder, to go back to our earlier discussion, is this tapping into something that Paul's kids in New Haven have that he could bring out, or is it actually something that we have to work hard against our nature to inculcate. And if so, that's an interesting thing: to try to leverage ourselves so that we do things that don't come naturally to us, for example, to be happy for people that beat us at a tennis match (i.e., at Wimbledon!).

Paulson: Next question from the audience. "When thinking about autobiographical memory, how does revisionist memory affect the sense of self?"

Baumeister: Well, it serves it. As your interests change you may revise your autobiography. I think Pat Robertson at one point published an autobiography saying "God had told him not to run for political office." Then, later on he ran for president and there was a new edition of his autobiography omitting the divine injunction to keep away from politics (*participants laughing*).

Paulson: I guess the question is, is that just a minor tinkering of revising the narratives we tell about ourselves, or might there be something more fundamental about changing who we are as new memories or new revisionist memories come into play?

Baumeister: The past is supposedly fixed and something that objectively happened. But as it lives in our memory the past can be reinvented in light of current goals and interests. We think we remember our lives, but it's kind of shocking the extent to which we actually don't. Remembering different things will come up if you go through a religious conversion or some other change. You may remember different aspects of your life. I've heard people tell different versions of the same story at different times, and noticed that key details change.

Flanagan: It's an interesting question. An ordinary example of this would be that you see someone you haven't seen in 10 or 15 years, and last time you saw this person he/she was brokenhearted over something, and now if you bring it up he/she says, "I never loved her anyway."

What's that about? It's very common, though. What do you psychologists say about that? Is it kind of a self-serving spin that you put on later, or is it forgetfulness? I mean, it sure seemed like he loved her and was devastated.

Bloom: I'll just say two things. First, there are extreme cases of memory failure. I was once at a dinner with my wife and I was telling a story of something that happened to me, and then later she pointed out that it had happened to her (*participants laughing*)! But my memory was perfect! It was a wonderful story!

The issue of life stories in general is a fascinating topic. Some psychologists argue that each one of us has a sort of narrative we tell—you know, if I said, "Tell me the story of your life." For some of us it would be redemption; for some of us it would be striving and success; for others, it would be being constantly betrayed. There's a small set of stories each of us has, and these stories color everything. If your story is that of striving and succeeding, you'll blot out your failures in memory.

Paulson: That example, to me, raises a question of whether, if you've been married for a long time, you and your spouse merge selves to some degree?

Bloom: It's a question that some philosophers like Andy Clark and others have wrestled with: considering the boundaries of self. A lot of the information I have in my life is in my iPhone. Is that information actually part of my memory? Is it different from the memory inside my head?

Baumeister: You can allocate memory—

Bloom: And so the boundaries get blurred . . .

Baumeister: But the boundaries remain. You still know who forgot whose birthday or who took the trash out and things like that. The selves are kept separate. And, you know, people are surprisingly attentive to things that matter when you have to keep track of important things in a relationship.

Bloom: But I'll push this a bit further. Go back to the issues of the elderly. One of the worst things that can happen to an elderly person is to be removed from his or her house and put into a new place. Suddenly the most capable person in the world can become lost and helpless. This is because at a certain age, memories are triggered by the environment around us. The person says to herself, "I'm not going to get old,"—so certainly an important part of a person's sense of self is in the head. But there is an interesting sense in which the self can then encompass other people and an environment.

Paulson: Next question from the audience. "Why is being moral important for being a self? You explained why self is important for morality, but not the other way around." So the question is, Why is being moral important for being a self?

Flanagan: I'm not sure it is, actually. I mean, the concepts come apart. There are the psychopathic or sociopathic selves. We kind of agree they have selves. And so "I'm not being moral" is important for being a self.

Luckily for us it's typical for members of the species *Homo sapiens* to have the sparks and kind of gregarious social life that orients us toward some kind of *modus vivendi*. There are philosophical tales about the state of nature. Thomas Hobbes, for example, says in Chapter 13 of *Leviathan*, you know, at the beginning when the ice melted at the end of the Pleistocene, we were all aware, in Roy's sense, that we were individuals—this is a Western story—and each of us wanted the stuff in the middle of the room, and we all looked and saw that everyone else wanted the same stuff and we realized that there would be a war of each against each if we acted totally according to our nature. So the idea is that in a situation of scarcity, egoism will come out. But then *reason* makes us shake hands and say, "let's not go there." However, the egoistic impulse is always there.

And this is of course Freud's view in *Civilization and Its Discontents*. That's why we're always discontented, because we can't always get what we want.

But I guess the Rolling Stones said that too. . .

Baumeister: I would give a different answer. We develop self so that we can be part of a particular cultural group with its systems. The earliest concepts or distinctions are between self and others and between good and bad. The purpose of what goes on inside, as the disparate brain sites create a self as a member of a group, is to be good and seen by others as good. That they feel that you're good, which means they like you, and if they don't like you, if nobody likes you, then you will make changes to yourself to try to get along.

Second, you want to be respected, which involves other ways of being good, for example, being seen as competent and as moral. Competent means that you're able to do your job—again, culture is a system where people have different roles and tasks to perform. You want to be respected for being competent at what you do, and as being moral or ethical, so you follow the rules, you treat others well, you reciprocate, you keep your promises and so on.

Thus, one of the basic tasks by which the self secures acceptance in the group, and thereby ensures the survival and reproduction of the body to which its attached, is to become accepted morally by the group, and to do that you have to get the group to see you as good.

Paulson: Next question. "Do you think it is possible that 'self-evident truths' do exist but that a majority of people in a given society or time just are not aware of them or don't incorporate them into their legal systems?"

Baumeister: In that case they wouldn't be very self-evident!

Bloom: Right. All sorts of mathematical truths could be revealed if only we were smart enough. But they aren't self-evident in the sense that they would come to us normally. They have to be reasoned about. And this includes moral truths. Consider the evils of slavery. This might seem perfectly obvious to somebody living now, but anybody with just a hint of historical knowledge or knowledge of how things go on in other parts of the world realizes that our understanding about the evils of slavery is a *contingent fact*. Not self-evident in any interesting sense. And again, I think it has to be the product of something like reason.

Baumeister: And, according to Orlando Patterson and others, slavery originated as a substitute for being killed in war. It was seen as a moral good thing that instead of killing your enemy you allowed him/her to enter your household and serve you. So, at that point it was seen as a positive thing.

Bloom: Right. Slave owners would argue, "Look, isn't it better to own somebody than to rent them?" because you treat something better if you own it.

Baumeister: Or they would say it is better to own a person than to kill him or her.

Paulson: We're almost out of time and so I'm going to ask one last question to each of you, sort of put you on the spot here. Given this whole question about the self, the scientific investigation of the self, if there is one question that you want an answer to about some of these issues that we're talking about, what would it be? Owen?

Flanagan: Boy, that's a tough one. I think I'd be interested in getting to the bottom of the question—or having someone else get to the bottom of the question—of the degree to which selfhood is linguistic. I have very powerful intuitions that it shouldn't be linguistic because I just have trouble thinking that nonhuman mammals don't have a sense of their own lives. But there are a lot of linguists and a lot of philosophers, going back to Descartes, who think that animals don't have inner lives because they're not fully conscious, and that they're not fully conscious because they don't have language. I'd love to know how someone would sort this out and not just leave us with these powerful intuitions.

Paulson: Okay. Paul, your big question?

Bloom: My question is not unrelated to Owen's. It's this: when does the notion of self emerge in human development? Not just the date or the time of development, but what triggers it? I'm tempted to think that it might just grow naturally, and that when a brain reaches a certain degree of complexity a notion of self kicks in and the baby says, as it were, "I think, therefore I am." Perhaps that's mistaken and that something else, maybe language or a certain empathetic relationship with another, is needed to trigger that notion and that's what I wish I knew.

Paulson: Roy?

Baumeister: For me the great puzzle is, again, how is unity of self created? It's experienced as a unity; it's socially meaningful as a unity; and yet we know the brain and mind consist of many separate little places and processes. With none of them in charge, how do they compete? How do all these different parts manage to get themselves together and make a being that can keep its promises and maintain relationships and be the same person over a long period of time as part of society?

Paulson: I think we have the makings of another panel discussion in the future. I want to thank you Roy Baumeister, Owen Flanagan, and Paul Bloom.

Ann. N.Y. Acad. Sci. ISSN 0077-8923

ANNALS OF THE NEW YORK ACADEMY OF SCIENCES
Issue: *Perspectives on the Self*

What do you think you are?

Christina Starmans and Paul Bloom

Department of Psychology, Yale University, New Haven, Connecticut

Address for correspondence: Christina Starmans, Department of Psychology, Yale University, New Haven, CT. christina.starmans@yale.edu

Here, what might be considered a universal belief in dualism is integrated with developmental perspectives on the emergence of identifying the mental and physical components of the self. Additionally, work to "localize" the self is introduced.

"Pig valves." Rabbit tries to hide his revulsion. "Was it terrible? They split your chest open and run your blood through a machine?"
"Piece of cake. You're knocked out cold. What's wrong with running your blood through a machine? What else you think you are, champ?"
A god-made one-of-a-kind with an immortal soul breathed in. A vehicle of grace. A battlefield of good and evil. An apprentice angel.

—John Updike, *Rabbit at Rest*

Humans have long wondered about the nature of our conscious selves. Are we immaterial souls, essentially different from material things such as chairs and trees and our own physical bodies? Or is mental life the by-product of the physical workings of the brain, in much the same way that the capacities of a computer emerge from low-level physical processes? (The usual slogan here is "The mind is what the brain does"). Perhaps the right theory of selves will be based on the interaction between our brains and our environments, especially our social environments. Or, as some skeptical philosophers would argue, Is the very notion of a self (and consciousness, and free will) an illusion, having no place in a mature scientific understanding of the universe?

This mystery is, perhaps fortunately, not the topic of our current paper. We are interested here in a simpler and more tractable question, one that runs parallel to the harder one: How do people naturally think of themselves? What is the commonsense conception of self?

It is possible that there is no answer to this question. Perhaps individuals have radically different conceptions, depending on their religious background, their scientific views, and their philosophical views, explicit or otherwise. It is also possible that most people have no conception of the self at all, simply because they have never given the issue any thought.

We will suggest here, however, that there is evidence for two universal beliefs about the self. These show up in all cultures, emerge spontaneously in development, and are hard to shake, even by those of us who consciously believe that they are mistaken.

The first belief is that the self is nonphysical (see Ref. 1, which is the basis for much of the discussion that follows). In other words, we naturally subscribe to the philosophical doctrine known as *dualism*, most elegantly articulated by Rene Descartes.[2]

Indeed, Descartes' most famous argument for the metaphysical truth of dualism was based on his own intuitions. In 1641, he embarked on his plan of philosophical skepticism. He knew that a lot of what he believed could be false; after all, certain lunatics, "befogged by the black vapors of the bile," believe that they are kings, or that their heads are made out of clay, or that their bodies are glass. Although Descartes refused to entertain the possibility that he himself might be a lunatic, he noted that when he slept, he dreamed the same things that lunatics imagine while they are awake. How could he be certain that he was not now asleep? Or that everything he perceived and knew to be true was a result of the diabolical manipulations of an evil demon? How, then, could he trust *any* of his intuitions?

doi: 10.1111/j.1749-6632.2011.06144.x

Ann. N.Y. Acad. Sci. 1234 (2011) 44–47 © 2011 New York Academy of Sciences.

Descartes concluded that the one thing he could not be deceived about was the fact that he, himself, existed: I think, therefore I am. He added: "So this self, that is to say the soul, through which I am what I am, is entirely separate from the body, and is even more easily known than the latter, so that even if I did not have a body, my soul would continue to be all that it is." Descartes concluded that he was not his body and could exist even if his body did not.

This does seem to make sense in certain discussions. Indeed, the afterlife beliefs expressed in many of the world's religions entail this dualist metaphysics, in which the self is separate from the body and can survive its destruction—we ascend to heaven, descend to hell, occupy another body, or enter a spirit world.

This metaphysical stance might be rooted in an early-emerging distinction between the mental and the physical. The psychologist Henry Wellman proposes that "young children are dualists: knowledgeable of mental states and entities as ontologically different from physical objects and real events" (p. 50).[3] His conclusion is based on a series of influential experiments. In one of them, young children were told stories involving mental entities versus physical entities. For instance, one tale was about one boy who had a cookie and another boy who was *thinking* about a cookie. Even three year olds understand the difference between a real cookie, which can be seen and touched by another person, and an imagined cookie; conversely, an imagined cookie can be mentally transformed by the person who is thinking about it, but a real cookie cannot be transformed.

Now this is not the same as Cartesian dualism; if children believe that these mental states are coextensive with physical states (specifically, brain states), then they are not dualists in the interestingly Cartesian sense.

There is, however, some evidence for a stronger dualism in children. Jean Piaget found that up until the age of about eight, the children he studied had little understanding of what the brain was for. Modern American and European children are more precocious than this. Five year olds know where the brain is, and they know that people and other animals cannot think without a brain. But they do not usually understand that the brain is needed for physical action, such as hopping or brushing your teeth, and they do not think the brain is needed for an activity like pretending to be a kangaroo. And if you tell these children a story in which a child's brain is successfully transplanted into the head of a pig, children agree that the pig would now be as smart as a person, but they think that it would still keep the memories, personality, and identity of the pig. Indeed, the natural conception of the brain by children, even after science education, is that it is a tool we use for certain mental operations. It is a cognitive prosthesis, added to the soul to increase its computing power.

Indeed, we doubt that this understanding is much different from that of many adults. Much excitement is generated by recent studies showing increased neural activity—certain parts of the brain "lighting up" in a scanner—when subjects think about such intimate and important topics as religion, or love, or race. The details of these findings are plainly relevant for theories of the location and time course of different mental activities, but people often seem fascinated by the mere fact that the brain is involved at all. We are astonished because we feel that *we* love and hate and believe in God, not our brains. Such astonishment betrays the dualist intuitions of even the most scientifically literate adults.

The proposal so far is that people think that they are immaterial; we are not identical to our physical bodies. But there is an interesting way in which our commonsense dualism departs from Descartes' dualism. Consider how Descartes summarizes his conclusion: "I realized that I was a substance whose essence, or nature, is nothing but thought, and which, in order to exist, needs no place to exist nor any other material thing." For Descartes, then, the soul "needs no place to exist." But we would suggest that our commonsense assumption is that it does have a place. More specifically, the second commonsense assumption about our selves is that *we exist inside our heads.*

There has been little empirical research exploring our intuitions about the location of the self. To our knowledge, the only study that has directly examined this question was done by a group of Italian researchers, who guided adult participants through a lengthy semistructured interview designed to generate a verbal report of their phenomenological experience of the location of the self.[4] Not only were people perfectly able to make sense of the idea of their self being "located" in a particular spot within the body, they also found it relatively easy to indicate a precise location, and their answers were highly consensual. The vast majority of participants indicated a precise point inside the head, midway behind the eyes, as the location for what the researchers called the "I-that-perceives."

Furthermore, the researchers also recruited eight subjects who were blind—some from birth, and some who became blind later in life. These subjects showed the same pattern of responses as the sighted subjects, suggesting that the experience of the self as being in the head, near the eyes, is not entirely related to vision.

What can we conclude from these findings? It seems that when asked directly, people have no problem asserting that their conscious self is located inside their head. However, it is highly likely that these adult subjects were aware of the common contemporary idea that the brain is responsible for producing all mental states. As such, it is possible that despite being instructed to focus on their phenomenal experiences, these participants were simply using their culturally acquired knowledge of the brain as the source of mental life to guide their responses. The overwhelming concurrence of the blind subjects may actually provide additional evidence that this is the case, as blind subjects obviously have different phenomenal experiences than sighted subjects, but probably have the same cultural knowledge.

We were interested in whether, aside from this cultural knowledge, there is an intuitive sense of the self as being located in a particular spot in the body. One way of getting at these intuitions is to look at preschool-aged children, who have little understanding of the brain as the producer of mental states.[5]

There is some indirect evidence to suggest that, in fact, children at this age do have intuitions about the location of the self. In a 1980 study investigating children's egocentrism, Flavell et al.[6] found that when 2.5- to 4-year-old children had their eyes covered, they judged that an experimenter could not see them. However, they acknowledged that the experimenter could see their arm, despite the fact that the child themselves could not, suggesting that they were capable of taking the experimenter's perspective at least some of the time.

In a related study, McGuigan and Doherty[7] found that 2- and 3-year-old children claimed that they could see a doll if its legs were occluded, but that they could not see the doll if its head was occluded.

The researchers interpreted this curious pattern of results as suggesting that children between the ages of about 2 and 4 may have a different notion than adults of what it means to "see" a person. McGuigan and Doherty[7] suggest that children may misconstrue the concept of "seeing" a human target as an activity that requires mutual engagement.

But there is another interpretation, first proposed in this journal by Neisser.[8] Perhaps children intuitively see the head or the eyes as the "location" of the individual and intend the claim that the experimenter "can't see me" to mean the experimenter "can't see my self." This hypothesis predicts that children would also claim that they could not see another person when that person's eyes were covered. A later study by McGuigan[9] finds exactly this result: 2- and 3-year-old children claimed that when a doll was blindfolded, another doll could not see it.

We are currently conducting three experiments to further investigate the hypothesis that humans have a natural inclination to think of the head, and perhaps the eyes, as the location of the self.[10] These experiments use two different implicit methods to probe the intuitions of 4- and 5-year-old children, as well as undergraduate adults. Both of these methods take advantage of the idea that we understand the referent of proper names such as "Sally" to be the person's self, which may correspond with some, all, or none of her physical body.

In one study we show 4- and 5-year-old children, and a group of Yale undergraduates, a stick-figure drawing of a girl named Sally, and ask them to erase as much of the drawing as possible while still leaving Sally in the picture. Both children and adults tend to erase the elements of Sally's lower body before those of her head. Children are equally likely to leave all the parts of Sally's head in the picture, while adults more often leave Sally's eyes in the picture than her mouth.

In another study, we introduce children and adults to a cartoon character who has a fly positioned on her body in different locations and ask them to judge when the fly was closer to her. Both children and adults judge the fly to be closest to the character when it is near her eyes. In a follow-up experiment, participants make the same judgments about an alien character whose eyes are located on his chest. Again, both adults and children think that the fly closest to the alien's eyes is the closest to the alien. This suggests that both adults and children have a strong sense that the self is located near the eyes, even when the eyes are not located in the head. Together, these three studies provide converging evidence that children and adults intuitively think of a person as being located close to the eyes, and lend support to the idea that we think of the self as occupying a physical location within the body.

The indirect nature of the methods used in these experiments suggest that these judgments do not result from a culturally learned understanding of the role of the brain in producing mental states, or of the location of the self. Participants were asked to make judgments about distance, and about the minimally essential parts of a person when depicted in a drawing. Neither of these questions should, *a priori*, cause participants to consciously reflect on the location of the self, or the nature of the brain, and yet, a robust agreement among participants aligns with findings from previous research to suggest that there is a commonly experienced sense of the self as being located near the eyes.

If participants consider the self to be equally distributed across the body, or if they think of the self as an abstract idea with no spatial location, then they should judge that an object is equally close to the person no matter where on the body it is positioned. However, participants in our study judged a fly to be closer to Mary when it was near her eyes rather than her feet. Thus we suggest that participants were using the name of the person as presented in the questions ("try your best to leave *Sally* in the picture"; "Which fly is closer to *Mary*?") as standing for Sally's/Mary's *self*, and that this self is seen as residing near the eyes.

While several questions yet remain about the precise nature of our intuitions about the location of the self, these studies illuminate a previously unknown intuitive bias to see the self as located near the eyes, and provide a useful method for further investigations into our intuitive conception of the self and its properties and capabilities.

Conflicts of interest

The authors declare no conflicts of interest.

References

1. Bloom, P. 2004. *Descartes' Baby: How the Science of Child Development Explains What Makes Us Human.* Basic Books. New York
2. Descartes, R. 1641/1968. Meditations. In *The Philosophical Works of Descartes*, Vol. 2. E. Haldane & G. Ross, Eds.: Cambridge University Press. Cambridge, MA.
3. Wellman, H. 1990. *The Child's Theory of Mind.* MIT Press. Cambridge, MA.
4. Bertossa, F., M. Besa, R. Ferrari & F. Ferri. 2008. Point zero: a phenomenological inquiry into the seat of consciousness. *Percept. Mot. Skills* **107:** 323–335.
5. Corriveau, K., E. Pasquini & P. Harris. 2005. "If it's in your mind, it's in your knowledge": children's developing anatomy of identity. *Cogn. Dev.* **20:** 321–340.
6. Flavell, J., S. Shipstead & K. Croft. 1980. What young children think you see when their eyes are closed. *Cognition* **4:** 369–387.
7. McGuigan, N. & M. Doherty. 2006. Head and shoulders, knees and toes: Which parts of the body are necessary to be seen? *Brit. J. Dev. Psychol.* **24:** 727–732.
8. Neisser, U. 1997. The roots of self-knowledge: perceiving self, it, and thou. *Ann. N.Y. Acad. Sci.* **818:** 19–33.
9. McGuigan, N. 2009. Does the direction in which a figure is looking influence whether it is visible? *J. Genet. Psychol.* **170:** 227–233.
10. Starmans & Bloom. In preparation.

Ann. N.Y. Acad. Sci. ISSN 0077-8923

ANNALS OF THE NEW YORK ACADEMY OF SCIENCES
Issue: *Perspectives on the Self*

Self and identity: a brief overview of what they are, what they do, and how they work

Roy F. Baumeister

Department of Psychology, Florida State University, Tallahassee, Florida

Address for correspondence: Roy F. Baumeister, Department of Psychology, Florida State University, 1107 Call Street, Tallahassee, FL 32306-4301. baumeister@psy.fsu.edu.

The human self exists at the interface between the animal body and the social system. Solitary beings would hardly need or have selves, but social and cultural systems define identities, and the human animal acquires selfhood in order to function in these systems. Self begins with the physical body, with acting and choosing as a unity, and as a point of reference distinct from others, and it acquires meaningful content by participating in the social system. The self is not contained in the brain, but rather the human brain learns to operate a self.

Keywords: self; culture; social environment

The self is at once an utterly familiar and surprisingly elusive thing. People say *self* dozens if not hundreds of times every day, without problem or misunderstanding, yet furnishing a precise definition is quite difficult. On another level, researchers face similar problems, such as having been unable to match selfhood to a specific location or process in the brain, which has led some researchers to deny the reality of selves[1]—yet apparently without irony these same authors list them*selves* as authors of the published works that claim selves do not exist!

The injunction to "know thyself" is variously attributed to Socrates, Heraclitus, Solon, the Oracle at Delphi, and other ancient Greek sources, but the phrase does beg the questions, What exactly is there to be known? and Why it is important to know? Back in the days of the Greeks, "know thyself" probably did not mean *having an identity crisis* or *undertaking psychoanalysis*, or even *getting in touch with your feelings*, but simply *acquiring a working knowledge of one's capacities* for pragmatic reasons. Quite possibly it meant *know your place and act appropriately*. Many cultures and eras since then recognized that there are obstacles to accurate self-knowledge—perhaps especially in the form of narcissistic self-enhancement—but the idea that gaining self-knowledge is a long, difficult, yet vitally important and rewarding task is a characteristically modern one.[2,3]

In this short article, I undertake to provide an overview of what the human self is, based on what research has been uncovered about its contents and operations, what its specific functions are, and how it comes into being. I shall indicate the importance of avoiding certain common and tempting mistakes, such as equating *self* with *self-concept*, positing multiple selves for each individual, and assuming that the self must be a part of the brain. Contrary to those who suggest there is no such thing as a self or that there are multiple selves for each individual, I hope to persuade the reader that a single self per individual is a scientifically viable reality that is essential for psychological theory to acknowledge.

What self and identity are: toward working definitions

Rather than wrestling with the problem of precise definition, I shall begin with a quick overview of what is needed to understand self and the related concept of identity. Intuitively, self is what one means when one speaks (as most people frequently do) of "myself" and "yourself" and the like. This way of thinking is intended as more than a dodge or cop-out: in an important sense, selfhood partly originates as a point of reference. For example,

doi: 10.1111/j.1749-6632.2011.06224.x

Ann. N.Y. Acad. Sci. 1234 (2011) 48–55 © 2011 New York Academy of Sciences.

ownership entails that items belong to a self, which thus functions as a distinct point, without postulating mental or physical properties of the self. Likewise, grammar and language distinguish selves as distinct points of reference without making strong assumptions about what they contain.

Several years ago, while attempting an integrative summary of the vast research literature on the self, I sought a single conceptual or experiential root to explain the self but was unable to settle on one, needing instead three,[4] which serve not only as a way of organizing the empirical findings but also of understanding human selfhood. The three are as follows.

First, self is a *knowledge structure*, based on the experience of reflexive consciousness. People are capable of self-awareness, and by using their self-awareness they build up extensive stores of information about themselves. The term *self-concept* has been popular for decades but makes some researchers uncomfortable because it implies simplicity and coherence, whereas in empirical fact most people's self-knowledge contains a wide assortment of loosely associated beliefs, only some of which enter awareness at any given time, and some of which may even be contradictory. Self involves not so much a single concept as a large stock (i.e., multiple pieces) of information. The term *knowledge* also raises some objections among philosophically rigorous thinkers who insist that knowledge entails correctness (or truth); many people's beliefs about themselves contain ample quantities of distorted and even false claims. Thus, the stock of self-knowledge is not a strong, coherent unity, though it is united in the point of reference, insofar as all the beliefs refer to the same self (at least for most humans).

Second, self is *an interpersonal being*. Focusing on self-knowledge can create the misleading impression that selfhood arises in isolation, such as through navel-gazing introspection. In practice, selves emerge from interpersonal relations. Selves adapt and modify according to interpersonal processes. As we shall see, many of the self's most important functions involve relating to others. A forever solitary being would not need—much less have—a self, in most senses of the word. Even the self as point of reference is partly defined by contrasting it with others. The example of ownership illustrates this. That is, saying that an item belongs to someone is only meaningful vis-à-vis other people who are not entitled to have and use that item. A creature living a solitary life on a deserted island would not need, or likely even have, any notion of ownership.

Third, self is *an agent with an executive function*. In other words, a self is not simply a being but a doer. A self makes choices, initiates action, exerts control over the environment, and regulates its own responses and inner processes. Without this, the self might know itself and be connected to a social environment, but it could not really *do* anything.

My earlier efforts to synthesize analyses of human *identity* emphasized continuity and differentiation as essential, defining criteria, and these apply to *self-hood* as well.[2,3] Identity means being the same person across time—different from others. Unity and continuity of selfhood are, however, complicated problems, and I shall return to these later. Identity is defined partly by one's place in the social system, including one's roles and attachments.

A person has an identity only in relation to other people and other roles. *Attachments*, by definition, link different people together, and *roles* prescribe how multiple individuals do/should interact (teachers have students, leaders have followers, helpers have recipients, lawyers have clients, physicians have patients, and so forth). Identity exists longer than the biological self, in the sense that a person's name and home might be ready before he or she is born, and a person's remains will still be identified as that person after death (usually labeled in burial). In both cases, the continuity of a persona's identity beyond the boundaries of physical life is created and sustained by the culture in which the person lives. In between birth and death, the identity accumulates its meaning in society in terms of what it contributes or inflicts, thus fleshing out who the person ends up being. All these patterns reflect how individual identity depends on the social group and its systems and information (i.e., its culture).

One final and important point, implicit in the above, is that the self is not really contained inside a brain or body. Rather, while the self depends on processes inside a body/brain, it also depends on relations to the social system and social environment. Hence the self exists at the interface between the physical body and the social system, including culture. The next section will elaborate this.

Culture as context for understanding human selfhood

I assume that the basis for human selfhood, like that of psychological capabilities and tendencies generally, was produced by evolution and therefore selected for its survival and reproductive benefits. Although all species face the common problems of survival and reproduction, they use different strategies to solve them. Humankind has developed a very unusual strategy. The human strategy involves sharing knowledge and information through social groups, developing systems of interlocking roles to cooperate on tasks, and the like. In other words, culture (a new kind of social life) is humankind's biological strategy for dealing with life, up to and including survival and reproduction. The distinctively human traits, such as the capacity for language, can best be understood as adaptations for this new strategy and the social environment it comprises.[5] Insofar as there is any genuine psychological process behind the folk notion of free will, it too would likely be an adaptation of the self for behaving in culture.[6]

Cultures consist of shared information and systems. They depend on communication to develop shared understandings so that information can be accumulated and integrated *collectively*. The last point is important, because in a given culture information is preserved in the group and thereby passed along to new generations. Noncultural animals keep their information (the results of their learning) in their own minds; but cultural animals share what they learn and what they learn outlives them, unlike for other animals.[7]

All mammals use sensory information, but humans rely heavily on symbolic information, including representations of knowledge that is built up across generations. Human self and identity become heavily infused with symbols, including names and numbers and other complex representations of how each particular animal body is linked to a particular cultural system by occupation, status, residence, and membership in various groups and categories. Human selves are also elaborated with narrative histories that not only record events but interpret them symbolically.[8]

Human cultural systems include division of labor, group decision making (e.g., corporate and political systems), exchange of goods and services among specialists (economic systems), and even systems for finding and organizing knowledge (religion, science). Human selves reflect the complex demands and opportunities of this advanced form of social life. Indeed, I think human selfhood evolved precisely for the sake of participation in cultural groups, and so the forms and outcomes of participation go a long way toward defining each self.

What the self is for?

How much self and identity would a solitary creature (even a human) need or have? Above, I suggested that the answer is not very much at all. There would be no roles in systems of complementary roles: A solitary being would not be a teacher, a consultant, an employee, a friend, a cousin, a dentist, because all these roles only exist within structured social groups. *Ownership* matters only in a group, in the sense that something belongs to one person as opposed to being at the disposal of someone else. Self-knowledge for a solitary creature would derive from relatively few sources, insofar as all the usual social and interpersonal ones would be missing. Public self-consciousness—understanding oneself based on how one appears to others—would not happen. A loner could not have a reputation (because that requires a group in which people know each other), and so all self-presentational and other, related concerns would not exist. Moral responsibility would have no basis or meaning. And although self-regulation might be useful for delay of gratification, its more common uses of adapting to the norms and rules of the social group would be absent. It is hard to see a complete loner as even needing a name—let alone a social security number, job title, or street address. At most, a vague sense of bodily unity and perhaps a bit of introspection regarding feelings would serve.

Most humans, however, are not loners and do not live alone. Insofar as belonging to a social group (with culture) is central to the way humans evolved to survive and reproduce, the human self is an important tool "designed" to facilitate social acceptance. Hence the self evolved to secure a *place* within a social group and, thereafter, to maintain and (perhaps) improve one's place in the group. Many selves do this multiple times and with different groups: for example, getting into schools and organizations and building families.

The concepts of good and bad are among the most basic, universally understood, and frequently used concepts—and among the earliest ones children learn.[9] I suspect that that is because they form the basic dimension of evaluation, and evaluation is fundamental to much human thought and feeling, thus to the majority of psychological phenomena. Motivation is the core driving force of psychological phenomena partly because motivations are linked to the basic needs of individuals to obtain things that sustain life. Motivation is the natural basis for evaluating things as either *good* or *bad*, and among humans such evaluative hedonism is augmented by moral systems that define good and bad in more sophisticated ways, that is, in relation to the goals of the group rather than the selfish individual.

The reason I bring up good and bad is that I have contended that the self fundamentally and inherently strives for social acceptance; and being accepted socially is good. Indeed, increases in acceptance and belongingness are central to the majority of emotions that feel good, and decreases in acceptance and belongingness produce the emotions that feel bad.[10] More importantly, for a person to be accepted in a group often depends on being regarded by others as good. It is thus natural for the self to want to be good, or at least to be regarded by others as good. This motivation takes several forms. For example, one way to be regarded as good is to have other people *feel* that you are good: this means that they like you and/or love you.

A second way to be regarded as good is to be respected, which rests on more than feeling: others must *think* you are good. In human culture, there are two main bases for respect: competence and morality.[a] *Liking* is presumably social; the social self is thus partly designed to earn others' liking. This entails getting other people to form a positive emotional attitude toward one's self. Social psychologists recognized early on that a great deal of human behavior is aimed at being liked.[11] Presumably, a self

will alter its patterns of behavior in order to increase the chance of being liked.

Respect may be essentially cultural, as opposed to merely social. Among humans, at least, respect depends on being good in the sense of performing well one's roles in a cultural system; this entails both *competence* and *virtue*. A "good" plumber, lawyer, or merchant, for example, has two characteristics: he/she is competent at performing tasks (the plumber can actually fix the leaking pipe) and is ethical, in the sense of being honest and trustworthy (the plumber charges a fair price, fixes the leak in a manner that will last instead of falling apart a week later, and so forth). The human self finds its place in the social system. Then it becomes regarded as good by performing that role competently and ethically. Its success at doing that earns respect, thereby improving its prospects for survival and reproduction.

Self or other?

A basic question is whether one first learns about oneself or about the selves of others. It is easy to imagine that understanding one would facilitate the other. For example, people may use self-knowledge to guide how they understand others;[12,13] alternatively, they might begin to have self-understanding by copying or adapting what they learn by understanding other selves, such as by social comparison processes.[14,15] Both possibilities seem plausible based on the limited empirical evidence available.

My hypothesis, however, is that understanding oneself is ineluctably intertwined with understanding other selves, and indeed development does not proceed by understanding one and then the other. Rather, the crucial developmental step starts with distinguishing one from the other, so that both are simultaneously understood as different. At a simple level of awareness, there may be no effective distinction between my pleasure and yours but simply an awareness of indistinct pleasure of the world at that moment. Experience is only *mine* or *yours* to the extent that the perceiver can appreciate the distinction. Once the distinction is grasped, there is a rudimentary basis for understanding self and other separately.

Indeed, I propose that a vital impetus motivating the brain to operate a coherent self is the (self) perception that one is known to others. A human

---

[a]To be sure, one may also use the term *respect* for relationships based on fear, in which the weak seemingly respect the strong out of fear of being hurt. This may be common in social animals and probably occurs among humans also. Whether that truly deserves to be called respect is debatable, and I will omit it for the sake of brevity.

being, whether so inclined or not, must pragmatically recognize that it *has* a reputation. That is, other people have a concept of a certain entity, so to speak, with your name on it, and your future outcomes (up to and including survival and reproduction) depend on that socially shared concept. It therefore behooves you to maintain that reputation in good shape, so that others will treat you well. That fact of life is an environmental contingency that is fundamental to the self.

The unity of self

Each person has one self. The only possible and partial exceptions may be people suffering from multiple personality disorders and similar pathologies. But unity is part of the essential nature of selfhood and a defining aspect of identity. The self's pronoun "I" is singular, each person has one name, and the point of reference that defines ownership and perspective is likewise a unit.

The unity of self may seem obvious, but over the years many profound and influential theorists have been tempted to propose that there are multiple selves.[16,17] Popular discourse sometimes expresses similar notions ("I was a very different person back then"), and introductory philosophy classes often pose the *sameness of self* as a paradox, such as based on the notion that all the molecules in someone's physical body are gradually replaced by new ones over time, thereby seemingly removing a physical basis for the unity of self. The notion of *multiple selves*, especially with reference to sameness across time, is sometimes used to express valid and important insights—but, in my view, to express them incorrectly. Discussions of multiple selves call attention to the very real phenomena of division, inconsistency, and alternative possibility within the self. But all your possible selves are possible versions of you. They are not separate, like strangers passing one another in a mall.

People do change; and their sense of self may feel different afterward. Nonetheless, an important element of continuity remains, indeed enforced by the social system. If you borrowed money twenty years ago and never paid it back, you still owe it, and you will not dissuade your creditors by claiming "I was a different person back then." Likewise, if you passed a driver's test or earned a college degree, that credential still works for you regardless of any turnover of the molecules in your body.

Unity comes from both inside and outside. The body itself operates as a unity, even if it does change very gradually over time. One property of life itself is the demarcation of boundaries. Each living thing separates itself from its environment, sustaining life by means of processes that integrate its parts. Most obviously, a person can go from one physical environment to another; and such an action moves the entire person while leaving the environment behind.

Meanwhile, the requirements of social life define each person as a single, unified self. Your possessions belong to your entire self. Moral responsibility for your actions accrues in your entire self, not just in a hand or foot. When you promise, marry, graduate, or vote, these actions reflect your unified social being, not just some part of it. Indeed, it is difficult to imagine how promises, ownership, graduation, or voting would even be possible in a world of multiple or changing selves.

Perhaps the most recent and profound challenge to the unity of selfhood comes from brain research. As noted above, brain researchers have not been able to localize the self to a single part of the brain, causing some to speculate that selves do not exist at all.[1] The latter speculation can perhaps be dismissed as implausible and overstated: not everything that is real exists as a specific place or event inside the brain. But there is an important question associated with the brain research. Although the brain is in a sense the central processing unit of the human body, the brain itself apparently does not have a central processing unit. It is organized rather as a collection of separate, interactive parts that function in parallel and sometimes in concert, but without hierarchical organization, though (to put it crudely) much of the front of the brain is for managing and overriding the back.

Brain researchers, such as cognitive scientists, understand phenomena as parallel systems and subroutines, which makes such scientists uncomfortable with the idea of a single unity of self. In contrast, social psychologists find united selves indispensable. The differences in theoretical outlooks between subdisciplines are highly revealing. Selves are not needed for private, intrapsychic functioning (cognitive neuroscience), but social life would be incoherent without them (social psychology, economics).

Part of the answer, as I have already said, is that the self is not in the brain, but rather exists at the interface of the brain/body and the social system. Yet, that is not a fully satisfactory answer. How do this brain and this mind—-consisting of parallel, distributed processes—-create a self that is experienced as unified and that acts as one when dealing with the social and cultural environment? To put this another way: a core problem of selfhood is to understand how the disparate parts of brain and mind manage to work together to operate a self that has the unity and continuity required by the external social system.

Consciousness may provide an important part of the answer. Multiple theorists have argued that a major intrapsychic function of consciousness is to facilitate communication and coordination across the various sites of brain and mind.[18–21] An incoming sensory stimulus might go straight to one specific brain site, where it activates a behavioral response. When that happens, there is not necessarily any integration of information from dispersed sites, and the action would not necessarily reflect the full, integrated self. Indeed, if challenged by another person, the self might disown responsibility by saying something akin to "I did not mean to do that."

By contrast, an incoming stimulus might cause the mind to engage in a conscious mental simulation of the action before performing it. The mental simulation allows all the various sites in brain and mind to furnish relevant associations, such as alternative possibilities for execution, possible refinements of the plan, and moral and legal considerations. An action performed after such consideration does, in an important sense, reflect the full self. It is a product of potentially all relevant parts of the self, rather than just one.[22]

In short, consciousness performs integrative functions that make the self possible. It is no accident that courts of law assign higher responsibility for premeditated actions than for impulsive ones, because premeditation implies that the full self is responsible. The person had time to understand the consequences and implications and decided to commit the deed regardless of them. This occurred because the person consciously simulated the action in advance, had time to elicit all his or her associations as to possible implications, and went ahead after being able to consider all these implications.

Understanding the processes by which a brain without a central, unified control center operates a social being that is unified (such as a moral agent) remains a challenge. There is no single "decider" that chooses among competing impulses or that even controls which thoughts, generated by the unconscious mind, will enter consciousness. Somehow the competing ones "jostle" and "compete" until one (at a time) emerges as the winner. When a person reflects for a while on a possible action, a series of thoughts can be entertained, of course. The thoughts do proceed in some sequence, as if there were a central decider that looked over the applicant thoughts and arranged which ones enter consciousness and in what sequence. Yet, one must assume there is not a centrally powerful decider. For example, sometimes crucial thoughts "arrive" late, such as when a person is already en route to a place and suddenly realizes it will be necessary to return to fetch a checkbook or passport, or when someone realizes he/she is going the wrong way and must change course. Why do those thoughts often arrive so late? However, when they do, the successful operation of the full self is facilitated even by the late incorporation of thoughts into plans of action.

Continuity across time

Among the most famous studies on consciousness were the ones by Libet, which showed that brain activity begins prior to the precise time of a self-reported conscious decision to initiate an action.[23,24] Some researchers have interpreted those findings as disproving the possibility of free will and as indicating that conscious thoughts have no causal role, because it seems the brain is already carrying out an activity before the conscious mind is made up. Such interpretations have multiple conceptual flaws and mistakes.[25] Nonetheless, there is a broad sense in the research community that the burden of proof shifted. Whereas in the 1970s it was common to assume that all human behavior was guided by conscious thoughts, some expert opinion gradually came to question whether consciousness has any causal impact at all, or any beyond occasional and trivial input into minor actions.[26–29]

Responding to that challenge, a recent literature review sought to compile experimental studies that established conscious causation of behavior, based on employing a research design with random assignment among conditions defined by manipulation of conscious states or events and with overtly behavioral-dependent variables.[30] A wide assortment of findings met those criteria. Libet's findings notwithstanding, consciousness does cause behavior.

The relevance of this work to the present discussion of selfhood is that one of the main patterns, running across multiple sets of research findings, was that consciousness facilitates integration across time. That is, conscious thoughts are highly relevant to supporting continuity. They help current behavior be guided by past events (e.g., by means of accurate and counterfactual replays) and by future possibilities (by means of mental simulation of various options and consequences). They connect present to future (such as by making plans to be enacted later). They integrate future and past (e.g., by ruminating about past events and what might have happened, so as to extract lessons that will be useful in the future).

Thus, again, conscious thought is important for facilitating one of the key aspects of self. I have proposed that continuity across time is central to human selfhood. This is not simply a matter of experiential continuity, such as in knowing that I emptied the garbage or promised to visit Joanne next week, as opposed to merely knowing that *someone* emptied or promised. Remember, experiential continuity, though compelling to individuals, is of minor interest to the social system; instead the requirements of continuity are rooted in what has to be done to make the social system function. Social systems rely on continuity of action, such as people owning up to their past deeds, keeping promises, fulfilling obligations, and performing assigned roles reliably over possibly long periods of time and resuming after interruptions. Human consciousness appears to be an important facilitator of such cross-temporal integration.

Conclusion: selves within systems

My emphasis in this brief article has been to reject the traditional and easy assumption that selves come into being from inside the person and are ultimately contained *inside*, such as inside a brain. Bodies are indeed separate units from other things, and selfhood begins with some understanding of bodily integrity. But the power, extent, and complexity of human selfhood move far beyond the unity of an animal body. Human selfhood is in large part an adaptation to the demands of the social environment, which in the case of humans includes culture. Selves are a vital part of the interface between the physical animal body and the cultural social system.

Culture is a system of interlocking and coordinated roles. One's personal identity is determined by being a node in that system and by being defined by a specific set of tasks that one must perform so that the group can achieve its goals. Culture also depends on shared information, and selves are built from that shared information and indeed become part of it.

Even a point of reference, which I proposed is a basic origin of selfhood, exists only within a system and, essentially, contrasts with other points. The very concept of reference, in other words, entails multiple beings (points), some of which refer to other beings (points) as separate. In my view, the core insight reached at many different times and places—such as by the Buddhist philosopher Nagarjuna and others who denied the reality of self, or at least insist that it was "empty"—is that the self is nothing by itself and only exists in a world of relationships.

Animals have bodies that seek to sustain life and brains that help accomplish this goal. Humans survive and reproduce by participating in elaborate social and cultural groups. Each human self and identity connects one animal body to these cultural groups. Selves are part of the animal/culture interface, and their functions and processes are for enabling bodies to participate in social groups.

Conflicts of interest

The author declares no conflicts of interest.

References

1. Metzinger, T. 2009. *The Ego Tunnel: The Science of the Mind and the Myth of the Self*. Basic Books. New York.
2. Baumeister, R.F. 1986. *Identity: Cultural Change and the Struggle for Self*. Oxford University Press. New York.
3. Baumeister, R.F. 1987. How the self became a problem: a psychological review of historical research. *J. Pers. Soc. Psych.* **52:** 163–176.
4. Baumeister, R.F. 1998. The self. In *Handbook of Social Psychology*. Gilbert, D.T., S.T. Fiske & G. Lindzey, Eds.: 4th ed., 680–740. McGraw-Hill. New York.
5. Baumeister, R.F. 2005. *The cultural animal: Human nature, meaning, and social life*. Oxford University Press. New York.
6. Baumeister, R.F. 2008. Free will in scientific psychology. *Perspectives Psych. Sci.* **3:** 14–19.
7. Tomasello, M. 1999. *The Cultural Origins of Human Cognition*. Harvard University Press. Cambridge, MA.

8. McAdams, D.P. 1985. *Power, Intimacy and the Life Story: Personological Inquiries into Identity*. Guilford Press. New York.

9. Cassirer, E. 1955. *The Philosophy of Symbolic Forms* (Vol. 1: Language). Yale University Press. New Haven. Original work published in 1921.

10. Baumeister, R.F. & M.R. Leary. 1995. The need to belong: Desire for interpersonal attachments as a fundamental human motivation. *Psych. Bull.* **117:** 497–529.

11. Jones, E.E. 1964. *Ingratiation*. Irvington Publishers. New York.

12. Lewicki, P. 1984. Self-schema and social information processing. *J. Pers. Soc. Psych.* **47:** 1177–1190.

13. Lewicki, P. 1983. Self-image bias in person perception. *J. Pers. Soc. Psych.* **45:** 384–393.

14. Festinger, L. 1954. A theory of social comparison processes. *Human Relns.* **7:** 117–140.

15. Wills, T.A. 1981. Downward comparison principles in social psychology. *Psych. Bull.* **90:** 245–271.

16. Bloom, P. 2008. *First Person Plural*. The Atlantic Online, 1–7.

17. Markus, H. & P.S. Nurius. 1986. Possible selves. *Am. Psychol.* **41:** 954–969.

18. Baars, B.J. 1997. *In the Theater of Consciousness: The Workspace of the Mind*. Oxford University Press. New York, NY.

19. Baars, B.J. 2002. The conscious access hypothesis: origins and recent evidence. *Trends Cogn. Sci.* **6:** 47–52.

20. Humphrey, N. 1986. *The Inner Eye*. Faber & Faber. London, UK.

21. Morsella, E. 2005. The function of phenomenal states: Supramodular interaction theory. *Psych. Rev.* **112:** 1000–1021.

22. Baumeister, R.F., & E.J. Masicampo. 2010. Conscious thought is for facilitating social and cultural interactions: How mental simulations serve the animal-culture interface. *Psych. Rev.* **117:** 945–971.

23. Libet, B. 1985. Unconscious cerebral initiative and the role of conscious will in voluntary action. *Behavior. Brain Sci.* **8:** 529–566.

24. Libet, B. 2004. *Mind Time: The Temporal Factor in Consciousness*. Harvard. Cambridge.

25. Mele, A.R. 2009. *Effective Intentions: The Power of Conscious Will*. Oxford. NY.

26. Bargh, J.A. 1997. The automaticity of everyday life. In *The Automaticity of Everyday Life: Advances in Social Cognition* Vol. 10. Wyer, R.S. Jr., Ed.: 1–61. Erlbaum. Mahwah, NJ.

27. Dijksterhuis, A., & L.F. Nordgren. 2006. A theory of unconscious thought. *Perspectives Psychl. Sci.* **1:** 95–109.

28. Wegner, D.M. 2002. *The Illusion of Conscious Will*. MIT. Cambridge.

29. Wilson, T.D. 2002. *Strangers to Ourselves: Discovering the Adaptive Unconscious*. Harvard. Cambridge

30. Baumeister, R.F. *et al.* 2011. Do conscious thoughts cause behavior? *Annu. Rev. Psych.* **62:** 331–361.

Ann. N.Y. Acad. Sci. ISSN 0077-8923

ANNALS OF THE NEW YORK ACADEMY OF SCIENCES

Issue: *Perspectives on the Self*

The pursuit of immortality: From the ego to the soul

Lisa Miller, Kenneth Miller, John Haught, and Nancey Murphy

Moderated by Lisa Miller from *Newsweek*, evolutionary biologist Kenneth Miller (Brown University) and theologians John Haught (Georgetown University) and Nancey Murphy (Fuller Theological Seminary) discuss the questions Are we immortal? Do our souls exist beyond our bodies? and What scientific evidence is there for mystical experience? from a cultural, historical, and scientific perspective. The following is an edited transcript of the discussion that occurred March 23, 2011, 7:00–8:15 PM, at the New York Academy of Sciences in New York City.

L. Miller: I'm going to introduce the esteemed panel. On my left is John Haught, a theologian at Georgetown who's been interested, for a long time, in the intersections of science and religion. He is possibly the only theologian who has ever received the Friend of Darwin award. Next to him is Nancey Murphy, a philosopher of science at Fuller Seminary. She is also interested in the connection between science and theology, and her most recent book is *Did My Neurons Make Me Do It?* To her left is Ken Miller, a cell biologist at Brown. He is the coauthor of the most widely used high school biology textbook in the country, and his most recent book is *Only a Theory: Evolution and the Battle for America's Soul*. So please welcome our panel and let's get started.

This event was advertised as a conversation about immortality and the soul and their connection to the self, broadly. So I just thought I would jump in with the first question, which is, Do we have immortal souls and are they separate entities from our bodies? John, would you like to start?

Haught: I don't like to use the word *soul* without describing the context in which I'm using it. I think Nancey will agree with me that we've had too dualistic an understanding of humans—that, on the one hand, soul is something like a spark that accidentally came from some other world and was imprisoned in matter. That's the old myth of the exiled soul, and a lot of people still have that idea.

But from the point of view of my own studies of science, of evolution and cosmology, I follow the great Jesuit paleontologist Teilhard de Chardin, who suggested that we should think of the soul not so much as a spark that falls accidentally from some other world, but as a flame that breaks out after a long cosmic process of fermentation. The soul is one kind of flame. There are other flames that break out too. There are other kinds of self, or subjectivity, than our own that we recognize. But I like to think of the soul as tied *into* the universe. So when we ask about the soul, at least in the theology that I'm comfortable with, we're asking simultaneously about the destiny of the whole universe.

L. Miller: Nancey, you have a wonderful quiz in your book about what people actually think the soul is and where it resides. And I wonder if you could share with us the quiz and maybe invite the audience.

Murphy: Will I be able to ask them to raise their hands?

doi: 10.1111/j.1749-6632.2011.06183.x

Ann. N.Y. Acad. Sci. 1234 (2011) 56–69 © 2011 New York Academy of Sciences.

L. Miller: Yes, of course!

Murphy: All right. Well, here's the quiz. It's multiple choice. Which of the following comes closest to your view of human nature? Humans are composed of (a) one part, a physical body; (b) two parts: a body and a soul, or a body and a mind; (c) three parts: a body, a soul, and a spirit; or again, (d) one part, but a purely spiritual substance. And I always put in some sort of escape question at the end, like, Who cares? (*Participants laughing.*)

And so [to the audience] I want you to raise your hands. How many of you would choose one part, a body? Two parts: either a body and a mind or a body and a spirit or a body and soul? Quite a few. How about three parts: body, soul and spirit? How about one part: a spiritual substance? And finally, Who cares? (*Participants laughing.*)

I usually go on then to argue that the position of the Bible is actually the last option, who cares? or why are you asking this question?

L. Miller: What do you personally think, Nancey? Do you think that we have a soul? And, if so, is it separate from our body and what is it made of?

Murphy: No. I am either famous, or infamous, depending on where I'm speaking, for denying that there is such a thing as a substantial soul. It is a concept that has a variety of sources in various religions, in various philosophies, but I think that the ancient Hebrews were rather unique in seeing themselves as psychophysical unities with an emphasis on the physicality—for example, they're made out of the dust of the earth. The *dualist conception* of human nature actually entered into Christianity sometime after the life of Christ and it came primarily from the philosophical and religious milieu of the Mediterranean world.

L. Miller: Okay. I have another question I'll put on hold and ask Ken for his idea about what the soul is.

K. Miller: Well, as a scientist, as a biologist, I have a really easy answer, which is that since the soul is generally construed to be immaterial and science deals with matter, I have nothing to say about it (*participants laughing*).

L. Miller: Cop-out, cop-out! (*Participants laughing.*)

K. Miller: But don't worry, I know I can't get away that easily (*participants laughing*).
What I can tell you—what any biologist will likely tell you—is what the soul is not. And what the soul is *certainly* not is the animation that puts the spark in life.

I think the latter is a conception that many people have—that we are animal in nature and the soul somehow is what makes us human, what gives us the capacity for ethics, for making moral judgments, for writing poetry and music. However, as a biologist, I really don't think there's anything that goes on in our minds that is not ultimately explicable in terms of the laws of physics, chemistry, and cell biology of the neuroconnections in the brain. Now, to many people, that means I'm reducing humanity to *mere* chemistry and physics. And my answer to that is, I am. But what I object to is the word mere, because chemistry and physics are far more marvelous than we generally think they are.

Today as we investigate more and more about the physical universe, we come to realize that the sort of dimensions that one thought of 100 years ago in physics—that we can map out space in a Cartesian sense, that we can understand matter and energy as quantities to be measured and simply set aside, that we can say what there is and what there isn't—these conceptions have become obsolete. We talk now about existence as being composed of 10 or 11 dimensions, and about being trapped in a three- or four-dimensional universe ourselves and of being unable to conceive of or communicate with other universes. If you went back 150 years and threw these concepts out to very learned people, the concepts would sound spiritual in nature to those people. They would sound almost mystical. And yet that's the view of the physical universe that science has increasingly converged upon.

L. Miller: Okay. But I'm stuck with being a literal-minded person, and I know that as Christians you all have to believe that some part of yourselves lives forever after you die.
   So what is that thing?

Haught: Well, I'm not opposed, as a theologian, to thinking of the soul as, at least partly, an *animating principle*, which comes from the Latin word *anima*, which means soul. We get the word *animal* from it. I think we need to be more democratic in spreading this animating principle around to other species as well.
   But I can't help recalling the fact that the whole notion of the soul came into our consciousness as human beings long before the scientific revolution, at a time that the great Jewish philosopher Hans Jonas refers to as *panvitalist milieu*, when everything was thought of as alive, not just animals and plants but the whole environment including the stars. Even Aristotle thought there was an animating principle in the stars. So the whole world was full of life. Everything pulsed with life.
   At that time, in that context, the problematic thing was that if everything is so alive, how can anything be dead? So, imagine yourself in a tribal setting, and somebody in the tribe dies and there's an inert corpse lying before you. It doesn't make any sense at all. Life is the norm, death is the unintelligible exception.
   And then something very interesting happened: modern thought separated matter from mind very, very severely. Now, matter is on one side of the divide and mind on the other, which implies that matter is essentially mindless and lifeless too. This realm of matter, which had been divorced from mind, became the metaphysical foundation of modern science and much modern thought. We now live in a world—and science, by discovering vast tracks of lifeless space and time has added to this—where the assumption has been, until recently, that if everything is dead, how can anything be alive? So it's very tempting to turn back to a kind of dualism and say, well, there's this principle (the soul) that's separable from matter because we thought of matter as inanimate.

L. Miller: Right.

Haught: And then we allow at death that the soul goes off to some other world. That idea is very dangerous. But I think there are a lot of interesting things that have happened in contemporary science that now allow us to recover a kind of post-critical or post-scientific panvitalism. For example, the discovery by astrophysics and other sciences that we live in a world, a universe, that has been pregnant with life—or at least with the material to give rise to life—and with mind since the first microsecond of the Big Bang.
   And I'm not drawing any theological consequences directly from that. I just want to point out that science itself is moving away from the idea that matter is essentially lifeless and mindless and the assumption that we live in an essentially mindless and lifeless universe.

L. Miller: Does anyone want to add to this discussion of the substance of the thing that lives forever for a Christian?

K. Miller: Well, I'll take the bait (*participants laughing*).

L. Miller: Okay.

K. Miller: I've been outspoken in my career on evolution as the central organizing principle of biology. And I defended that in public, in the stuff I've written, and I've even defended it in courtrooms, as has John [Haught]. And I see sort of a grand vision—and "grandeur" is the way that Charles Darwin put it—in thinking that we are part of the fabric of life that covers everything on this beautiful planet in which we live I think that's an extraordinary thing. We are part of that fabric of life. Many people would say that we as a species emerged from nature. I prefer to say we emerged *with* nature, because we are part of nature and we are part of the natural world.

So, what to make of the concept of a soul? We are animals, but I don't think we are *just* animals. I think there's something absolutely unique about the human species. There are differences that we have in quality and in kind compared to other organisms, even compared to our most closely related primate siblings on the evolutionary tree. There is something genuinely different about the human species. We're the ones organizing this event. We're the ones building buildings. We're the only ones thinking of great questions. To me, the soul is kind of a spiritual reflection of our individuality as beings.

Any Christian, by definition, has to be a follower of Christ. I regard Christian teachings written down in the Gospels, imperfect as they are, as containing a promise. It's the promise that is captured in the verse where Jesus is in the process of being crucified, with a thief on either side of him, and one thief says something that most of us would say, "Hey, if you're so important, get me down from this cross." And the other one is saying, "Lord, just remember me when you come into your kingdom." And Jesus turns to him and says, "This day you will be with me in paradise."

I don't pretend to know what paradise is, but I do think that's a promise available to each of us. To me, that promise, of being with the Creator at some point, is really what the essence of the soul means.

Murphy: Well, I take quite a different line.

L. Miller: Good.

Murphy: Because I don't believe that there is a soul—there isn't some part of us that is left over after death.

There have actually been two major conceptions of life after death in the West. One is the concept of an immortal soul. But already beginning 200 years before Jesus' day, the notion of bodily resurrection came into Hebrew thinking. And so while Jesus was alive there were three possibilities: one could be a body–soul dualist and pin one's hope on the immortality of the soul; one could have the older Hebraic view that when we're dead we're just dead—we only live on in our progeny; or the third option, one could believe that some strange transformation happens to our bodies after death and we are, in a sense, recreated as imperishable living beings. If you just stop at Jesus' promise on the cross, you haven't gotten to the good part of the story, which comes three days later when Jesus is reported to actually have been resurrected and transformed.

L. Miller: And actually his body is seen in all different kinds of forms by all different kinds of people.

Murphy: Yes. And some people say that the inconsistencies of the descriptions of his resurrected body argue in favor of it being mere fiction. But if we recognize that the language we've got to describe what a person would be like after this transformation into whatever comes next in God's plans, we simply don't have any adequate language for that. And the best way to convey what that is going to be like is by having slightly contrasting stories to indicate that this is not just an apparition, it's not a ghost, it's not a resuscitated corpse, but it's something genuinely new.

And so my understanding of hope for the future—and I share this with Muslims, with a number of Jews, and with a number of Christians—is that we will be resurrected at some future point. But importantly, this concept of resurrection calls for the idea that the entire creation will be transformed. Because while we've got the stories of Jesus actually traipsing around on the surface of the earth after his resurrection, we know, for instance, that earth is going to get fried in four billion years. And so we can't hope to be traipsing around on earth four billion years from now even in resurrected states.

So I believe that there are hints in scripture that say that the entire cosmos is going to be transformed in a similar way that Jesus' body was transformed on Easter.

L. Miller: So nothing we do or don't do actually gets us there? In other words, are we all going to be in this renewed world independent of our actions—whether or not we help old ladies across the street or believe in Jesus Christ or give to charity?

Murphy: Equally competent theologians have various positions on that. One view is called *universalism*—that somehow or another we all get transformed. Another view, which I find very off-putting, is that only some of us get transformed, while others get resurrected but only for punishment—this doesn't fit with any concept of God that I could possibly believe in. And the third possibility is called *annihilationism*, which sounds nasty but it just means that those who really choose to be with God and God's people, and have been looking out for the good all of their lives, will be resurrected, transformed, but others will simply have passed away.

L. Miller: Ken, this is right in your backyard, no? "My neurons made me do it"? If we are all just a mass of neurons and chemicals and things firing in our brains, then what decisions are we making? What choices are we making? Where is morality and how does that connect to our future destiny in some new renewed earth?

K. Miller: Well, you ask a series of interesting questions. As I mentioned, as a scientist, I'm a materialist. What I see is that life simply emerges out of the properties of matter itself and the capacity for life is built directly into matter. We haven't solved, for example, the problem of how life first originated on this planet, but that's not to say we don't know anything—we actually know a great deal. But I don't see any particular reason, either scientific or theological, to doubt that life arose on this planet spontaneously, by ordinary actions of chemicals. What we know about the prebiotic atmosphere and the prebiotic composition of the earth supports that view.

Now, the question ultimately is, How did life emerge from the first primitive cell to cells that dominated this planet for most of its history? It took life about two and a half billion years to figure out how to become multicellular and another seven or eight hundred million years to figure out how to build an animal. From the first animal to us, it actually went pretty quickly, as it turns out.

We are collections of not just the molecules that make us up but of the cells that make up our bodies. And these collections have *emergent properties*. What I mean by emergent properties is that the hundred trillion or so cells that make up a human being, together, are capable of doing things that no one in their right mind would ever look at a single cell and think it was eventually going to do those things. I've never looked at a cell in an electron microscope and said, "you know, that's the cell that can compose a symphony" or "that's a cell that can hit a baseball." Out of these emergent properties comes not just the ability to make moral decisions but the ability to ask questions like, What is the truth and why should we seek it?

Ultimately, I've always been a very strong proponent of the idea of free will. But many people have argued, certainly with me and with others, that if we are material beings and we're governed by ordinary physical law, there can be no such thing as free will simply because we are machines made up of molecules. Anyone who really thinks that passionately wasn't paying attention to physics in the first two decades of the twentieth century, where it became apparent that at its finest level matter has an inherent unpredictability. This fact certainly doesn't explain free will but it definitely brings doubt to the notion that any inherent mechanical system is ultimately predictable. I don't think we are predictable. I think that capacity to make choices is ultimately wired into the circuitry of our brain. And that's how we have become autonomous beings, how we make judgments, and how we decide to seek the truth and make moral decisions.

Haught: I think your question raises the issue of how to talk about these issues in science and theology at all. And how we can make a place for both, or can we make a place for both?

I think if there's going to be a meaningful conversation here, we first of all have to develop a taste for what I call *layered explanation*, that is, explanation made at multiple levels. For example, if you asked me the question, Why are you up there [on stage] thinking right now? one answer is, "well, because my neurons are connecting the synapses and the neurons are firing" and so forth, doing all the things that the neuroscientist talks about. But I could also answer the question by saying that, like the rest of us, "I'm simply trying to understand." At an even deeper level, if I ask the question, Why am I capable of thinking at all? I would have to say partly because the universe is intelligible.

So we have three different answers, and the point I want to make is that they don't contradict each other. In others words, I don't say I'm up here thinking "because I'm trying to understand" *rather than* "because the neurons are moving." Yet, we live in a culture that's influenced by *scientism*, not science, but scientism, which is infatuated with *explanatory monism*—that is, that there's only one valid level of explanation. You see a lot of this in literature from the neurosciences today. Scientism is a commitment to explanatory monism, which is not science but a belief system.

My view is that you're going to have a better chance of catching the rich texture of reality if you adopt as many different levels of approach as possible—which is *explanatory pluralism*. My point is, taking the understanding of the material description of what's going on in the brain as the only explanation leaves a lot of other important descriptions out.

L. Miller: Nancy, did you want to say something?

Murphy: I just wanted to comment to Kenneth that I think the one point you're leaving out of your account is *culture*. I don't think that you have a full-fledged human being unless you consider his/her social nature and the huge extent to which brains are endowed with capacities for thought, for the pursuit of truth and morality, which then, in turn, activates our freedom to choose alternative paths, unless you pay attention to the huge endowment that we get through language and culture.

K. Miller: Yes, I couldn't agree more with you. I think any anthropologist would argue that an important element in becoming human is our extraordinary capacity as a species to form coherent social groups. There are a number of primate species that form social groups, but we excel at it. And you look at the enormous human societies that form and cohere around culture, tradition, and language and all of these things shape our development as individuals. I'm with you one hundred percent, Nancy.

Murphy: Good.

L. Miller: I'm going to change the subject a little bit away from the soul.

When we were waiting for this panel discussion to begin, we were having a really interesting conversation and I want to recreate it here if we can. It deals with the questions of near-death experiences and visions of another world. Are these real experiences or are they, again, sort of neurological firings and chemical accidents? And what does that mean about the way we think the next world looks, because in a Western tradition, all of our visions of what heaven looks like come from these firsthand accounts.

So, Nancey, you were reading a book recently that talked about near-death experiences. Maybe you can tell us a little bit about what it said and then we can go from there.

Murphy: Whenever I lecture on human nature and claim that there is no soul, somebody in the audience asks me, "well, what about out-of-body experiences? How can you have those if there isn't something besides your body that gets out, such as the soul?" So I figured I really needed to study up on the topic. I just reviewed a book by Michael Marsh called *Out-of-Body and Near-Death Experiences: Brain-State Phenomena or Glimpses of Immortality?* and, ironically, found it an overwhelmingly convincing account of how out-of-body experiences are merely experiences caused by assault to a person's brain and therefore don't have theological significance beyond that.

Now that sounds very iconoclastic and disappointing, but the author did his doctoral research in this area and looked at a wide body of literature and the extent to which other authors tended to cherry-pick cases that supported such conclusions as that is a lot of agreement about what happens during out-of-body experiences and that a high percentage of the people have tremendous moral transformations as a result of them. Marsh makes it pretty clear that the evidence gets cherry-picked.

On the other hand, his background is in medicine and he's able to take each of the phenomena that typically gets reported in an out-of-body experience—such as seeming to see your body from a point up at the ceiling—and gives a number of documented cases of that happening where it's known exactly what's going wrong in the brain that's likely causing the experience.

If you put together the incongruity of the reports of the experience with what our mainline theologies would expect them to experience and find a mismatch, and on the other hand, put the experiences together with a huge body of knowledge on neurological causes of identical or similar phenomena, you pretty confidently conclude that these are consequences of brain injury.

L. Miller: Do either one of you want to comment?

Haught: Well, I don't base my hopes for my ultimate destiny on reports like this, but I do want to be as open as I can about them. I don't think that simply from measuring the neurological level of what's going on—whether it's pathological or not—we can thereby jump to a conclusion that these experiences are *not* referential, that they don't point to something real. Such a conclusion would have to be established on some other basis. From a theological point of view, the great traditions of the world, and not just Christian, have always maintained that one of the criteria of authenticity of any sort of reports about transcendent reality is the degree to which it has transformed your life. And that's very, very hard to measure.

One thing that the great teachers—whether Zen masters or Christian spiritual advisors—insist upon is that a process of transformation is required. Grace does not come cheaply, nor does enlightenment come cheaply. You have to go through a process of attaining, as the medievals used to call it, *adaequatio*—you have to become adequate to the particular level of reality before talking about it appropriately. Even Jesus spoke about how the only ones who are going to see God are the pure of heart. And who are the pure of heart? Those who have learned to become like little children.

What I mean is, there's a process involved as a condition for being put in touch with certain dimensions of reality. So that's still a question that would arise after you've seen these reports.

K. Miller: I haven't read Marsh's book; I just heard about it tonight. But I'm going to read it because it sounds very interesting. I've never had a near-death experience—I guess that means I'm lucky. I've actually never talked to anyone personally who has had such experiences. Of course I've read about them as many people have.

But there is one thing about this that Nancey related from the book that I found profoundly unimpressive, and that is that there are certain drugs, anesthetics and others, that can mimic these near-death experiences. Well, that's hardly surprising. I hate to keep using the word "chemical," but the brain is a chemical machine. So everyone right now in this room who sees me and hears me as a result of a chemical reaction that's taking place inside the sensory systems. There are chemicals we can give ourselves that make us happy; there are chemicals that will affect our brain and make us angry or anxious. Does that mean that happiness, anger, and anxiousness are not real? Well, the answer is, of course not.

L. Miller: Right.

K. Miller: So, the very fact that you can simulate some of these experiences by artificial means doesn't necessarily take away their authenticity—again, I don't have a dog in this fight. But I'm skeptical of any near-death experience in the way that any scientist would be skeptical of it. The fact that they can be replicated chemically is hardly surprising, because just about every other sensation and every other perception can be replicated that way as well.

L. Miller: I'm going to switch gears here and talk about the way that the atheist-science community talks about religion in the mainstream press. Because this is a conversation that seems to go on endlessly and to which there is no good answer. I have never seen an atheist and a believer have rhetorical combat and then one of them just put down their sword and go, "You know what, you're right, I don't believe in God," or "Jesus is Lord." The two sides are just so entrenched and they go at it seemingly endlessly.

So, the question is, what do the new atheists—and you know the people and the groups I'm talking about—what do they misunderstand about the way religious thought and theology and Christian philosophy works? What is it they're not getting?

Murphy: I think one of the things they're missing is how self-critical we actually are—how many years does one go to school to become a theologian? Can I list all the major intellectual crises that the Christian tradition has faced over its history? You bet I can. Do I see them as very severe intellectual problems? You bet I do. So those who think that religious people are highly gullible simply haven't learned as much about the history of our own self-criticism as those of us who study Christianity and related religions have.

But the one thing that they [new atheists] are getting partly right and that we really have to listen to is the extent to which religions have been implicated in violence. And so here is, you might say, an intellectual crisis that they are rightly bringing to us. We have to ask ourselves, what have we been doing wrong over the centuries so that the new atheists can be on target, not always, but in many cases, in accusing Christians and other religionists of participating in evil.

L. Miller: John?

Haught: Yes. I think that one level of discussion is the moral issue. The problem is that discussions of the morality of religion are always inconclusive because no matter what side you're on, you're always going to think of a new item to add to your list of reasons for rejecting or accepting the new atheism.

As an academic, my approach has been to ask whether the new atheist books are intellectually respectable. What are the intellectual foundations of the new atheism? And they're very clear, in fact they're self-avowed; they would acknowledge this themselves. The first item is what we call *scientism*, a term that Richard Dawkins, for example, accepts. It's the belief that science is really the only reliable road to gathering truth about the real world. From scientism follows *scientific naturalism*, which is the view that reality consists only of that which is in principle available to scientific experience and ordinary experience.

What the new atheists have added is a third item that you might call *evolutionary naturalism*, and that's the belief that evolutionary biology now provides sufficient reason for why we are moral, intellectual, as well as religious. And so a new atheist might ask, "Now that we have a purely empirical explanation for everything living, why do we need theology?" And my reply is along the lines of what I said earlier. I could go into it in great detail, but my proposal is to think in terms of layers of explanation.

For example, we can account for religion at several levels of explanation. Yes, at one level, we are religious because religion has been adaptive; it's helped our genes get from one generation to the next. But even from a secular point of view, you could also add we are religious because it gives us a sense of community and happiness and so forth. But you could also add, at least in principle, without contradicting the scientific levels of explanation, that we are religious because we have been addressed by the infinite, and that from a theological point of view, the ultimate milieu in which the whole universe evolves, is *infinite being, infinite truth, infinite goodness, infinite love*. This transcendent dimension has always exercised an attractive force or causality on the whole cosmic process.

When humans come along in the cosmic process, we respond consciously to this transcendent environment: "Yes." And that's what soul means to me. I like the word *soul*, for soul is that space within us which responds to the mystery of being, it is the goodness that pervades everything, the unity, the coherence, the meaning, the truth, the beauty in which the universe is bathed. Goodness, truth, and beauty are what philosophers and theologians traditionally call the transcendentals—they all belong together. So, at one level, you can tell the evolutionary story of how morality, mind, religion came along. And I want to push those explanations as far as possible. But you could also say, at another level of explanation, in general that the whole cosmic process is a *response* and not just a series of events pushed from behind by mechanical causation.

K. Miller: While I think many of the new atheists get certain fundamental points wrong, I admire their writing, I admire the challenges they put to religion; I tell every Christian I know, unless you can read *The God Delusion* by Richard Dawkins and come away still a Christian, you haven't confirmed your faith. I mean, it is important to read these challenges. I think Sam Harris carries out a similar service. I was very pleased a couple years ago to debate Christopher Hitchens in print and go back and forth on the issue of whether or not modern science has made the concept of God obsolete, and I think Mr. Hitchens and I had an interesting exchange of views which is still available on the Web, and I enjoyed it a great deal.

To me, the new atheist stereotype of religion and religious faith as being the *enemy* of science, first of all displays a kind of historical ignorance of the roots of Western science, which actually come from the whole tradition of Western monotheism, which basically views man as being separate from nature and therefore gives you a kind of objective platform from which to study that nature. And that objective platform basically is what we try, always imperfectly, to replicate in science.

L. Miller: Theology was a science...

K. Miller: The Western view of the relationship between man and nature leads directly to the emergence of Western science, upon which the new atheists base most of their critique. That's one thing. The other thing that new atheists get wrong is the notion that religious faith is inalterably opposed to science because it involves accepting dogma without evidence, which flies in the face of the kind of humility that I think truly religious people show with respect to great questions.

One consequence these stereotypes lead to, unfortunately, is the personal judgments they can lead us to make. The example we were talking about before we came on stage is that about a year and a half ago President Obama nominated Francis Collins, a very distinguished geneticist, to head the National Institutes of Health. Sam Harris wrote an op-ed piece in the *New York Times* arguing, with some passion, the following line of argument: Francis Collins is a Christian; Christians believe a lot of stupid things; no one who believes a lot of stupid things (namely, Francis Collins) should be allowed to run the National Institutes of Health. And that was the essence of Harris' argument.

The reality is that Francis Collins, although an evangelical Christian, is an extraordinary scientist who brought in the Human Genome Project two years ahead of schedule and about $150 million under budget, and he has proven to be an extraordinarily capable administrator of the National Institutes of Health.

About forty percent of the members of the American Association for the Advancement of Science, the group to which pretty much all practicing scientists belong in the United States, profess some sort of belief in a supreme being. And that in itself argues, simply in terms of demographics, that the notion of religious faith being fundamentally antithetical to the scientific enterprise is simply wrong.

L. Miller: Right. I agree with you about Francis Collins and I also wrote a piece supporting him. I don't think that one's religious belief should be a litmus test for a position as the head of a federal agency.

K. Miller: Not the least of which is because the Constitution says that, right.

L. Miller: That's right. On the other hand, a staggering number of Americans do not believe in evolution right now.

K. Miller: Of course.

L. Miller: Something like fifty percent. And those Americans do not believe in evolution in the name of [because of] their religious faith.

K. Miller: For the most part, that's correct.

L. Miller: So, Ken, Sam Harris' argument that these Americans are waving the flag of ignorance or that they are anti-science because of religion is not wrong. Are you then saying that these American's are not true Christians?

K. Miller: No, I'm not saying that; I'm not saying that at all. I'm saying they're wrong about science.

K. Miller: Uh. huh.

K. Miller: It's absolutely true that the principal obstacle toward acceptance of the theory of evolution—you certainly see this in public education, where there are battles I've been involved in for two decades now—is a kind of fundamentalist belief that the Bible should be read as a book of science and not just a book of spiritual revelation. That's something I think the early Christians— and I put Augustine in this category and a little bit later I put Aquinas in this category—would not have understood. They would not have understood this kind of reading.

The kind of modern fundamentalism that we see that regards the Bible as scientifically authentic had to wait for science to develop. It's not a traditional belief. It's something that took hold in the United States in the 1870s and 1880s. So it's really a recent development. That's why I don't equate it with what I would regard as traditional Western monotheism.

Haught: Yes. If you read the new atheists, Sam Harris' *Letter to a Christian Nation*, for example, you'll find, as also in the case of Hitchens and Dawkins and others, that they share with their creationist and intelligent design adversaries the assumption that somehow if religious literature has anything worth paying attention to it should be that it gives us reliable *scientific* information. And that's exactly the same assumption that creationists have. The creationist looks at Genesis and sees a story of origins and then takes that narrative as the true science.

Of course, the new atheists reject the Bible as true science, but they still asssume that if religious literature is to have any substance to it at all—as Harris puts it—it should be to tell us something about the periodic table, the structure of DNA, the age of the universe and so on. "Since you Christians don't have that information in your Bible," he says, "why are you paying any attention to it." And this goes back to what I said earlier: the fundamental assumption underlying the new atheism is scientism. Scientism says to take nothing on faith. Yet it takes enormous faith to embrace scientism. So there's a kind of intellectual self-subversion going on at the very foundation of all the new atheism that I've read.

Murphy: I have a symbolic way of reflecting that same comment: I put creationists, intelligent design people, and new atheists all on the same bookshelf together.

L. Miller: We have a question from the audience. "If the human species had never evolved a proclivity for a spiritual faith and all humans were always philosophical materialists, would society have developed moral and ethical codes and structures? In other words, is spiritual faith a necessary precondition for morality?"

K. Miller: I'll give a quick answer to that, and that is: atheists are some of the most moral people I know. From my own observations—I have a lot of friends who are nonbelievers—is that someone in a society like ours, which is a predominantly religious society, who can confidently declare themselves a nonbeliever has probably thought longer and harder about issues of religious faith than someone who casually says, "I'm a Christian."

L. Miller: In fact, studies show that atheists are more religiously, biblically, literate than many so-called believers.

K. Miller: Yes, I think that's actually a condition in our society. Because to make that declaration in a predominantly Christian society, you've got to think pretty hard before you're willing to do that. I'm not sure that would apply in some Western European countries where disbelief is more the rule than the exception. So of course a nonbeliever can be moral.

Here's an answer that relates directly to the way the question was worded. Evolution has given us an answer as to why human beings have evolved a moral sense, as to why we cooperate in societies, and even why religious traditions are there. E.O. Wilson wrote about these 35 years ago in his great book *On Human Nature*. And he argued that the religious impulse, which is in all of us, enables us to cohere around myth, symbolism, and ritual. This gave early human societies the ability to do things that helped us survive, raise food, raise children, make war—and all the things that human social groups do. Therefore, a moral sense provides an adaptive advantage.

So in answer to the question, Is spiritual faith a necessary precondition for morality? I think in an evolutionary sense, the answer is no. The religious impulse comes in parcel with the development of an ethical and moral sense. That's not the same thing as saying you've got to be religious to be moral. But in an evolutionary sense, I think these things come as a package.

Haught: I would just add to that that I make a crisper distinction between ethics and religion. I think religion comes into our discourse at what I would call limits of our ordinary experience. For example, when you're doing science, you go along, you try to solve a problem and someday you're driving home and you say, "Why am I doing this? Why am I seeking truth?" Such questions thrust you into another kind of discourse. I'm not saying religion is the only answer to these questions. But with morality the question arises. We spend so much of our public discourse debating whether stem cell research or abortions are moral, but sometimes we need to stand back and ask, "Well, why should we be responsible at all?" That's not an ethical question, that's a question that thrusts one into a worldview-type of discourse. And this leads me back to the issue of materialism.

I have no doubt that the atheists are good, moral people. The question is whether their materialist worldview can provide a satisfactory answer to the limit question "Why should I be responsible at all?" For example, can it provide the basis for the belief in human dignity? Steven Pinker, representing a materialist worldview, wrote an essay recently saying that the whole idea of dignity is foolish. Once we get into the issues of justification for upholding the notions of human dignity, of freedom, of the inviolability of personality, my question is, will a purely materialist worldview provide a rational and complete justification of respect for life and for personality?

That's a long debate which we can't get into, but that's the question that's at issue here.

L. Miller: Yes. Nancey, you were sort of on the brink of answering this question already, so I'm going to ask it. "At what point in human history did souls start going to heaven? Do lobsters have souls that go to heaven?"

K. Miller: I'm a New Englander; I really like boiled lobster. I don't have a clue! (*Participants laughing.*)

L. Miller: The lobster part is more of a throwaway. But the history part, At what point in human history did souls start going to heaven?

K. Miller: The history part also gets that same answer, which is I don't have a clue. And I'll give you an example. A couple years ago, I and a couple other evolutionary biologists were invited to give a lesson on evolutionary biology to a committee of the Conference of Catholic Bishops. There were something like six bishops there and we were lecturing on evolutionary biology. They were all very interested in the topic and most of them had some science background. A couple of them were engineers before they entered the priesthood. They read *Scientific American*—these are all good signs.

And at one point Harold Morowitz, from Yale, and I went out for lunch and sat down with four or five of these fellows and we decided to talk about stem cell research. I was trying to explain what a blastocyst and an inner cell mass are, what the motivation is for this type of research, and why I don't necessarily share their [the bishops'] particular concerns on this issue. And then I said something like, "Well, I know the Church teaches that the soul is infused at the moment of conception," and one of the bishops grabbed my arm and said, "No, we don't." And I said, "What, have I not been paying attention?" He said, "What we teach is that *we don't know*. We don't have any idea."

L. Miller: Bishops do sometimes disagree.

K. Miller: That's right. But this was the consensus. The other three bishops were nodding, "He's right, he's right." The Bishop continued saying, "Since we teach that we don't really know, we decide to err on the side of caution." And that might be a distinction without a difference. But if you think very, very literally about the soul as being this spark that's fired down from heaven, you get into all sorts of difficulties, which is one of the reasons I sort of sidestep this and Nancey rejects the concept all together. Take the example of identical twins.

Identical twins come about by fertilization of a single ovum by a single sperm, which usually divides into what's called an early morula stage, a little cluster of cells, and then something happens and that causes this to split into two. If the soul is infused at the moment of fertilization, what happens when single morula splits? Does the soul split too? (*Participants laughing.*) Does the one soul go with one cluster of cells and another soul have to come down for the other cluster of cells?

These questions get a little goofy, and that's one of the reasons I prefer to say I really don't have the faintest idea. To some people in the audience that probably means the whole idea is a ridiculous concept. To me, it means the question doesn't attend a simple explanation, such as here's when a soul shows up in conception or here's when souls showed up in the evolutionary history of the human species.

L. Miller: Another question: "The Buddhist philosopher Jack Kornfield has said that immortality would be the worst thing that could happen to us. He meant that only by accepting our suffering and impermanence can we find meaning. How would you respond? Would you personally like to be immortal?" That question also seems to contain another question: Does your individual self exist as you in eternity?

Haught: When people tell me that they would be bored with immortality and heaven, I tell them, "Well, use your imagination, surely there are things you could come up with" (*participants laughing*).

For example—anybody who's fallen in love already has as an idea of an ultimate destiny! I don't think I would find that boring or offensive. I would want to be with my beloved eternally if I truly loved them and cared for them; I would want their fulfillment along with mine.

But at the same time, going back to what I said earlier, all these angels-dancing-on-a-pin type of theological discussions are pointless. My view is that if you don't find something inherently transformative about a theological discussion of immortality then it's not worth talking about.

Murphy: I have no desire to be immortal, in the sense of this life lasting on and on. And as I was saying before, if you expect there to be a transformation and for the kingdom of God to be realized in full, we don't have any clear ideas of what it would be like. Jesus used the image of a wedding banquet quite often to refer to the next life. There are a few things I think we can say for sure: it's going to be social, but we can't answer questions such as whether we're actually going to be drinking wine or not.

One of the things that's given me a way of imagining why I would like life to go on and on is that we have conversations like the one we're having here; we start a topic and then branch, branch, and branch. Yet in this life we never have time to go back and finish up everything we wanted to say to one another on those topics. And so the idea that the kingdom of God allows for ongoing conversation with interesting people discussing significant ideas, and we never have to quit at a prescribed hour, that sounds pretty good to me (*participants laughing*).

L. Miller: That's right, that's right.

L. Miller: Belief in reincarnation in America is growing very, very fast, and belief in resurrection is falling. I wrote a story about this because Americans tend to sentimentalize what reincarnation means, "you know, life is really great, we can go to the supermarket and buy whatever we want; we can have dinner with our intelligent friends and drink a lot of wine—reincarnation, to come back and do that again, would be great."

But of course in real Buddhism and Hinduism reincarnation is terrible, and the whole point is to get out of it.

Murphy: Uh huh. Yes.

L. Miller: It's a terrible cycle. But it's so uniquely American to simply want more of what we've got.

Murphy: You might come back as a lobster (*participants laughing*).

L. Miller: Do we have time for one more question? "As a scientist, I value experiment, repeatability, and evidence. Is there any evidence or repeatable experiment demonstrating the existence of what you call a soul?"

K. Miller: Not that I'm aware of.

Haught: Well, I think when you're talking about evidence and religion and science, you have to distinguish between two different kinds of evidence. Science operates according to what you might call *spectator evidence*, the kind of evidence that you can share publicly. It comes rather easily; the same thing happens in Japan as in the United States under the same experimental conditions; it involves the kind of sense of control or objectification of the subject. But when you're talking about soul or any religious idea, you're talking about something I call *transformative evidence*—which is that we really are not in a position to declare whether it's there or not unless we have risked ourselves on a journey of transformation.

The great theologian Paul Tillich says that in religion there's no truth without the *way* to the truth. There's no depth without the *way* to depth. This way involves some sacrifice and perhaps some suffering as well. Only such experience can put people in a position where they are adequate, to use the term I used earlier, to comment on the reality of ideas such as soul or immortality. People who have not gone on a kind of journey are not competent really to talk about these things. So, transformative evidence is not so much that of grasping, but the evidence of *being grasped by*. I know many people can testify to that experience as the most real thing in their lives.

K. Miller: Let me expand on what I just said. When I said that I'm not aware of experimental evidence of souls.

I was reminded of the story of someone looking for their car keys, which they've lost, and they're crawling all around the house and then they tell a friend, "I can't find them." The friend replies, "But you haven't looked over there and over there and in that room," and the person says, "Well, it's dark in there so I can't see anything."

That's what asking for scientific evidence of the soul is like. Because science can see in certain places. Science is the only tool we have to answer questions about the material and physical universe. But by definition, the soul isn't physical and it isn't material, so it's an error of category to expect science to provide evidence for it. Analogously, because there are dark places in the room where you can't see doesn't mean your keys aren't in one of them.

L. Miller: This is a good place to stop because we started with the soul and we ended with the soul.

I want to thank John and Nancey and Ken for being here, and you all for coming out on this terrible night. Thank you.

Ann. N.Y. Acad. Sci. ISSN 0077-8923

ANNALS OF THE NEW YORK ACADEMY OF SCIENCES

Issue: *Perspectives on the Self*

Science, self, and immortality

John F. Haught

Georgetown University, Washington, District of Columbia

Address for correspondence: John F. Haught, Woodstock Theological Center, Box 571137, Georgetown University, Washington, DC 20057-1137. haughtj@georgetown.edu

The following considers the concept of scientific naturalism in relation to life after death and contrasts three alternative perspectives on immortality of the soul, including naturalistic fatalism, otherworldly optimism, and long-suffering hope.

Scientific naturalism—by which I mean the modern belief that "nature is all there is" and that science is the only sure way to understand it—insists that our consciousness will not survive our dying. At death, according to many scientifically minded people, our consciousness vanishes into the void forever. And because ages from now our universe itself will fade into oblivion as a consequence of energy exhaustion, there will be nothing or nobody to remember any trace of the consciousness that has recently emerged in evolution.

Duke University philosopher Owen Flanagan, in his recent book *The Problem of the Soul,* admits that most people believe that the human soul or self will live on after death. But such beliefs, he claims, are irrational, since science can provide no evidence to support them. Not only are they irrational, they are also an annoying impediment to the spread of naturalism, the only acceptable contemporary philosophical option. He explains:

> Most philosophers and scientists in the twenty-first century see their job as making the world safe for a fully naturalistic view of things. The beliefs in nonnatural properties of persons, indeed of any nonnatural things, including—yes—God, stand in the way of understanding our natures truthfully and locating what makes life meaningful in a nonillusory way. . . . Furthermore, historical evidence abounds that sectarian religious beliefs not only lack rational (i.e., scientific) evidence or support, but they are at least partly at the root of terrible human practices—religious wars, terrorism, and torture. Yes, I know the answer; such calamities come at the hands

of fanatics. Even if this is true, the fact is that fanatics are fanatics because they believe that what they believe is indubitably true.[1]

Flanagan and many other contemporary naturalists usually embrace a philosophy that is usually indistinguishable from what used to be called "scientific materialism," the belief that "matter" is all there is. The great American psychologist and philosopher William James said that materialist naturalism implies the following:

> That is the sting of it, that in the vast driftings of the cosmic weather, though many a jeweled shore appears, and many an enchanted cloud-bank floats away, long lingering ere it be dissolved—even as our world now lingers for our joy—yet when these transient products are gone, nothing, absolutely *nothing* remains, to represent those particular qualities, those elements of preciousness which they may have enshrined. Dead and gone are they, gone utterly from the very sphere and room of being. Without an echo; without a memory; without an influence on aught that may come after, to make it care for similar ideals. This utter final wreck and tragedy is of the essence of scientific materialism as at present understood.[2]

Flanagan and other materialists, by the logic of their own commitments, have to agree with James's assessment. Nothing, absolutely nothing—including the whole history of consciousness—will remain when the whole cosmic show is over, if the materialists are correct.

Most people, both in the past and today, however, consider the final extinguishing of consciousness to

doi: 10.1111/j.1749-6632.2011.06131.x

 Ann. N.Y. Acad. Sci. 1234 (2011) 70–75 © 2011 New York Academy of Sciences.

be the greatest of evils. Moreover, no scientific evidence exists to support Flanagan's claims. Flanagan's claims are no less the product of belief than are the ideas of religious people.

I have explored the question of cosmic and personal human destiny in a number of publications, especially the following:

- *Making Sense of Evolution: Darwin, God, and The Drama of Life*[8]
- *God and the New Atheism: A Critical Response to Dawkins, Harris, and Hitchens*[9]
- *Christianity and Science: Toward a Theology of Nature*[10]
- *Is Nature Enough? Meaning and Truth in the Age of Science*[11]
- *Deeper Than Darwin: The Prospect for Religion in the Age of Evolution*[12]
- *God After Darwin: A Theology of Evolution.*[13]

In these works I argue that human rationality is supported, not diminished, by the ageless human hope that consciousness can survive death. I also argue that the contemporary declaration that belief in immortality, or for that matter religion in general, is adaptive in an evolutionary sense says absolutely nothing about its veracity. Darwinian naturalists nowadays allow that the propensity to extend ourselves imaginatively toward endless life beyond the grave originates in the genetic information that sculpts our brains. Our genes trick us into harboring religious illusions. Hope for immortality is just one of countless ways by which strands of DNA work to get passed on to the future. Consequently, since it now appears to many evolutionists that the roots of religion lie more fundamentally in biology than in culture, they no longer expect historical or cultural change alone to eradicate our pious fantasizing. Even during an age of scientific enlightenment, phantasms of deity and immortality will more than likely linger on if for no other reason than that human genes continue to create brains inclined to entertain such "counterintuitive" conceits.[3,4]

So the new Darwinian interpreters of religion are not nearly as hostile or unsympathetic to religious believers as were earlier critics of religion. This is because the new debunkers of religion are aware that they carry around the same genetic make-up as their religiously deluded human predecessors. The new Darwinian enthusiasts, especially evolutionary psychologists, are reluctant to judge religious tendencies too harshly since they realize that without religion's adaptive effectiveness in their own biological history they would not be here today. Even though they are convinced that the idea of immortality is entirely fictitious, some of them are willing to condone this illusion's flourishing among the scientifically ignorant masses of people.

Beyond all reach

Belief in immortality, of course, is inseparable from what we commonly refer to as religion. But just what is religion? Religion, as the philosopher Alfred North Whitehead has put it,

> . . . is the vision of something which stands beyond, behind, and within, the passing flux of immediate things; something which is real, and yet waiting to be realized; something which is a remote possibility, and yet the greatest of present facts; something that gives meaning to all that passes, and yet eludes apprehension; something whose possession is the final good, and yet is beyond all reach; something which is the ultimate ideal, and the hopeless quest.[5]

Whitehead thinks of God as a dimension of everlastingness that saves everything that appears to our limited vision to be merely transitory. Consequently, if we ourselves are not to perish absolutely, then that which "gives meaning to all that passes" must be able in some way to preserve everlastingly our own subjectivity along with the whole history of consciousness in the universe. Why, though, does the final good and the greatest of present facts have to be beyond all reach, including especially the reach of science?

An obvious, but too often overlooked, reason for all of our uncertainty in the realm of religious awareness is that the universe, in which our lives and our religious aspirations are now absorbed, is still in process. Since everything is in process, including our own awareness and knowledge, at least for now, it is not surprising that we can discern only dimly what this universe and the whole history of consciousness are really all about. As in the case of any drama that is still unfolding, in order to understand it, we shall have to wait—perhaps for an indefinite amount of time.

It is difficult, though, for humans to put up for long with the uncertainty of an unfinished cosmos. So we strain in various ways to make it seem complete. For example, as far apart as religious literalists, intelligent design proponents, and evolutionary materialists are in other respects, they share an impatient, perfectionistic, and unreasonable demand for present certainty about all the big human questions. However, their shared impetuosity does not fit a cosmos whose full intelligibility still lies far out of sight. One of the constant temptations of religions is obsession with certitude. But scientific materialists, as James calls those who think all being is reducible to mindless physical stuff, exhibit a similar obsession with certitude. Their assumption that contemporary scientific clarity has finally put us fully in touch with the foundational level of all reality is one of modernity's most problematic but persistent habits. It still undergirds most contemporary attempts to wipe the ambiguities of religion off the map of contemporary intellectual culture, as exemplified in the work of the so-called new atheists. It leads to such claims as the following by Owen Flanagan:

> . . . if you want more [than what naturalism allows], if you wish that your life had prospects for transcendent meaning, for more than the personal satisfaction and contentment you can achieve while you are alive, and more than what you will have contributed to the well-being of the world after you die, then you are still in the grip of illusions. Trust me, you can't get more. But what you can get, if you live well, is enough. Don't be greedy. Enough is enough.[6]

Perhaps if we were sure that our universe had reached the final epoch of its evolution, it might be appropriate to follow Flanagan's demand for an end to all ambiguity. However, as long as the world is still coming into being, we cannot realistically expect at present to make out clearly what it is all about, let alone what lies "beyond, behind, or within" the transient flux of events. It is inevitable, therefore, that what Whitehead calls "the greatest of present facts" will lie beyond all reach. Present uncertainty about our own destinies is tied up with cosmic incompleteness.

True, in the context of a still unfinished universe, the reasons for despair may often seem more persuasive than those that enkindle hope. With the 19th century poet Algernon Charles Swinburne, we might even conclude cheerfully that all perishing is final:

> We thank with brief thanksgiving
> Whatever Gods may be

> That no life lives forever;
> That dead men rise up never;
> That even the weariest river
> Winds somewhere safe to sea.

Perishing: three possible perspectives

Such lyrical resignation, however, is not the usual manner in which people approach death. Human reflection on the fact of perishing has generally taken three distinct forms. Let us call these three options: *naturalistic fatalism, otherworldly optimism,* and *long-suffering hope.* (I abbreviate these sometimes in the following discussion as *fatalism, optimism,* and *hope*).

Fatalism views all loss as permanent and final. As William James points out, scientific materialism is fatalistic in claiming that the totality of cosmic achievements, including consciousness and culture, is destined for complete nothingness. It follows, therefore, that the cosmos is not purposeful but "pointless." Fatalists also agree that human life has no lasting purpose, although it idealizes a kind of tragic heroism that faces up to the finality of death and final cosmic meaninglessness. Scientific materialists may allow for moments of human flourishing, but these are just passing flashes of light. Only an inflexible fatalism squares realistically with the pointless universe uncovered by physics, biology, and astronomy.

Otherworldly optimism, on the other hand, acknowledges the fact of perishing, but its proponents claim to have come in touch with a dimension of permanence beneath or behind the transient flow of events. For the otherworldly optimist the finite physical universe is a kind "veil" that temporarily covers up the timeless splendor of the eternal and the infinite. Time and history by themselves only lead us away from the domain of unchanging perfection. Accordingly, salvation entails finding our way beyond the scientifically accessible world into the world of eternity to which science cannot penetrate. This way of transcending the experience of loss, an approach that has had enormous influence in Western and Eastern cultures alike, claims that the meaning of our lives consists of placing ourselves in the presence of an imperishable realm of being that some major religions refer to as God. Since time itself leads eventually to loss, otherworldly optimism seeks the eternal that lies beneath, behind, or beyond time. This means that the authentic human life is one that struggles mightily to neutralize or vanquish the erosive passage of time.

Otherworldly optimists today are often educated and scientifically informed. However, they generally consider modern science, including evolutionary biology, to be religiously insignificant. Since science is concerned only with the temporal world, its discoveries, including those of evolutionary biology and astrophysics, are inconsequential. The only world that really matters lies beyond the reach of empirical method.

A third way of dealing with perishing is *long-suffering hope*. This approach is fully aware of the world's perpetual perishing, but it rejects the fatalist's unsupportable claim that perishing is final and the cosmic process "pointless." It also criticizes otherworldly optimism, for it believes that the forward and irreversible flow of time, including the whole history of consciousness, moves toward a climactic future fulfillment at the end of time. This perspective is concerned not only with the individual's survival after death, but with the ultimate destiny of the entire universe. Whereas otherworldly optimism is not interested in questions of cosmic destiny, long-suffering hope is inclusive of the entire natural course of events. Its hope does not try to nullify time and history but instead portrays the entire unfolding of the universe as being taken into the all-renewing life of God. There, both the individual's story and the cosmic story are transformed and woven everlastingly into the infinite beauty of God.

Even though from the point of view of physics and cosmology the universe may eventually run down completely, the totality of *events* that make up the cosmic *story* can be preserved everlastingly within the compassion of God. Of course, such an understanding requires that contemporary believers move beyond the image of ultimate reality as a one-planet deity.

What is permanent to the eyes of hope is not an eternal divine stillness lurking outside the flow of time, but a fully incarnate deity who suffers and struggles along with creation and whose compassion ultimately redeems all things from the threat of nothingness—hope then entails both a patient openness to the new and a refusal to relegate the cosmic and historical past to complete oblivion. Hope foresees the future redemption of all events that have faded into the past. As events pass by, they do not vanish into absolute nothingness. Instead the moments of time keep adding up and accumulating. They remain ingredients in each new present and lie open to being retained everlastingly by the God who lies "beyond all reach."

Fatalism, optimism, and hope all have ancient pedigrees. Fatalism's remote exemplar is ancient Greek tragedy and stoicism. Optimism is foreshadowed by Platonic thought with its emphasis on an unchanging ideal world existing above time, untouched by perishing. And hope finds its classic expression in the Abrahamic religious traditions with their sense that time, even in all its transience, is filled with the promise of a fulfillment beyond all reach. Abrahamic hope associates God with the fulfillment of time, history, and creation rather than with an unchanging completeness untouched by the flow of perishable events.

I believe that in addressing the question of immortality and the self we have to choose one or the other of the three options I have just laid out. Is it fatalism, optimism, or hope that best accommodates the discoveries of science? No doubt, in any individual consciousness there may be a hybrid version of the three options. In the history of religion as well, fatalism is often tinged with optimism, optimism laced with hope, and hope contaminated with impatience. Moreover, in any person's lifetime there may be a flitting from one option to another during different periods.

Still, there are logical distinctions that require justification of whatever perspective one decides to take. For example, fatalism on the one hand is logically incompatible with otherworldly optimism and hope on the other. One is logically compelled to decide between a view of things that discerns a saving permanence behind appearances and the claim that all perishing is final. Moreover, if one rejects fatalism, one still has to choose between otherworldly optimism and long-suffering hope. The former aspires to lift the shroud of impermanence abruptly in order to expose the permanence it conceals. The physical world, in this perspective, is an obstacle to salvation. Hope, however, views the stream of perishable events in nature and history as a path to the eternal, not an obstacle in the road. Accordingly, the world of becoming is a stream into which we must insert or own lives and particular callings. For the eternal lies not "beneath" or "behind" the passing flux of immediate things so much as "up ahead," as the goal of the whole universe's temporal passage.[7]

Hope shares with optimism an intuition of the permanence beyond all change; but instead of taking a headlong hurdle out of the flux, it stays patiently with the flow of events that carries the entire universe—and perhaps multiple universes—along with human persons and history, into an always new future. The name of this ever-faithful future—a future that no passage of time can ever erode—is God. God, as the Roman Catholic theologian Karl Rahner puts it, is the absolute future. God is the biblical name for the ultimate source of the future that is always dawning for all of us. It is this reading of the cosmos that I personally defend as more compatible with science than either optimistic impatience or naturalistic pessimism.

Will I survive?

However, the pressing question, at least for many people today, is whether subjective consciousness will live on in some way after our deaths? Is such an expectation a mere fiction devised by our genes for the sake of evolutionary adaptation, or is it (also) possibly true? In response, I would say that the fatalist's claim that human hope for immortality must be an illusion because we now realize that it has an adaptive function is a logical *non sequitur*. Second, this *non sequitur* itself is rooted not in science but in scientific materialism, a belief system that is still the metaphysical framework of much contemporary intellectual life. Third, and finally, I propose that the question of personal, subjective immortality must be treated as part of the larger concern about the ultimate destiny of the universe itself. What follows is a very brief sketch of a position I have defended in much greater detail in the books listed earlier.

(1) The Darwinian naturalist interprets the persistent human hope for immortality as an evolutionary adaptation, or perhaps a by-product of other evolutionary adaptations. On this basis, the fatalist often assumes therefore that the idea of immortality is sheer illusion. But such a judgment makes a logical mistake. It is an instance of what Holmes Rolston III has called the "if functional, therefore untrue" fallacy. It does not follow, logically speaking, that if belief in immortality is adaptive in the biologi-

cal sense, that this belief has no relationship to reality. If the fatalist is correct that hope for immortality is pure fiction, then such a judgment would have to be confirmed independently of whether such a belief is adaptive in the evolutionary sense. There is no reason why the irrepressible human hope for immortality cannot have *both* an evolutionary *and* a theological explanation simultaneously and without contradiction. Perhaps humans have believed in immortality not only because it is biologically adaptive, but also because they are correct in trusting that there is a scientifically inaccessible dimension of everlastingness underlying all that exists. In any case, there is no logical or scientific reason to rule out such a proposition.

(2) The Darwinian naturalist's exclusion of immortality is the consequence of an underlying dogmatic fatalism rather than of actual research. No doubt, during the last 30 years, Darwinian naturalism has been increasingly enshrined as the ultimate and adequate explanation of all manifestations of life, including ethics and religion. There is no reason, however, to conflate good biology with scientific materialism. Such a fusion, after all, is no less objectionable than creationism's confusion of the book of Genesis with a scientific understanding of origins. Much of the alleged scientific opposition to belief in immortality comes not from science but, instead, from the belief system that Whitehead refers to as scientific materialism, and that I refer to in my own work as scientific naturalism.

(3) Nevertheless, evolutionary biology and other sciences have clearly demonstrated that we humans are fully part of the larger story of life and the cosmos. Consequently, the individual's concern for survival of death is inseparable from the question of cosmic destiny. Until now the doctrine of immortality has been formulated apart from concern about the outcome of cosmic process in a larger sense. As long as the material universe was thought of as the soul's temporary habitat, it mattered little what happened to the physical universe itself. Geology, biology, and cosmology, however, have now extended the story of nature back into a nearly unfathomable past, and scientists now think of

the universe as having an indeterminably long future ahead of it before it collapses of energy exhaustion eventually.

Human beings are part of this universe. Our past and future merge with the universe's past and future. Since our conscious subjectivity is intimately woven into the historical unfolding of an entire cosmos, we cannot help but be concerned, and perhaps even disturbed, about the eventual perishing of the cosmos that has given birth to us. So, if the universe as a whole is drifting toward complete extinction, the significance of our own lives is placed in question also. The otherworldly optimists do not care about this prospect since they separate human existence from what is going on in the physical universe. But now that science has so thoroughly immersed human subjectivity in the flow of events that make up the universe, our religious questions about whether we can expect to survive death are inescapably connected to the larger concern about what the cosmos is and where it will end up. Today, theological discussion of personal survival beyond death links up with the question of whether the universe itself has a point and whether it is redeemable.

The intuition that the *whole* of things has a meaning and that it can be saved may be easier to entertain if we learn to think, along with Whitehead, that cosmic process is composed fundamentally of temporal events rather than spatially distributed chunks of stuff. Material bits eventually become atomized and dispersed, whereas events can add up—that is, they may accumulate, one event on top of the preceding. In this way, what happened in the past is still preserved in some way in the present state of things, just as the present will always remain at least faintly ingredient in the cosmic future. Correspondingly we may think of God, not in spatially static terms, but as the repository of all the events that take place in cosmic history. Moreover, if God is the absolute future, we may think of God simultaneously as the infinite source of possibilities by which the world becomes new from moment to moment.

Cosmologically speaking, without God's preservation of the whole series of events that make up the universe the whole would be ultimately pointless. Furthermore, our own brief experience of conscious existence would amount to nothing in the end as well. But if the world's absolute future is indeed also absolute compassion, then there would be sufficient theological basis for our hope as well. Although what I have just said is not capable of being proven by science—and indeed science would be out of place even trying to do so—there is nothing here that stands in contradiction to the very best scientific information available today.

Conflicts of interest

The author declares no conflicts of interest.

References

1. Flanagan, O. 2002. *The Problem of the Soul: Two Visions of Mind and How to Reconcile Them*. 167–168. Basic Books. New York.
2. James, W. 1964. *Pragmatism*. 76. Meridian Books. Cleveland.
3. Boyer, P. 2001. *Religion Explained: The Evolutionary Origins of Religious Thought*. Basic Books. New York.
4. Atran, S. 2002. *In Gods We Trust: The Evolutionary Landscape of Religion*. Oxford University Press. New York.
5. Whitehead, A.N. 1967. *Science and the Modern World*. 191–192. The Free Press. New York.
6. Flanagan. p. 319.
7. Teilhard de Chardin, P. 1999. *The Human Phenomenon*. Translated by Sarah Appleton-Weber. Sussex Academic Press. Portland, Oregon.
8. Haught, J. F. 2010. *Making Sense of Evolution: Darwin, God, and The Drama of Life*. Westminster/John Knox Press. Louisville.
9. Haught, J. F. 2008. *God and the New Atheism: A Critical Response to Dawkins, Harris, and Hitchens*. Westminster/John Knox Press. Louisville.
10. Haught, J. F. 2007. *Christianity and Science: Toward a Theology of Nature*. Orbis Press. Maryknoll.
11. Haught, J. F. 2006. *Is Nature Enough? Meaning and Truth in the Age of Science*. Cambridge University Press. Cambridge.
12. Haught, J. F. 2003. *Deeper Than Darwin: The Prospect for Religion in the Age of Evolution*. Westview Press. Boulder.
13. Haught, J. F. 2000 (Second Edition, 2007). *God After Darwin: A Theology of Evolution*. Westview Press. Boulder.

Ann. N.Y. Acad. Sci. ISSN 0077-8923

Immortality versus resurrection in the Christian tradition

Nancey Murphy

Fuller Theological Seminary, Pasadena, California

Address for correspondence: Nancey Murphy, School of Theology, Fuller Theological Seminary, Pasadena, CA 91182. nmurphy@fuller.edu

For those in contemporary society who believe in an afterlife, there are a number of views available. The most common may be based on belief in an immortal soul. However, the early Christian account was, instead, bodily resurrection. As Christianity moved throughout the Mediterranean world, apologists and theologians adapted their teaching on human nature and the afterlife to Greek and Roman philosophies. By the time of Augustine (d. 430), the doctrines of body–soul dualism and immortality of the soul were firmly entrenched in Christian teaching. The incorporation of the concept of an immortal soul into Christian accounts of life after death produced a hybrid account. The body dies, the soul (at least of those who were to be saved) travels to heaven. At the end of history, there would be a general resurrection, and the souls would be reunited with their bodies, although the bodies would be in a transformed, indestructible state. This hybrid account of life after death went largely uncontested until the twentieth century. In this essay, I describe this history and argue for a return to the early Christian view of humans as a unity, not a duality, and for belief in resurrection of the body as the appropriate expectation for eternal life. This would not only be truer to Christian sources, but, valuable, I believe, in focusing Christian attention on the need to care for the environment.

Keywords: afterlife; ecological ethics; dualism; immortality; physicalism; resurrection

Introduction

One of the strange things about our culture is that different people hold radically different views about what a human being, most basically, is. Are humans nonmaterial beings (minds or souls) temporarily housed in physical bodies, or are they fully physical beings, essentially enmeshed in the natural world? Stranger still, many people are unaware of these radically different views. I believe that this lack of awareness is the cause of a number of strident ethical disagreements. Why do opponents of stem cell research argue that it involves killing our offspring? Because they are *dualists* and believe that the soul is present from the moment of fertilization.

Dualism may be playing a similar role in many Christians' lack of concern for the natural world. While Christian teaching at its best has denied that the human soul is divine, theologians have always been working against the assumption that souls are bits of "Godstuff."[a] This tendency has made it all too easy to identify that which is distinctively human with God, *the* sacred one, and to contrast it with all of nature.

I speak often on the topic of human nature, and because of the remarkable silence on the dualism–physicalism issue, I have had to resort to informal polling of my audiences to find out what they believe. I have found that among laypeople (those who are neither theologians nor scientists), the vast majority are either dualists or trichotomists (that is, they believe humans are composed of body, soul,

---

[a]This is Daniel C. Dennett's parody in *Freedom Evolves*.[1] But see Harold Bloom's argument to the effect that the "the real American religion is and always has been in fact. . . . gnosticism" in *The American Religion: The Emergence of the Post-Christian Nation*.[2]

doi: 10.1111/j.1749-6632.2011.06132.x

and spirit). Now, I need to insert a note on terminology. At the beginning of the modern period, the words *mind* and *soul* could be used nearly interchangeably. It has only been in the past century that they have taken on different connotations. Now, if I am correct that trichotomism and both body–soul and body–mind dualism support a disregard of nature, then it is encouraging that discussions of these issues are now taking place in a variety of spheres, and that the direction of change is very much toward physicalism.

A short history of dualism

When I first began to study the place of dualism in Christian theology I was disappointed to find no comprehensive history of the relevant issues. The relevant terms, *soul*, *immortality*, and *resurrection*, did not even appear in the indexes of major histories of doctrine. I therefore resorted to patching together my own account of the history by consulting reference works from various periods.[b] Here is my account:

First, there is no concept of the soul anything like that of today's Christians in the ancient Hebrew scriptures. This conclusion has been widely agreed upon for half a century. Also there was no clear concept of life after death until close to Jesus' day, at which time some Jews expected bodily resurrection at the end of history and some others had adopted body–soul dualism along with belief in the immortality of the soul. However, New Testament authors largely adhered to the ancient Hebraic concept of the person. Thus, they were closer to contemporary physicalism than contemporary body–soul dualism.[c]

---

[b]This was fifteen years ago while preparing to write the Introduction in Warren S. Brown, Nancey Murphy, and H. Newton Malony, eds., *Whatever Happened to the Soul: Scientific and Theological Portraits of Human Nature*.[3] Since then two particularly helpful books have appeared: Raymond Martin and John Barresi, *The Rise and Fall of Soul and Self: An Intellectual History of Personal Identity*;[4] and Joel B. Green, *Body, Soul, and Human Life: The Nature of Humanity in the Bible*.[5] My own account is published in *Bodies and Souls, or Spirited Bodies?*[6]

[c]The arguments here focus largely on Paul's anthropology. The best source, I believe, is James D.G. Dunn, *The Theology of Paul the Apostle*.[7]

Postbiblical teaching shows the gradual development of the dualism that remained central to Christianity for centuries. Early teaching on the afterlife, such as that of Clement of Rome (ca. 95 CE), focused on immortality as a gift from God, and as a consequence of resurrection of the body, with no mention of a soul. The fate of those who were not saved was simply death. The first mention in Christian teaching of an immortal soul was in the *Epistle to Diognetus* (ca. 130). Athenagoras was the first to link a philosophical conviction of the natural immortality of the soul with a Christian doctrine of the punishment of the wicked and to conclude that the damned would suffer eternally. By the time of Augustine (354-430) the doctrines of body–soul dualism and immortality of the soul were firmly entrenched in Christian teaching.

From Augustine's day until that of Thomas Aquinas (1225-74), Christian dualism was based on Platonic philosophy. Thomas developed a moderate Aristotelian dualism, according to which the soul is the form of the body. This remained an influential account of human nature through the Renaissance and is still the official Roman Catholic position. Meanwhile, during the Reformation, Protestants tended to return to Augustinian theology with its Platonic account of soul and body.

The return of physicalism

Christian scholarship, philosophy, and science have all played a role in the discrediting of dualism and the promotion of a physicalist anthropology. The theory of evolution has had wide-ranging effects on human self-understanding but relates to the dualism/physicalism debate, in that it raised, for some, the question of why humans should be thought to have souls if their close animal kin do not. Others responded with an emphasis on dualism as the very thing that distinguishes us from animals.

The most important scientific impact is taking place right now due to the influences of contemporary neuroscience. It is becoming increasingly obvious that the functions once attributed to the soul or mind are better understood as functions of the brain. These developments in neuroscience, along with the judgment that no account can be given of mind–body interaction, have resulted in a near total rejection of dualism in philosophy of mind. Current debates in philosophy focus on the issue of reductionism—is there any way to argue for the causal efficacy of the mental, or is it really brain functions that determine human thought and behavior. This has been the main focus of my own research for the past ten years, but I will not address it here (see Ref. 8).

While it is fair to say that developments in neuroscience provoked the shift to physicalism for many philosophers, it would be a mistake to say the same for Christian scholars. While the science has brought new attention to the issue, the rejection of dualism began exactly a century ago in biblical studies. In 1911, biblical scholar H. Wheeler Robinson argued that the Hebrew idea of personality is that of an animated body, not that of an incarnated soul.[d] From that point on, a variety of scholarly developments favored the rejection of dualism as the position of the Bible. In the mid-twentieth century, theologians made a sharp distinction between Hebraic and Hellenistic conceptions in Christian teaching and strongly favored the Hebraic. They also argued for the centrality of the resurrection (rather than immortality) in Christian teaching. A decisive contribution was Rudolf Bultmann's claim in his *Theology of the New Testament* that Paul uses the Greek word *soma* ("body") to characterize the human person as a whole.[10] In 1955, Oscar Cullmann gave lectures titled the "Immortality of the Soul or Resurrection of the Dead: The Witness of the New Testament." Here, he contrasted biblical attitudes toward death, along with expectation of bodily resurrection, versus Socrates' attitude, given that he expected his soul would survive the death of his body.[11]

Thus, in the minds of many, the issue was settled in favor of physicalism as original Christian teaching. Of course, this account is incomplete, in that many conservative Protestants either ignored or attempted to refute these developments; the issue is only now receiving the attention among Evangelicals that it received from liberals fifty years ago. Roman Catholics are divided as well: biblical scholars tend to be physicalists, while some theologians subscribe to the Thomist theory. In any event, it is clear from my informal surveys that, however thoroughly dualism has been rejected in the academy, this information did not reach the Christians in the pews.

Now, if it is the case that body–soul dualism is foreign to the Bible, how is it that Christians for centuries could have been so wrong in believing dualism to be biblical teaching? A crucial distinction comes from New Testament scholar James Dunn. Dunn distinguishes what he calls "aspective" and "partitive" accounts of human nature. Greek philosophers tended to be interested in a partitive account: what are the essential parts that make up a human being? By contrast, the biblical authors were interested in an aspective account. Here each "part" stands for the whole person thought of from a certain angle.[e] So, for example, Paul's distinction between spirit and flesh is not the later distinction between soul and body. Paul is concerned with two ways of living: one in conformity with the Spirit of God, and the other in conformity to the old aeon before Christ.

Dunn's insight explains how Christians for hundreds of years could have taken dualism to be scriptural teaching. The Old Testament was translated into Greek (called the Septuagint). Both the Old and New Testaments then contained the Greek terms that in the minds of philosophers referred to constituent parts of humans, and Christians have obligingly read them and translated them in this way for centuries. The clearest instance is the Hebrew word *nephesh,* which was translated as *psyche* in the Septuagint and later translated into English as *soul*. More recent translations use a variety of English words. For example, Genesis 2:7 used to read: ".... The Lord God formed man of the dust of the ground and breathed into his nostrils the breath of life and man became a living soul." Recent translations say that man became a living *being* (NIV), or a living *creature* (REB).

So I conclude that there is no such thing as the biblical view of human nature insofar as we are interested in a partitive account. The biblical authors, especially New Testament authors, wrote within the context of a wide variety of views, probably as diverse as in our own day, but did not take a clear stand on one theory or another. What the New Testament authors do attest is, first, that humans are

---

[d]H. Wheeler Robinson, *The Christian Doctrine of Man.*[9] While Robinson's account of Old Testament teaching struck a blow against dualism, it did not support physicalism directly since Robinson interpreted theories of human nature in terms of his idealist philosophy.

---

[e]Dunn[7] attributes the aspective/partitive account to D. E. H. Whitely, *The Theology of St. Paul.*[12]

psychophysical unities; second, that Christian hope for eternal life is staked on bodily resurrection, not an immortal soul; and, third, that humans are to be understood in terms of their relationships—relationships to the community of believers and especially to God.

Human nature and nature

I claim that physicalism is a theologically, scientifically, and philosophically sound theory of human nature and shall now relate it to the topic of the moral and theological status of nature. There are both scientific and theological features of physicalism that make it particularly relevant. First, scientific knowledge is making it increasingly obvious that humans cannot be understood apart from their embeddedness in nature. Developments in ecology show that we are not only physical beings, but "ecophysical beings."[f] I shall come back to this later.

A second reason that physicalism is important for thinking about nature is theological. I have noted that while immortality is the expectation for life after death associated with dualism, physicalism calls for eternal life conceived in terms of bodily resurrection. When expectation for the resurrection of human bodies is considered within the context of our ecophysicality, the implication is expectation for cosmic transformation, of which the resurrection of Jesus is a foretaste. And if the entire cosmos merits transformation and eternal preservation in the eyes of God, does this not argue for the importance of human care for it?

I have already noted the change in translation of Genesis 2:7; in recent translations the word *soul* has disappeared. What even the new translations fail to show is a literary device in the Hebrew that adds emphasis to the materiality of the human. The term *man* translates to *adham*, which is not a man's name but a generic term for humans. The word for *ground* is *adamah*. So the pun, "*adham* formed from *adamah*" is a literary device that highlights the dusty origin of the species. We can recapture the imagery

in English by describing ourselves as *humans* made from *humus*. This dust of the ground we now know to be, ultimately, star dust.

John Mustol argues more persuasively than I can summarize in this short piece that ecological ethics must become central to Christian ethics. Humans are a part of the Earth's ecology; the laws of ecology are as significant to our survival and that of our biosphere as are the laws of physics. They must be taken into account as we strive to live in closer accord with them. Mustol states:

> As physical organisms, we humans are subject to all the patterns, principles, limits, and "house rules" that govern the existence of all organisms living with us on earth. We must work within the "interdependencies, resources, and constraints" imposed upon us by the biosphere and all its systems. We are bound up within a system of "checks and balances, controls and feedback loops" that we must learn about and obey. Even in this day of our enormous technical and energetic power, these ecological realities circumscribe our existence.[g]

The "house rules" that Mustol lists include the recycling of finite resources, the facts of energy flow and exchange, the webs of food chains, population dynamics, and the concepts of carrying capacity and ecological footprint.

Mustol argues that adequate attention to these facts of life will require a significant change in human consciousness. We have evolved to focus our attention on groups of our own species; to extend that focus to our ecological setting requires a significant shift in self-perception. I have already introduced his term *ecophysical humans*. A second terminological shift is to abandon the distinction between ourselves and "our environment" since it implies that we humans are somehow at the center and that all else is what surrounds us. We are a part of an ecology. As James McClendon wrote, we cannot properly do Christian ethics if we do not take with full seriousness the fact that we are "organic constituents of the crust of the planet."[16]

---

[f] This is John Mustol's term, developed in his "Physical Humans in an Ecological World: The Implications of a Physicalist Anthropology for Christian Ecological Ethics."[13]

[g] Mustol,[13] quoting Sallie McFague, *A New Climate for Theology: God, the World, and Global Warming*[14] and Holmes Rolston, III, "Kenosis in Nature," in *The Work of Love: Creation as Kenosis*.[15]

Ecology and the theology of "last things"

When I speak about physicalist anthropology to dualists, they often hear it as bad news regarding what happens at death, since their hope for the long-term future is based on the survival of an immortal soul. However, I believe that physicalism sounds a more hopeful note. Physicalism and dualism are each bound up with an entire worldview, and I see the worldview of the physicalist as bearing great promise for the future of our species and our planet.

Dualism belongs to a worldview that owes a great deal to Plato. The title of a chapter on Plato's philosophy aptly characterizes his central contribution: "This World Is Not Our Home."[17] Plato invented the notion of a nonmaterial realm transcending this corruptible material world. The dualist view of the person mirrored this cosmic dualism. The human soul, immortal, belongs to the transcendent realm of the Forms (or Ideas), and life in the body is temporary imprisonment. Value resides in the other world; in fact, some of Plato's followers counted matter as essentially evil.

The Western imagination has been formed by a storyline that incorporated into Christian teaching Plato's otherworldliness and the ubiquitous ancient idea of a golden age in the past, followed by a catastrophic fall. Human misery and all natural evil and imperfection are attributed in one way or another to this fall. While original Christian teaching about the end of the story centered on bodily resurrection, later Christians have focused more on a Platonic hope for the soul's escape, to live forever in a transcendent heaven.

It is a mistake, of course, to think that evolutionary biology denies divine creation. However, evolution, along with current theories about the history of the universe as a whole, does contradict this ancient storyline from original perfection to fall to restoration. Science provides the backbone for a new storyline and calls for a strikingly different worldview. The new story sees no perfection in the past, at least not in terms of human values. Rather, the universe immediately after the Big Bang was chaotic and composed of the simplest of ingredients—for some time, composed merely of gasses.

Neither cosmology nor biology alone can provide criteria for assessing progress—for example, biology cannot say why it is better to have mammals and humans than a lot more insects. But from our human point of view, we cannot deny that the evolutionary process involves progress—in particular, progress to the point where its products can raise questions of value! There are long-standing disagreements over the question of whether evolution provides grounds for optimism about the future—that is, it may or may not entail progress in human history. But we can say at least that the new story frees us from the sense of tragic loss associated with the traditional story with its catastrophic fall.

In contrast to the Platonic worldview, as noted above, the sciences tell us that this world is very much our home—not just planet Earth, but the whole universe. The traditional storyline attributed toil, suffering, and death, human and animal alike, to the fall. Much suffering, of course, is the direct result of ubiquitous human sin. But in this new worldview we must raise questions afresh: Why are we so bent on sinning, if not because of a disorder in our souls caused by Adam's defection? And why are there natural disasters, if not because of the fall of the angels?

The old storyline says that animal nature was corrupted by human sin. But here is an interesting twist on the relationship between animals and human morality taken from the writings of ethologist Frans de Waal. He speculates that sharing and other positive social behaviors first evolved among animals that needed to form packs for hunting and killing prey. He says: "If carnivory was indeed the catalyst for the evolution of sharing, it is hard to escape the conclusion that human morality is steeped in animal blood. When we . . . ship food to starving people, or vote for measures that benefit the poor, we follow impulses shaped since the time our ancestors began to cluster around meat possessors."[18] This statement shows an ironic reversal of the traditional view that carnivory only began with human sin.

A deeper explanation for the toils and trials of human and animal life is found in physics. The second law of thermodynamics determines that any system will degrade, decay, or run down, if not supplied with energy from outside. This law is intimately involved in all biological processes—it is part of the fine-tuning that makes life possible—but it is the ultimate cause of hunger, of the need for shelter, for hard work, and, ultimately, death. The surface of the Earth itself needs constant replenishment—so earthquakes and volcanoes are necessary for life.

In sum, the character of the natural world is not the product of sin, human or angelic, but, through a theist's eyes, it can be seen to have been precisely designed for creatures like us. The suffering from nature and within nature can be seen as unwanted yet necessary by-products of the very laws of nature that make our existence possible.

The old storyline from creation to fall to restoration must yield to a storyline from creation, through slow and painful development, from the simple and chaotic to the complex and orderly. But then what? What is the final end of this process? Has it a goal or purpose? Here science provides no help and we must turn specifically to religion. How, in this new context do we retell the story of God's purposes and plans for the universe and the human race?

Here I need to be a bit speculative. I believe we can tell the story of the universe as a story of God creating something that was not God, something at first formless and chaotic—as unlike God as anything could be. God's creative hand has gradually brought order out of chaos and increasing complexity out of lower forms of order. But to what purpose? So that, ultimately, from that which is non-God there would emerge beings who are images of God, mirrors of the divine likeness—dust-creatures with the capacity to know and appreciate the universe (this includes doing science), and especially to know and respond in love to the Creator.

Proper Christian hope for the future is based not on "soul-ectomy," the surgical removal of the immortal soul, but rather on resurrection.[h] We say "resurrection of the body" but we should say resurrection of the person, the whole person. And the only vision of the end of the world that is fully consistent with the hope of resurrection is a transformation of the whole cosmos, a transformation of which the resurrection of Jesus on Easter is first fruits. We can say nothing of what this transformation will be like in scientific terms because all science is based on the way things are in this aeon. But we can say much about that new world in moral terms. This will be a world whose character Isaiah evoked in his prophecy:

> For I am about to create new heavens and a new earth. . . . I am about to create Jerusalem as a joy, and its people as a delight. . . . No more shall the sound of weeping be heard . . . or the cry of distress. They shall build houses and inhabit them; they shall plant vineyards and eat their fruit. . . . Before they call I will answer, while they are not yet speaking I will hear. The wolf and the lamb shall feed together, the lion shall eat straw like the ox. They shall not hurt or destroy on all my holy mountain, says the Lord. (Is. 65:17–25 *passim*.)

Note that this is a social vision—the recreation of city life. It is a vision of unimpaired, immediate relation to God. And it is a vision of a whole new cosmos—new heavens as well as new earth—in which humankind and all of nature will be reconciled.

Jesus' teaching about the world to come focused more narrowly on human reconciliation and reconciliation with God. A common image for the kingdom of God is a wedding feast to which all are invited to share the bridegroom's bounty. But the apostle Paul notes that the whole creation waits in eager longing to be set free from its bondage to decay (Rom. 8:19–23).

If we reject the neoplatonic vision of the "flight of the alone to the Alone," and return to the biblical view of the Rule of God "on earth as it is in heaven," we find a vision of end of time that shows the ultimate value of sociality; that shows that history is meaningful, because past achievements are not left behind but transformed, past sorrows add poignancy to present joy. Finally, it is a vision that shows there to be ultimate value in our care for and harmony with the whole of nature.

Conflicts of interest

The author declares no conflicts of interest.

References

1. Dennett, D.C. 2003. *Freedom Evolves*. Viking. New York.
2. Bloom, H. 1992. *The American Religion: The Emergence of the Post-Christian Nation*. Simon and Schuster. New York.
3. Brown, W.S., N. Murphy & H.N. Malony. 1998. *Whatever Happened to the Soul: Scientific and Theological Portraits of Human Nature*. Fortress. Minneapolis.
4. Martin, R. & J. Barresi. 2006. *The Rise and Fall of Soul and Self: An Intellectual History of Personal Identity*. Columbia University Press. New York.
5. Green, J. B. 2008. *Body, Soul, and Human Life: The Nature of Humanity in the Bible*. Baker Academic. Grand Rapids.
6. Murphy, N. 2002. *Bodies and Souls, or Spirited Bodies?* Cambridge University Press. Cambridge.

---

[h]This is Lutheran theologian Ted Peters's whimsical term.

7. Dunn, J.D.G. 1998. *The Theology of Paul the Apostle*. Eerdmans. Grand Rapids.

8. Murphy, N. & W.S. Brown. 2007. *Did My Neurons Make Me Do It? Philosophical and Neurobiological Perspectives on Moral Responsibility and Free Will*. Oxford University Press. Oxford.

9. Wheeler Robinson, H. 1911. *The Christian Doctrine of Man*. T & T. Clark. Edinburgh.

10. Bultmann, R. 1951. *Theology of the New Testament, Volume 1*. Scribner. New York.

11. Cullmann, O. 1958. *Immortality of the Soul or Resurrection of the Dead?* Epworth Press. London.

12. Whitely, D.E.H. 1964. *The Theology of St. Paul*. Blackwell. Oxford.

13. Mustol, J. 2010. "Physical Humans in an Ecological World: The Implications of a Physicalist Anthropology for Christian Ecological Ethics." ThM thesis. Fuller Theological Seminary.

14. McFague, S. 2008. *A New Climate for Theology: God, the World, and Global Warming*. Fortress. Minneapolis.

15. Polkinghorne, J. 2001. *The Work of Love: Creations as Kenosis*. Eerdmans. Grand Rapids.

16. McClendon, Jr., J.W. 1986. *Ethics: Systematic Theology, Volume 1*. Abingdon. Nashville.

17. Diogenes, A. 1985. *Philosophy for Understanding Theology*. John Knox Press. Atlanta.

18. De Waal, F. 1996. *Good Natured: The Origins of Right and Wrong in Humans and Other Animals*. Harvard University Press. Cambridge.

Ann. N.Y. Acad. Sci. ISSN 0077-8923

ANNALS OF THE NEW YORK ACADEMY OF SCIENCES
Issue: *Perspectives on the Self*

A self-fulfilling prophecy: linking belief to behavior

Esther Sternberg, Simon Critchley, Shaun Gallagher, and V.V. Raman

Moderated by Esther Sternberg (author of *Healing Spaces: The Science of Place and Well-being*), philosopher Simon Critchley (the New School for Social Research), cognitive scientist Shaun Gallagher (University of Central Florida), and physicist V.V. Raman (Rochester Institute of Technology) survey how the self is shaped by interactions with the environment; how free will, responsibility, and other traits emerge; and how character and virtue become targets for constructing the self. The following is an edited transcript of the discussion that occurred April 28, 2011, 7:00–8:15 PM, at the New York Academy of Sciences in New York City.

Sternberg: I want to thank the Nour Foundation and the New York Academy of Sciences for hosting this extremely interesting and provocative series. I think we'll find out that tonight's question is even more interesting and provocative, perhaps the most among all of them. I'm going to introduce first our panelists.

Simon Critchley is chair and professor of philosophy at the New School for Social Research. He's the author of many books, and he is running a philosophy column for the *New York Times* called "The Stone." And he's going to welcome all of you to contribute your comments to his philosophy column on the Web. I think that's quite a groundbreaking thing, for the *New York Times* to have a philosophy column!

Professor V.V. Raman is a philosopher, writer, and physicist; he's the author of many books. His highly acclaimed, most recent book is *Truth and Tension in Science and Religion*. He's a senior fellow at the Metanexus Institute in Philadelphia and the International Society for Science and Religion in Cambridge, in the United Kingdom. He's a meritorious professor of the humanities at Rochester Institute of Technology in Rochester, New York.

And Professor Shaun Gallagher is professor of philosophy and cognitive sciences at the Institute for Simulation and Training at the University of Central Florida. He has many books to his name. He's editor of *The Oxford Handbook of the Self*—so we'll look to him for all the expertise on self—and editor in chief of the journal *Phenomenology and the Cognitive Sciences*.

When I was first given the task to moderate the panel on "A Self-Fulfilling Prophecy: Linking Belief to Behavior," I really wasn't sure what I was going to say. My background is as a rheumatologist-immunologist. I drifted into study of the brain when I discovered that the part of the brain that controls the stress response is important in susceptibility to arthritis. But I hadn't really grappled with the question of self, other than in the context of the immunology concepts of "self antigens" and "foreign antigens." But then I thought of a story to tell you of my own experience with a self-fulfilling prophecy that I actually never understood until I started to think about this panel.

In 1997, my mother was dying of breast cancer and in her last days in the hospital, I was writing an article for *Scientific American* on stress and illness, often sitting by her bedside and editing the article. One day I walked into her room and she had posted by her bed, in large, black, capital letters, a sign on a piece of paper that said, "No self-fulfilling prophecies admitted here!" And I said, "What does this mean?" I didn't understand it.

doi: 10.1111/j.1749-6632.2011.06184.x

She had an Orthodox Hasidic nurse and the two of them would gang up on me and say, "Why are you only writing about stress and illness? Why aren't you writing about belief and wellness?" This was 1997, and I had all kinds of very clever answers as to why belief had nothing to do with wellness, and that we could explain stress and illness in scientific terms but we couldn't explain "belief," what it is and, certainly, how beliefs affect wellness.

But in a very real sense, my mother was right. The *placebo* effect, which is the role of belief and wellness, and the *nocebo* effect, which is the opposite, the belief that something is going to harm you and make you ill, are in fact self-fulfilling prophecies. This comes to the core of such questions as What is a prophecy? What is self? How do expectations affect healing? because the placebo effect is a combination of expectations and learned conditioned responses. It is an example of a self-fulfilling prophecy that affects health. So the question of this panel is, How do those learned self-fulfilling prophecies affect our physical self and, then, behavior?

I'm happy to report that since that time (the 1990s), we do have the neuroscience to understand how beliefs can affect wellness, of how brain stress hormones and nerve chemicals, and positive nerve chemicals and hormones, can actually affect the immune system to help heal.

With that introduction, I want to ask the panelists to comment on whichever aspect of this you feel is within your domain. In the biological sciences, when we think about expectations, they're generally internally generated. And that's how I think about the placebo effect: it's an internally generated self-fulfilling prophecy. But maybe it's not *all* internally generated; maybe it's externally generated? Are there examples in theology of *externally* generated self-fulfilling prophecies? Revelations? Miracle cures? And where in the brain is the self? Is there a spot? Is there a self "place" in the brain, and if so, how does it develop during early development in response to exposures and environmental experiences? When we have expectations of the future, will that shape our thinking, our behaviors, and our health?

I know there are a lot of questions in there, but I think each of you has expertise to address different parts of this. Maybe we can start with you Shaun.

Gallagher: I could start by saying something about the concept of self and the idea that it's internally generated. I think you are pointing to something a little bit different too: that who you are or who you want to be is also very much dependent upon whom you have around you. It's a social phenomenon as well. A lot of us think of the self as just this singular thing—that I, myself, am something distinct from everything and everybody else. But in fact, the self is something social, and what our expectations will be, what we might think of as a self-fulfilling prophecy, might be the product of the people around us and the environment that we are in.

So, the question about where in the brain is the self, I think, is not exactly the right one. I think we should say, "maybe the self isn't in the brain," it's more distributed in terms of our body and the environment that we find ourselves in. The brain is very important, of course, but also, I think, the kind of place we're in—the kind of people that surround us, our interactions with those people—these are very important things as well for understanding what the self is.

Sternberg: It's interesting, because the immune system is like that too. It's very distributed, and it depends on your external environment. Maybe that's the minimal self?

Gallagher: Well, minimal. Certainly at the level of the immune system it's difficult for philosophers to get hold of the idea that there is something like a self there. But in fact there's a differentiation between "self" and "other," a very basic one, built into our biology and the biology of every animal, and this may be the starting point for something like the self.

Critchley: I guess the thing that I wanted to say tonight is *the self is not in the head* (*participants laughing*).

Sternberg: So that's the answer to the question of the location of the self?

Critchley: Kind of. What I mean is that it might *feel* that the self is in the head and the head is obviously important to the way we usually think about the self. And of course what is inside the head is also important, that is, the brain is certainly important. But in my view, while the brain might be a *necessary* condition for understanding the self, it is not a *sufficient* condition for explaining something like the experience of the self. The self is something that's "out there" among things. It's a social phenomenon. It's an interactive phenomenon. It's a relational phenomenon. It's the experience that you were talking about in relation to your mother—what it is to go through suffering of someone you love who's in a perilous situation, or the experience of grief, or experiences that take us outside of ourselves, right? So while formal debates make it sound as if the self is in the head, we often experience the self as "out there".

Sternberg: So in a very real sense, in an importance sense, the self lives on after death. I'm still having a conversation with my mother. . .

Critchley: Yes. Uh huh.

Sternberg: I wrote one of my books to answer my mother's question and I thought I was going to continue to disagree with her. But I found eventually there was enough evidence there to say, "Yes, you were right, Mom."

Critchley: I have no objection to that. The experience of grief for me is an exemplary experience that undoes us. Right? We're undone. We're in pain with grief. We don't know what to do. The love that grief embodies lives on. And other ancestors live on. This is not a substantial idea of immortality but it's an idea of memory living on or surviving, which I think is very important.

Sternberg: V.V. Raman, I want to bring you in to the conversation.

Raman: Well, I don't know about others. I have to tell you, quite frankly, I don't know who I am! . . . (*participants laughing*).

There are several perspectives on self. If I go from the perspective of the Hindu tradition, for example, each of us is simply a fragment of a cosmic self and we are going through the six—during a bracket of eternity, and then what happens to that self is anybody's guess as far as I'm concerned. But from a scientific point of view, it seems to me that all we know is that, evolutionary speaking, humans have acquired extraordinarily complex brains. And in the human brain is some kind of a framework that we call "the mind," which we believe is the source of all our thoughts and, more important, of the conviction that there is what may be called *insularity*—the conviction that we have an *individuality* into which no one can break and from which we cannot escape.

The totality of all our thoughts and feelings and our urges and inhibitions, all these things together go to make what the self is. And I agree completely with the statements that it is as much an overall effect of the neural network in the brain as the interactions with the outside world that constitute the self. Together, all of these things constitute what we call the self. And associated with that concept of self are many other questions, such as the possibility of free will and other things.

Sternberg: So is there a collective self, then? Because all of you have said that the social world is essential, that is, one's interactions with the social world are essential to a narrative of self. You [Shaun Gallager] talk in your writings about a *narrative of self*, and you have different narratives with different individuals. . .

Gallager: Uh. huh.

Sternberg: But is there a collective self?

Raman: From a social, cognitive point of view each self is related and connected to our environment, whether it is on a local level of the family or community, on a national level, or on the level of humanity. And then from the metaphysical perspective of the Hindu world, for example, we are also part of a much larger cosmic self. So, in that sense, there are both narrative and collective conceptions of self.

Gallagher: There are different senses of what you might mean by a "collective self." And one might be the idea of a cosmic self—I'm not sure about that, myself. But I think that to the extent that we are, in some sense, products of our interactions with others, then it's hard to draw a real sharp line between one distinct self and another one. I wouldn't call the self a wholly collective self, but I would say definitely that our cultural life enters into constituting what the self is.

For example, your idea, Esther, that in some sense your mother is still living with you . . . I think that's a very, very good, deep thought. I think that, in some sense, we *are* the significant other people we meet and interact with in our lives; we become something like them. Infants, from the very beginning of their lives, are interacting with others and are shaped by those interactions. But I wouldn't therefore say that the self is *only* a collective self. Instead I would say the self is a social self; it's something bigger than just a single brain in a single body.

Sternberg: So do you think that emotions are the glue of these social selves? If we think of what it is that brings people together—love, hate—do these things create *emergent* selves between different individuals who connect?

Critchley: It can, yes. We are dependent creatures. We are rational, for sure. We may often feel alone and alienated, but most of all we are dependent creatures. We're vulnerable, we're fragile— *The weakest reed in nature*, as Pascal said. The merest thing can destroy us: a virus, a questionable piece of shellfish. And yet we have this idea of ourselves and the self as something fortified and strong, something potent and invulnerable. But that's the wrong picture! At a minimum, we're dependent, rational creatures, and we can forge groups; and we can sometimes get along.

As I said, I'm not sure about the cosmic self. It sounds great, but I'm not sure about it. We can certainly think, as a practical example of what's happening right now, about the way in which grief has become a political factor in what's happening, for example, in North Africa and the Middle East. We have the shocking situation of people being shot at during funerals. Funerals, acts of collective grieving, become occasions for people to be linked together into forms of alliance. There are certain experiences like grief which can be affective or emotional ways of forming a collective, a group. Whether that adds up to something bigger than that, I'm not sure. It's something that we do.

Sternberg: Well, maybe that's the reason for ritual.

Raman: But let me explain, once again, the idea of the cosmic self. I'm not suggesting there is one; I was presenting *one* perspective on the self.

You can approach the self as a philosopher, as a mystic, as a neuroscientist, and there are several perspectives. The Hindu metaphysical approach is the assumption that there is a cosmic self of which we are a part. I think this is a beautiful, poetic idea, which I find very meaningful. But there is no guarantee that you are going to meet any such thing later on. That's an open question. But it's nice to know that there are these different perspectives.

I think that sense of the self we are talking about is related to the brain and its many antics, and I don't know if we can pinpoint them. I'm afraid the ancient injunction of Socrates is still an incomplete project.

Gallagher: Absolutely.

Raman: And I don't think we will ever know all the acceptant terms or definitions of what ultimately the self is.

Gallagher: Can I follow up on that?

Sternberg: I was actually going to ask you to talk about the neurobiology. . .

Gallagher: I think it's very important, what you [Raman] just said about the idea that in order to understand the self, that it takes more than one discipline. If you only study the brain you can work out a comprehensive explanation of how the brain works, but you would get only an incomplete picture of what anything like the self is.

So, while I think you need neuroscience, you also need the other disciplines, and I would say both the sciences and the arts. Because the self is one of those very complex things that require many different disciplines in order to approach and to understand it. One discipline will give you an incomplete picture of what it is and you need to take other approaches that will give you more insight. But in the end I don't know if one can add up the individual pictures to get "a self," because that becomes a very difficult process. . .

Sternberg: So I'm wondering if we're talking about the self as if it's a thing "out there," as if it's a noun. Maybe it's a verb?

Gallagher: Uh huh.

Sternberg: It's constantly changing; it depends upon who we're interacting with, the environment, our memories. Maybe you can review the process of memory as we now understand it, that it constantly changes every time you pull out a memory.

Raman: It's an abstract noun.

Critchley: I think it is more like a verb: *to exist*.

Gallagher: That's nice, a verb. Yes. I think memory and narrative are closely tied to one another. Our memory depends, to some extent, on to what extent we can put it into language. And sometimes we construct our memories as we go and we adjust our memories and so forth. But the narratives that we use in order to remember, to recall who we are, and that help to constitute our personal identity over time, I think are not only our own but they also belong to others. And so, again, you have a social dimension entering in. I think our narratives help to constitute ourselves; we tell different stories to different people. We have different perspectives on who we are and that's just one of the basic facts about the self.

Sternberg: Maybe we can switch a little bit here to *agency*, because somebody mentioned agency earlier. And that speaks to the words "self-fulfilling prophecy." Because prophecy, to me, implies a theological aspect to it, *a prophet*—something that's going to happen in the future. You can either be a prophet for your own future, and that's internally driven, or it could be externally driven. And that speaks to agency: how much of where you're going or what you think about yourself comes from the external versus the internal, and how much control we really have over ourselves?

Raman: Yes. Contrary to previous beliefs on self, before the emergence of modern science, most religious traditions believed that with each of us is associated with an abstract entity called "the self," which had several properties, one of which was the capacity to *choose* between right and wrong. And there is a reason for this development, it seems to me.

But all that we can say is that this doesn't seem to be the case. We make hundreds of decisions in the course of our lives, and they are governed by many other factors over which we have either conscious or no control. And I was going to begin by thanking all of you for being here—probably most of you, all of you, have come here of your own free will, I think (*participants laughing*). But "free will" is a difficult concept.

All we know is that there of at least one constraining factor that we call the genes, which gave us our initial personhood when a sperm and an ovum fused in the darkness of the fallopian tube, and that's how we came to be an organism. But equally, from the first shriek of the baby, released from the cozy comfort of the womb, I think we have been inundated by countless inputs, and all these together have made us what we are. It's like a big painting that is constantly being tampered with or abridged, beautified, uglified—by a red dot here, a black shade there, etc. So it's constantly changing.

Sternberg: Did you want to talk about future? You've written about the future.

Critchley: I was going to bring up agency. Agency is action, right? It's something we do. The self is revealed in action. That's very important. And I wanted to tell a story that you will know about prophecy. It needn't necessarily be overtly religious.

I'm teaching a course on Greek tragedy at the moment (for reasons of complete personal indulgence). We know the story of Oedipus. There's a prophecy about Oedipus, and the prophecy is that he will marry his mother and kill his father. At the beginning of *Oedipus the King*, we see someone who's an agent who believes himself free; he comes on stage and says, "I'm Oedipus, some call me great. You know who I am, I solved the riddle, now what seems to be the problem?" So he's in this position of a self who seems to know at the beginning of the play.

However, as the play unravels and he goes through these relationships with Tiresias, with others, it becomes clear that he doesn't know who he is. Oedipus moves from a delusive idea of freedom based on an unemcumbered view of the self to an idea of freedom as responsibility for who he is—the prophecy that's made him the being that he is. And I think that's still instructive; the ancient Greeks knew a thing or two, right? It is an idea that we don't know ourselves unless we come to know ourselves through a drama. The drama that is a life. And we will rage against that, we'll fight against that, denounce the people that seem to be telling us the truth, and maybe eventually we'll come to some recognition. So there's a lesson here that the self that we think we know and that we have is not necessarily the true self. It's something that has to be explored in relationships with others.

Sternberg: Well, that speaks to studies by the cognitive neuroscientist Michael Gazzaniga showing that the left brain is trying to explain what the right brain is doing even though it doesn't really know.

Gallagher: Right. So confabulation.

Sternberg: Do you want to address that?

Gallagher: I think you can take that a little bit too far. Take the idea too far that there is a kind of narrative center in the left brain that will confabulate—will fill in details—and your life becomes something like the fish story about how big the fish was that you caught. I think the idea that much of our mental story is confabulation can be taken to an extreme. Some people think, oh, well, that means that our whole life is an illusion, our whole self is an illusion; that there's no truth there at all.

But I think there's a mixture, probably, of truth and falsehood. We do live our lives and are aware, usually, as we go through our everyday living with others, and there's some truth there to hang on to. It's not, as you were saying, Simon, that we necessarily know clearly who we are, but we get clues from the people around us and we should come to some understanding of who we are as we move through our life, and it's not an illusion. It's something that has some truth to it.

Raman: But self-fulfilling prophecy, as I interpret it, is a lot of what we do and accomplish for the good or the bad in life depends on the framework from which we are working and the self, with a small "s", simply means how we view ourselves in the context of the world in which we live. And the kind of belief system that we adopt will enable us to do things, good and bad, and in that sense it will be self-fulfilling.

Gallagher: If we think through the idea that the self is a social entity, how should we think about free will in that context? A long tradition in philosophy has thought about free will in terms of it being a characteristic of the individual: either I'm free or I'm not free. But perhaps we should think of free will as being a matter of degree, and maybe with some people I'm freer than with others. Some people will put constraints on my actions, while others will open up possibilities for my action.

So, again, free will should not be thought of as just an individual-in-the-head kind of characteristic, but rather something that is generated in our relations with others and in actions, which are often interactions with others.

Sternberg: I think from a biological point of view, one could argue there's no such thing as free will. Because so much of what we do is driven by our emotions that we may not even be aware of. So again, the placebo effect and the nocebo effect: you can have a beneficial effect of a pill, a fake pill, on healing even if you are not consciously aware that that is triggering an association and nerve chemicals that affect how the immune system works.

There's a lot that's going on literally subconsciously in terms of the neurobiology and the mechanisms—the hormones and nerve chemicals that affect the rest of the body—that is changing how you function, that is changing your actions. That is not free will.

Gallagher: I agree that those subpersonal processes sometimes push us in a certain direction and we're not quite aware of what's happening. But I would say that's still only an incomplete story. There is certainly a point when we *do* become aware, when consciousness comes into play, and then we can use that opportunity to change course, to adjust our life. So it's not that we're just blindly driven by mechanical processes. I think there's something else involved.

Critchley: It's bound up with *responsibility*. Whether there is or is not free will, or there's a will, there are experiences in which we take responsibility for ourselves and responsibility for others. Right? And that's freedom. That's freedom that's not manifested, and there is an infantile idea of freedom, a *negative* idea of freedom, that my freedom is something I have in isolation from others in society, which is a very popular idea of freedom. And there's an idea of freedom that I think is more interesting, which is that freedom comes *through constraint*, through the norms that govern our lives. Which means the question of freedom is indistinguishable from the question of responsibility and the questions of ethics.

Sternberg: Do you think in our society today we're losing sight of that?

Critchley: I think there's a tendency in the United States for a certain negative idea of liberty to take hold—you know, liberty is something that you have in isolation from society. I think it's a battle that has to be fought.

Sternberg: So actually, this question from the audience relates to this. "How do your definitions of self relate to the concepts of ethics and morality?"

Critchley: A self is something that finds itself in action, right? An action where you can do certain things well. What Aristotle called excellences—which we call virtues.

I think there needs to be a distinction between a theoretical or scientific conception of the self and a practical idea of the self. I don't think that you can simply add the two up. And I think practical ideas of the self leading to questions of ethics are *not* reducible to scientific conceptions of the self.

Sternberg: Could you explain?

Critchley: I think natural science does what it does extraordinarily well. There's a risk always of allowing it to extend its domain over all phenomena, over social and practical phenomena, and that's where the business I'm in, the humanities business, has other things to say, other stories to tell.

It's a question of what areas of our life do we need to explain causally, scientifically, and in what areas of our life do we require something else, an interpretation, an elucidation, a reminder?

Gallagher: The idea that the self has a social dimension is related to Aristotle's notion of practical wisdom, which is what allows us to make the kinds of decisions we need to make in moral situations. Aristotle explains where this wisdom comes from. It is not something that we generate out of thin air, but rather it depends upon the way we've been raised, the kind of environment that we're raised in, and as our parents always told us, the company that we hang around with, e.g., our friends, who turn out to be extremely important for the way we live our lives. And that kind of deep insight into what the virtuous life is, according to Aristotle, really depends upon such things.

Sternberg: Well, I'm going to go from Aristotle to the very present day with this question. "How do social media narratives, which seem somehow more permanent, impact our conception of ourselves?" So that's really taking it into the blogosphere.

Raman: I think more than its impacting our concept of ourselves, it does a lot to fashion our values and our beliefs. We are absolutely, I don't want to say victims, but certainly products of what we hear, what we read, and what we are told—and even our political views depend largely on whether we read the *New York Times* or the *Wall Street Journal* or we listen to Fox News or to NPR. I think the media does plays a very important role on the concept we have of ourselves, and to the extent that we are aware of it, we can try to maintain what little chastity we still have. And that's my own view.

But I want to say one thing about how my idea of self affects my morality. This poetic vision, I said, of every human being being a fragment of the cosmic self. I often think of it when I interact with people and it gives me a different perspective on what the other person is, the so-called "other" I regard as simply another version of myself, in a way. And this has personally enabled me to understand other people's perspectives and to respect even people with whom I totally disagree. So, these kinds of hypotheses or views of the self can have a very positive impact.

The idea that we have free will is, I think, does not have have scientific corroboration. However, evolutionarily speaking, we have reached the stage in which I think nature is playing the script that we have this free will because it is enormously valuable in society, in civilization. And the deterministic forces that are under girding everything, we are unaware of those, thank goodness, because that enables us to make decisions at least at one level.

Sternberg: I agree with you that there is probably a continuum of free will. And I want to bring that together with the previous question about social media. Because if we've agreed that the self is "out there" or among us collectively, then social media amplifies *exponentially* the numbers of interactions we're going to have. Are we entering a new world, so to speak, of the evolving self?

Critchley: Well, there's a transformation, right? Cinema died at the hands of television. Television has died at the hands of social media. And it's a good and a bad thing. We shouldn't get carried away with social media, but it's very interesting what's happening, and it enables forms of collectivity to take shape. We think about the role social media played in what happened recently in Egypt and elsewhere. It's fascinating and enabling—for example, you get protestors in Egypt sending pizza to workers in Wisconsin! You get strange things happening that are fascinating.

But as I said, we mustn't get carried away with social media. I'd like people to get out a little bit more. So I'm pleased you all came this evening. . . (*participants laughing*).

Sternberg: Wait, there are people out watching us on the Web. Don't ignore them!

Critchley: But they really should be here (*participants laughing*). There's something to be said for getting out of the house and getting on the subway and going somewhere and meeting human beings in flesh and blood. Otherwise, we can be sucked in to a certain delusion about virtuality, which just means us sitting there glued to the virtual media.

Sternberg: To that extent, part of self is one's imagination, and when one is in the virtual world, there's a lot more imagination than when one is face to face with individuals in the flesh.

Critchley: I don't know about that. . .

Sternberg: No?

Critchley: I find that face-to-face encounters require much more imagination!

Gallagher: I agree to some extent with Simon. But I think also the virtual world opens up possibilities that weren't there before. And possibilities for creating culture. I think culture comes into play very heavily in terms of how we think about ourselves. In a certain way, social media may allow us to be more participatory in creating the kind of culture that we want to pay attention to, so that we are not simply the products of one dominant culture. It may be that we have a little bit more freedom by engaging with social media.

Sternberg: So I'm going to move on to this next question, "Is faith part of self—sometimes active, sometimes not active—or is it the self that goes in search of faith in some people?" That's a tough one.

Raman: Faith?

Sternberg: Faith.

Raman: Depending on to which faith one belongs, there are different images or views on self. I think in that sense faith plays a role, but it depends on whether we want to understand the role of self from a religious metaphysical perspective or from a scientific perspective. We may have heard of Benjamin Libet's work that our free will is actually predetermined by things going on in the subconscious. It's somewhat like saying that God had actually instructed Eve to do whatever she had to do to make Adam fall—meaning that this was all preordained, even the free will business. But I personally think that at the actual level, we *do* have this freedom, which is what matters ultimately for all practical purposes.

Critchley: May I?

Sternberg: Yes, sure.

Critchley: I think that the idea of faith as something you can add on to the self is ludicrous. And the idea of faith as some sort of faith in some metaphysical beyond is not what's interesting about faith. I think faith is an *enactment*, right? Faith is something that is done that brings ourselves into being. The paradigm example of that for me would be something like Saint Paul, who shifts from being Saul—Hebrew, born of Hebrews under the law, blameless Roman—into Paul, this other being through an act of commitment. Faith isn't something that a self might add on or not. Faith is something that *brings* a self into being for me. And that, for me, is the strength of religious approaches.

Sternberg: There's a question that follows on that. "How do you understand the notion of karma in Hindu philosophy and is it related to self?"

Raman: Well, karma, as I understand, is an interesting compromise between fatalism and free will, (*participants laughing*) because what it says essentially is that our present predicament has been predetermined by what we did previously, but that as of now, we have all the freedom to choose what we want to do. So, briefly put, it is an interesting metaphysical solution to the problem, in a way, of suffering, because it essentially says not only that we are responsible for our *current* experiences but also that we will be for our *future* experiences. And it also, in a way, exonerates God from interfering with our enjoyments.

Sternberg: That is the best explanation I've ever heard of karma. Maybe the *Back to the Future* movies are a popularization of that concept??

Here's another question, "Should the definition of self include a sense of purpose? Isn't the quest for finding a meaning in life the primary force that shapes and changes the self?"

Gallagher: Yes, the self is not something passive, something that's bestowed upon us, one to a customer, here you are and that's all you get (*participants laughing*). But we *make* ourselves through our actions and we can always *remake* ourselves. The idea of makeovers perhaps is not a bad thing—that we can engage in actions and, again, interact with people while we do that, and we can go different ways. And that's why we need something like practical wisdom to help us determine which way to go.

Sternberg: "How can we best grow and develop the self since the sense of self is extremely subjective and we may be unaware of it is most of the time due to our unconscious; how can we become more knowledgeable about who we truly are?" I would add to that, if we're talking about the self as evolving, whether we truly are anything—we're constantly changing. Would you agree?

Raman: Yes, certainly. It's awareness not only of ourselves but also of our roles in society and in the world at large. And that awareness is constantly growing and evolving and changing, and therefore, understanding the self not in an abstract metaphysical sense but in the sense of what we are, our role in society and in family and so on, can have a very positive influence on how we live.

Sternberg: To me the answer to this question speaks to the neurobiology of memory, again. If self is constantly evolving from multiple social interactions and other experiences in the environment, this is really memory. Memory is involved in our conception of self.

There's a question here about conditions in which that the sense of self is impaired: "If the self is a product of our interaction with others, how would you conceptualize the development of self in people with autism who interact with others in a different way from neurotypical individuals?"

Shaun, you actually write about schizophrenia. So, maybe you can comment about that.

Gallagher: Yes, I've written about autism as well. Of course autism is a very broad topic. It's a spectrum disorder, so there are different degrees of autism, so it's hard to generalize. The problem that some autistic people would have engaging with and relating to others would then have an effect upon how they think of themselves and who they are. So I don't think the self can be isolated; nor can it be said to reside someplace cut off from the kinds of problems that an autistic individual might have relating with others. Therefore, I think the self of the autistic subject would be affected.

Sternberg: Do mirror neurons come into play in our formation of self? And maybe you can comment on mirror neurons.

Gallagher: Well, mirror neurons—it seems today they're said to be responsible for everything; there are so many claims being made about mirror neurons. Mirror neurons are neurons that are activated when I reach to pick up something and take it to my mouth, for example.

Sternberg: And then I reach to do the same.

Gallagher: And you reach to do the same. And the very same neurons that were activated when I picked up the glass are activated when I see her do that. Those are mirror neurons.

So they definitely seem to be involved with our understanding of the other person's action. How far you want to extend this is a difficult question, and what kind of interpretation you give to the whole phenomenon of the mirror system in the brain is an important question to explore.

But whatever comes into our intersubjective relationship with other people will also have an effect upon the self. And if, for example, in autism there are problems with mirror neurons, then that's going to be something that shows up in the deficient modes of interrelating with others and also, I think, in terms of perhaps an impoverished conception of self.

Sternberg: Okay. Here's another question: "You said that the soul is not—that the soul is out there. If so, what is it that gives each individual a sense of ownership over what makes us think it is unique to us?"

Critchley: It *feels* unique. Whether it adds up to something unified has been a topic that's been debated in the history of philosophy. David Hume thought there were just bundles of perceptions that weren't in any sort of continuity.

But the self feels like something. To go back a little bit, there's an idea that the self is like something you grow, a culture you grow in a Petri dish. But it's not like that. And maybe we're using the wrong word. Maybe *self* is the wrong term. A verbal idea of the self might be just a better way of thinking about it. The philosopher Heidegger has a line that has stuck with me. I read it when I was 21 or something; he said, "We are always out there alongside things." Right? Always out there. We exist out there alongside things. So the idea of there being some Archimedean point of consciousness poised on the pineal gland, you know, sitting atop this brain system like a pilot in a ship is just the wrong model to explain how it is to be out there among things in the world. And we need different vocabularies to begin to capture that broader verbal picture of the self.

Sternberg: From a biological point of view, I would answer the question by saying that we're all unique. Every single one of us is unique because of epigenetics, which means that whatever we are at any point in time is determined by the genes that we are born with and the experiences that we are exposed to, which then in turn change our genes and how they function. That's epigenetics. So it's not just genes and it's not just environment; it's nature and nurture. Even identical twins who are exposed to different environments will be different. And so we are all unique. And to the extent that the self is all of the above, I would say that we're unique.

Raman: Yes. And I believe that uniqueness may be explained in terms of the fact that our brains—and I agree, we have more than the brains—but the brain consists of billions of cells, and what we are or we feel we are is like writing a book with a billion words; each is a different story and you use different ink, as it were. This uniqueness is essentially a nonrepeatable kind of randomness, one could say. And so it's not surprising.

But I also believe strongly—I'm inclined to believe—that this self notion and its freedom are evolutionary generated, because it is a much more enjoyable way of being an individual, a thinking individual, than if we feel that we are always subject to external forces. Except in rare cases where some feel they have to eat spinach or they have to smile at their boss and so on, normally we do things spontaneously, on our own, and it is a trick played by evolution, like sexual attraction, to perpetrate the species. This uniqueness is somewhat like that.

Critchley: That could all be true and I don't have the wherewithal to contest it, but getting back to where you began. Your uniqueness consists not just in your uniqueness, but in your relation to your mother, right? Your uniqueness consists in your unique relation of dependency on your mother, or my similar experience nursing my father before he died. Uniqueness doesn't exclude this dependency. I think what makes us unique are the bonds of love which bind us to others. And this is crucial I think to understanding what self might be.

Sternberg: I would argue that every one of these experiences makes one unique compared to what one was before that experience. I'm a different person now than I was at that time.

Critchley: Uh huh. Sure.

Sternberg: And my self has evolved and continues to do so until I die. Which brings me to a question here: "Is self different from the ego? If so, how do you distinguish them?"

Gallagher: Well, the term *ego* of course is Latin for "I." So is the self different from "I"?

If you think of "I" as just this individual internal thing that allows us to generate the pronoun "I," then I would say the self is larger than "I." So, again, still along the same lines of it being something social, something depending not just on the brain but on the body, the biology as you would say, and on the environments that we find ourselves in, which are both physical and social environments. All of that gets summarized in shorthand when I say "I" or when I say "ego."

Critchley: I think the words we use tend to substantify, or hypostasize, what is in fact a process in a series of actions. So, the ego, the self, the person.

Sternberg: The relationship. So, a relationship is also a verb.

Critchley: Yes: to be with others.

Raman: Sorry. Just a note, again, on Hindu philosophy or Hindu perspective, is that the ego is a created entity. It is created, from the metaphysical perspective of this cosmic consciousness thing.

There comes a time when in the process of this representation, one loses the connection with the cosmic consciousness. And it is that lack of connection or awareness of the connection that creates what's called the ego—*ahum*, which means "I," and *ahumkara*, an ego-creating entity which does this. Therefore, if we look at it from the spiritual perspective, which is just another perspective, then the moment that is removed, we become aware of this connection with a grander whole, and that is what one calls a mystical experience in the Hindu tradition.

Sternberg: So, in that sense, the ego is self centered.

Raman: Absolutely; yes.

Sternberg: And it's not *the* self.

Raman: Yes. It's very self-conscious as against other consciousness.

Sternberg: Here's another question that relates to what we were talking about: "What is the difference between the self and the soul? Since energy cannot be destroyed, is the soul infinite beyond death?"

Critchley: Wow...

Sternberg: In a way I was talking about that, but not in a concrete way—I don't believe that my mother is still living. Although in other traditions, there is a belief in living in the afterlife or living in another world. But I think, in many ways, my mother lives on in me. She lives on in my genes; she lives on in my early childhood development, and we know that early childhood development and maternal interactions with the offspring—whether you're a mouse, a cat, a rat or a human—are very important in setting the course of your life; she lives on in my memory; she lives on in my internal conversations, as do all the people whom I've interacted with in my life. So, in that sense, I think there is an eternity. It's a very biological view of eternity, but it is one view.

Gallagher: One can say something similar about narratives. That one's narrative can live on in what your children know about you and what your friends know about you. So even beyond death, there's still a bit of you there to be had in the narrative. And as you very nicely put it, some people just continue to live with us, even after they are gone.

If you want to call that the soul, then yeah. So that, that makes some sense. It depends on how you define what you call the soul.

Raman: The soul also may be looked upon as a third-person description of the self. We talk of the souls of other people, of any living being and so on; the self is the soul when it is in oneself. So one's own self is also a soul, but we refer to soul of other people.

Critchley: The question one is asked is, "Do you believe in the afterlife?" I believe in the life of those who come after, would be my answer. I believe in the life of those that come after.

I think the question of immortality has been hijacked by a certain selfish idea of the perpetuation of my existence, which is of some importance but not great importance. And this is where the Greeks knew a thing or two. There's a line in Sophocles, "Call no man happy until he is dead," right? Meaning that you could still screw up five minutes before it comes to an end. Your happiness consists in the stories that could be told about you after you die. And that's what the Greeks call glory, right? And that's an afterlife. An afterlife that consists in the narratives, in the stories that are told about you. It's an afterlife where you continue in the mouths and the breaths and the lives of others. That's a much more interesting afterlife than the indefinite continuation of my existence.

Gallagher: Aristotle takes it one step further. Because he says, even after you're dead, you can experience unhappiness, depending on what your children are doing.

Critchley: Absolutely.

Gallagher: So, if your children are not doing too well, you will be unhappy even after death.

Critchley: Yeah.

Raman: That's a question about afterlife about which I'm often surprised so many people speak with such authority (*participants laughing*). I believe I will find out about it but I'm not in a hurry (*participants laughing*).

Sternberg: "How does behavior constitute belief? What are the limits of self-fulfilling prophecy?" I would ask, does behavior constitute belief or does any aspect of behavior constitute belief? If I might change that question a little.

Raman: I think our behavior is largely determined by what we believe to be the truth. I don't know if the belief is determined by behavior. One may suspect the beliefs of others by how they behave, but our own behavior is determined by our belief.

Gallagher: There are some philosophers who turn that around and will say that whatever beliefs are, they are something like dispositions to behave or act in a certain way. Accordingly, we don't know what our beliefs are until we have to act upon them, and then definitely here they are in the action. *This* must be what I believe because this is what I've done. And that goes also to the question of ethics.

Sternberg: How does it go to ethics?

Gallagher: Well, we find out, in a sense, who we are by engaging in certain actions, and it's not always the case that we know beforehand how we're going to act in any particular circumstance. One would want to always be able to say, "I've acted in a good way," but sometimes we disappoint ourselves and find out that maybe our beliefs aren't what we thought.

Raman: And that's why what matters, as someone said I think, is not what we believe in but what we do with the beliefs.

Gallagher: Yes, precisely.

Sternberg: This is the last question I have from the audience. "What books or periodicals would the panel recommend reading linking belief to behavior?"

Raman: There is a book called *Truth and Tension in Science and Religion* (*participants laughing*).

Sternberg: By V.V. Raman. There's a book called *Healing Spaces: The Science of Place and Well-Being*, that I've written. And? (*Participants laughing.*)

Gallagher: I've just edited *The Oxford Handbook of the Self*, which has all the answers I'm told (*participants laughing*).

Sternberg: And you, Simon, have your column.

Critchley: I would spend some time with Mr. Sophocles. And maybe Ibsen and Chekhov, as well.

Sternberg: That's great.

Raman: Can I tell a short story about somebody who went in search of freedom of will, what it is, and took a long road, and there was a fork and a sign said, "If you believe in predestination, take this one; if you believe in free choice, take the other one." So he took the predestination choice. And then there was a cottage where an angel came and said, "Why are you here?" He said, "Because I believe in predestination, because when I saw this fork, I chose this." And the angel said, "You chose? You'd better go back" (*participants laughing*). And then he came back to the fork and went to the other cottage on the other road and the angel there said, "Why are you here?" And he said, "I had no choice" (*participants laughing*). So he had to be sent back. So often it's a no-win situation (*participants laughing*).

Gallagher: That summarizes our knowledge about these things very nicely (*participants laughing*).

Sternberg: That's excellent. Well, I think if there are no other questions, I've enjoyed this tremendously. So thank you all very much.

Ann. N.Y. Acad. Sci. ISSN 0077-8923

A self-fulfilling prophecy: linking belief to behavior

Esther Sternberg

Address for correspondence: www.esthersternberg.com. info@esthersternberg.com

The intriguing title "A self-fulfilling prophecy: linking belief to behavior" can be viewed from either philosophical or biological perspectives. This brief overview addresses the concept of *self-fulfilling prophecy* from the point of view of a neurobiologist-immunologist and shows how self-fulfilling prophecies might trigger behaviors that play a role in healing.

Keywords: self-fulfilling prophecy; conditioning; healing

The term *prophecy* can be viewed in its simplest form as an expectation: something that we predict will happen. Although we are often unaware of our expectations, our behaviors are constantly informed by them. Expectations can either have negative or positive connotations. We go to the doctor and expect that we will feel better. We take a pill and expect that it will heal. We enter a hospital for tests and expect that we will get bad news.

Where do we get such expectations? They are learned by association through multiple exposures pairing an emotional response to an event or experience. This form of learning is called *conditioning*. It is the same form of learning that dogs or cats—in fact any animals—do when they learn to associate a sound with food. This form of learning is called *Pavlovian conditioning*, after the Russian scientist Ivan Pavlov, who first described the phenomenon in dogs in the 1890s. When exposed to the sound of a bell a dog will not salivate. However, if you pair the bell with a steak for a few trials, then remove the steak and ring the bell, the dog will salivate. The dog has learned to associate the sound of the bell with the taste of the steak. The dog now has an expectation when he hears the bell, that he will get food. This causes an unconscious physiological reflex response of salivation, preparing the dog to eat. In this context, the expectation has triggered a behavior. It happens to humans all the time. Walk into a restaurant not feeling hungry, smell a pleasant aroma, and suddenly you are hungry and start to salivate. We

humans are subject to the same sort of learning that links experiences and physiological responses, as are all other animals.

Beliefs also contain an element of expectation. We believe that a pill will heal. We believe that if we pray we will be healed. Some believe in healing places—often spots where there is a long history of miracle cures. Such beliefs can affect healing in much the same way as the bell triggers salivation in a dog that has learned to associate the bell with food—except that in these human cases, the physiological response that occurs is one that involves neurochemical responses and hormones that affect the immune system.

When applied to healing, such beliefs are called the *placebo effect*. The term *placebo* often carries negative connotations: that it is not real, that it is fake or a trick. In fact the placebo effect is very real. It is the brain's own healing mechanism. Belief has powerful effects on the immune system, through nerve chemicals and hormones that are released when we believe in something. These can either lower the stress response, which in itself is beneficial to the immune system, or increase hormones and neurochemicals that improve mood and have beneficial effects on immune responses.

Whether or not we are consciously aware of them, such implicit expectations and beliefs can trigger central nervous system responses that can help or hinder healing. Thus, if we go to a hospital and expect the worst, the brain's stress and fear centers are turned on. This in turn causes the release

doi: 10.1111/j.1749-6632.2011.06190.x

of stress hormones, such as cortisol, which tunes down the immune cells' ability to do their job of healing. This negative aspect of belief and illness—the mirror image of the learned association of belief and wellness—is called the *nocebo effect*. By contrast, if we expect that a pill or place can heal, other brain regions are activated that reduce the stress response and release hormones and nerve chemicals that can enhance the immune system's healing properties.

In the same way, the prophecies that we make for ourselves—our expectations—also affect brain regions that play an important role in behaviors that affect healing. Beyond subconscious reflexes that are triggered by such associations, expectations can also shape our conscious behaviors in certain situations. These in turn can shape how we respond to others and how they respond to us. If we go into a situation—a hospital, for example—expecting the worst, we will feel stressed and fearful. Those emotions will affect our behaviors and health through those very same nervous system pathways that operate in the placebo and nocebo effects. A stressed and fearful person is less likely to interact with others in a positive way, further fulfilling his or her prophecy that the world is a dangerous and evil place. A person who is calm and at peace and expecting the best will be more open to new experiences and positive interactions with others, again confirming his or her pre-existing expectations. Such self-fulfilling prophecies, therefore, determine behaviors that can in turn amplify and internally validate preexisting expectations.

How do these principles inform what we can do about health? We can't necessarily change our expectations, since many of these are deeply ingrained. But we can modify our behaviors and expectations. These principles can even be used for therapy of certain disorders. Repeated immersion in an environment that an individual has learned to associate with fear, such as a battlefield, will cause even the tiniest environmental cues, such as noise that sounds like gunfire, to trigger a full-blown stress response. This is appropriate in a battlefield, as the stress response is life saving, allowing the individual to "fight or flee"—focus attention, increase vigilance, and gather the energy to run or do battle. If this response occurs in nonthreatening circumstances, it can interfere with healthy functioning back at home where the noise that sounds like gunfire is actually a truck backfiring. These negative stress reactions that were learned by repeated associations in a fearful environment can be unlearned to a certain extent by repeated immersions in a safe environment with exposure to similar cues. In this case the individual relearns to associate those same cues with safety rather than danger. Thus, using 3D virtual reality, researchers have been able to attenuate the fear and stress response in people who have experienced trauma, such as soldiers with posttraumatic stress disorder (PTSD) who experienced trauma on the battlefield. This approach is also used in people who are afraid of heights or airplanes. These practical examples show how self-fulfilling prophecies do shape behaviors and health and how they do it from a biological perspective.

Ann. N.Y. Acad. Sci. ISSN 0077-8923

ANNALS OF THE NEW YORK ACADEMY OF SCIENCES
Issue: *Perspectives on the Self*

The self in the Cartesian brain

Shaun Gallagher

Moss Professor of Excellence in Philosophy, University of Memphis, Memphis, Tennessee; and Research Professor of Philosophy and Cognitive Science, University of Hertfordshire, Hertfordshire, United Kingdom

Address for correspondence: Shaun Gallagher, University of Memphis, Memphis, TN. sgllghr1@memphis.edu

The following considers the role of our increased understanding of the neurobiological function of the brain in relation to classical Cartesian representations versus embodied self theories. The movement toward a multifaceted, narrative account of the self is discussed.

It seems odd that after 370 years or so, since Descartes published his *Meditations* (1641), we are still wrestling with his thought. Not just philosophers, but scientists who study the mind, as well.[1] By the time Descartes himself arrives at his Sixth Meditation, he is wrestling with his own thought. Insofar as he defined the self as a thinking thing (*res cogitans*) in the Second Meditation, he seems to be debating with himself as he attempts to work out how precisely the body comes into play with the mind. That the two things (mind and body) interact, he is sure. His theoretical dualism is still a problem, but practically speaking he knows that body and brain (at least the pineal gland) have something to do with cognition and self. And he is almost certain of this. The degree of certitude he has about bodily involvement in cognition, however, is not as great as the certitude he found in the Second Meditation concerning the self as a thinking thing. This seemed to him to be the one thing beyond doubt. He gains a high degree of certitude about the body, however, only by bringing God into the picture.

The very quick version of what happens between the Second and the Sixth Meditation is that Descartes attempts to prove (1) that God exists, (2) that (by definition) God is not a deceiver, and (3) that since our capacities for judgment are God given, we should trust our judgments as long as we are careful to follow proper methods. Hence our judgment that the body has something to do with the self and our cognitive life seems clear. The problem is, whether God exists or not, Descartes' argument for the existence of God is questionable, and we have good reasons to doubt its validity. Of course the very hypothesis that God exists is not something with which modern science wrestles. We have learned that this is simply a question that empirical science cannot address. As a result, absent Descartes' theological solution to his epistemological quandary, science and philosophy are thrown back to the earlier Meditations, and specifically, setting God aside, they find themselves wrestling with the evil demon.

The evil demon is a thought experiment devised by Descartes in the First Meditation to buoy up the extremely strong doubt that gets his meditations off the ground. There seems to be no way to know that our entire life experience and all of our thoughts have not been a large and complex illusion caused by an all-powerful demon (or if you are a fan of the *Matrix* films, an all-encompassing matrix). Descartes is not saying that this *is* the case—only that there is no way to tell that it is not. Hence, we should doubt everything. Except for the one thing that we cannot doubt, since even if the evil demon fools us into thinking that we are thinking, we are still thinking. *Cogito ergo sum.*

For some philosophers and scientists who think about the self, this is more or less where we still are. In place of the evil demon, however, we have the operations of our brains, which are seemingly something very real, but which, like the evil demon, generate an illusion or a set of illusions. Free will, for example, is one such illusion, as Daniel Wegner[2] argues, in part on the basis of the Libet experiments that purportedly show that brain activity (the readiness potential) correlated with a

doi: 10.1111/j.1749-6632.2011.06145.x

Ann. N.Y. Acad. Sci. 1234 (2011) 100–103 © 2011 New York Academy of Sciences.

particular action predates our conscious decision about performing that action by at least several hundred milliseconds.[3,4] Although we think that we are free, and although we have a sense of agency for our actions, this is an illusion perpetrated by the brain, perhaps to make our lives more interesting. It may also be the case that the world as we perceive it is a grand illusion, since, of course, that experience is sketchy at best and the product of certain neuronal representations (this is an argument that Noë[5] pieces together, attributes to, e.g., Blackmore *et al.*,[6] and then criticizes). Mess about with those neuronal processes and the world starts to look different, as it might to a person who is schizophrenic. Such internalist, neurocentric views pull the certitude that Descartes had found in the Second Meditation back into the doubt that reaches a crescendo at the end of the First. If we think certainly that we are thinking things, it turns out that we are "nothing but a pack of neurons," as Francis Crick[7] so nicely put it.

This is one influential position in regard to what we call "the self." Thomas Metzinger, for example, defends this view: "no such things as selves exist in the world: nobody ever *was* or *had* a self."[8] The self, if not an illusion, is something close to it; what we call the self (and seemingly experience as the self) is nothing but a "self-model" generated by the brain. The self that Metzinger denies is precisely the Cartesian self, the thinking *thing*, which, as construed by Descartes, is a thinking substance. There is nothing substantial about the self.

Galen Strawson[9] draws a different model of the self. In his view the self is nothing more than a momentary experience (perhaps no more than 3 sec in duration), which he defines as a distinct, mental, single, subject of experience. Its average life span may be around 3 sec because there is neurological evidence that the brain generates a coherent window of experience that is approximately that duration (see, e.g., Pöppel;[10] and Strawson,[9] pp. 9–10).

In a certain way, there is something very Cartesian about these self-models—not just in the sense that they are Second-Meditation "things," or First-Meditation matrix-like illusions, but because in a very real sense, and despite their residence in the brain, they are disembodied. Of course these selves may seem to be embodied, and we certainly experience ourselves as such, but if we start to look closer we find ourselves wrestling with the puzzles of the Sixth Meditation, this time without God, although

we still have our brains. And that is where we find our bodies. The prominent view in neuroscience and neurophilosophy is not that the brain is in the body, but that the body is in the brain, reducible in all important aspects to what Melzack[11] calls a *neuromatrix*. The idea that *the body is in the brain* is not simply another thought experiment dreamt up by philosophers, although there is such a thought experiment called "the brain in the vat";[12] no, it's also an idea to be found in the most recent neuroscience.[13–18] As Antonio and Hannah Damasio put it, "we (mentally speaking) exist in our bodies, and . . . our bodies exist in our minds"[19] (p. 15), and as they go on to show, this means that "the construction of the self would simply not be possible if the brain did not have available a dynamic representation of its body" (p. 21). Of course the claim that the body is in the brain is more rhetorical than metaphysical; no one claims that the physical body is literally in the brain, and there is plenty of evidence available to show that the body regulates the brain as much as the brain regulates the body. Neuroscience is rightly focused on understanding the brain processes that are involved in such two-way regulations. Still, the rhetoric sometimes leads the science and the philosophy when it comes to thinking about precisely what the nature of the embodied self is. The brain-in-the-vat thought experiment attempts to show that in principle (even if not in reality) to whatever extent the self is embodied, it is so only because the brain generates the representation in this way.[a]

In seeming opposition to the construal of the self as nothing more than a product of brain processes, some theorists have turned to narrative theory. In this view, "selves are inherently narrative entities"[20] (p. 395), where a narrative self, in contrast to the neural or minimal self, is defined as "a more or less coherent self (or self-image) constituted with a past and a future in the various stories that we and others tell about ourselves."[21]

There are various theories about the nature of the narrative self, but there is one that leads us right

---

[a]"A bodiless brain in a vat could certainly enjoy the phenomenal experience of holding a paper like this one in its own hands right now. The phenomenal content of your bodily self-representation is entirely determined by internal properties of your brain"[30] (3.3.2; see Gallagher[31] for discussion).

back to neuroscience. Daniel Dennett, for example, defines the self as a "center of narrative gravity"—an abstract and nonreal point of intersection where the various stories about oneself come together[22] (p. 418). Although this does not make the self an illusion, Dennett takes an ambiguous position on precisely what the narrative aspect of self is. On the one hand, narrative is the product of linguistic processes that are generated in the brain, get projected into the world, and loop back into the brain. On the other hand, Dennett sometimes describes the narratives as lines of subpersonal brain processes that compete with each other to rise to the level of consciousness. Michael Gazzaniga[23] follows this line more closely and suggests that narratives are generated in the neural processes of a left-hemisphere interpreter, which in many cases simply confabulates our story in order to make sense of experience. This comes closer to the idea that our narrative self is something of an illusion generated by the brain. Our self-model is a narrative model that is ultimately cashed out in brain processes.

The brain processes involved in generating a sense of self can be very complex, depending on what one means by the self. In a recent review article, Gillihan and Farah[24] show that even when studies focus on a specific self-related representation, such as self-face recognition (judged in contrast with another person's face, or morphed faces), different methodologies and different subject groups will identify different areas of the brain for this function, including the right hemisphere, left hemisphere, left anterior insula, putamen, and pulvinar; the right anterior cingulate cortex, and globus pallidus; left fusiform gyrus, anterior cingulate cortex, right supramarginal gyrus, superior parietal lobule, and precuneus; right middle, superior, and inferior frontal gyri; right insula, hippocampal formation, and lenticular and subthalamic nuclei; the left prefrontal cortex (inferior and middle frontal gyri), right middle temporal gyrus, left cerebellum, as well as parietal lobe and lingual gyrus. Indeed, it looks like the entire cortex is specialized for self-referential processing. Gillihan and Farah, however, suggest that studies of self-trait descriptions (what they define as a psychological component of self) provided no clear results for specialized brain areas because of various confounds. "The different ways in which the self–nonself distinction is confounded with other distinctions across studies are likely to

account for the different patterns of activation in different studies . . . even when the same aspect of the self is under study" (p. 94).[24] More generally, however, Legrand and Ruby[25] have shown that the diverse areas implicated in self-referential experience are, in fact, not areas of activation exclusively for self. The various brain areas frequently identified as self-specific brain are activated for cognitive processes that apply not just to self, but to other persons, and even to objects. It seems that the self is everywhere in the brain, or it is nowhere in the brain. This, however, entirely depends on how one defines the self.[26]

There are two points to make in regard to the neuroscience of the self. The first is that within neuroscience itself there is no clear picture of what one means by *self*. If, as the recent reviews seem to suggest, the self is everywhere and nowhere in the brain, it is only because there is no clear consensus operating in neuroscience about what *self* means. Is the self an illusion; is it an embodied reality; is it a narrative entity? These are only three possibilities. William James[27] defined four different conceptions of the self; Ulrich Neisser[28] defined five; Galen Strawson[29] identified 26 conceptions. It is not clear that this multiplication of selves is progress, but it is clear that the self is a complex phenomenon. It is also important to note that at least in some conceptions, the self is not something that depends solely (or solipsistically) on mental or brain processes that belong to the singular individual. If the self is social or intersubjectively constituted, as James, Neisser, and Strawson all suggest, then it has to be more than something that can be explained in terms of neuronal processes located in individual heads.

This leads to my second point. No one of these disciplines, whether neuroscience, philosophy, psychology, or any other, can claim to provide a full account of what seems to be a multidimensional and highly complex phenomenon. It is only a partial story to say that the brain is involved in the origins of the self. While there is no denying that the brain plays an important role, there is also no denying that to understand the self, like so many other complex phenomena, like consciousness, space, time, embodiment, or our relationships with others, one requires many different arts and sciences.

Conflicts of interest

The author declares no conflicts of interest.

References

1. Edelman, G. 2006. The embodiment of mind. *Daedalus* **135:** 23–32.
2. Wegner, D. 2003. *The Illusion of Conscious Will*. MIT Press. Cambridge, MA.
3. Libet, B. 1985. Unconscious cerebral initiative and the role of conscious will in voluntary action. *Behav. Brain Sci.* **8:** 529–566.
4. Libet, B., C.A. Gleason, E.W. Wright & D.K. Perl. 1983. Time of conscious intention to act in relation to cerebral activities (readiness potential): the unconscious initiation of a freely voluntary act. *Brain* **106:** 623–642.
5. Noë, A. 2002. Is the visual world a grand illusion? *J. Conscious. Stud.* **9:** 1–12.
6. Blackmore, S.J., G. Brelstaff, K. Nelson & T. Troscianko. 1995. Is the richness of our visual world an illusion? Transsaccadic memory for complex scenes. *Perception* **24:** 1075–1081.
7. Crick, F. 1995. *The Astonishing Hypothesis: The Scientific Search for the Soul*. Scribner. New York.
8. Metzinger, T. 2003. *Being No One: The Self-Model Theory of Subjectivity*. MIT Press. Cambridge, MA.
9. Strawson, G. 1999a. The self. In *Models of the Self*. S. Gallagher & J. Shear, Eds.: 1–24. Imprint Academic. Exeter.
10. Pöppel, E. 1978. Time perception. In *Handbook of Sensory Physiology*. R. Held, H.W. Leibovitz & H.L. Teuber, Eds.: Vol. 8. Springer. New York.
11. Melzack, R. 1990. Phantom limbs and the concept of a neuromatrix. *Trends Neurosci.* **13:** 88–92.
12. Putnam, H. 1992. Brains in a Vat. In *Skepticism: A Contemporary Reader*. K. DeRose & T.A. Warfield, Eds. Oxford University Press. Oxford.
13. Berlucchi, G. & S. Aglioti. 1997. The body in the brain: neural bases of corporeal awareness. *Trends Neurosci.* **20:** 560–564.
14. Berlucchi, G. & S. Aglioti. 2010. The body in the brain revisited. *Exp. Brain Res.* **200:** 25–35.
15. Dolan, R. 2006. The body in the brain. *Daedalus* **135:** 78–85.
16. Giummarra, M.J., S.J. Gibson, N. Georgiou-Karistianis & J.L. Bradshaw. 2008. Mechanisms underlying embodiment, disembodiment and loss of embodiment. *Neurosci. Biobehav. Rev.* **32:** 143–160.
17. Graziano, M. & M. Botvinik. 2001. How the brain represents the body: insights from neurophysiology and psychology. In *Common Mechanisms in Perception and Action, Attention and Performance*. W. Prinz & B. Hommel, Eds.: Vol. XIX, 136–157. Oxford University Press. Oxford.
18. Jackson, S.R., L. Buxbaum & H.B. Coslett, (Eds). The body in the brain: body representations, processes and neural mechanisms. Special Issue of *Cogn. Neuroscience*. In press.
19. Damasio, A. & H. Damasio. 2006. Minding the body. *Daedalus* **135:** 15–22.
20. Schechtman, M. 2011. The narrative self. In *The Oxford Handbook of the Self*. S. Gallagher, Ed.: 394–416. Oxford University Press. Oxford.
21. Gallagher, S. 2000. Philosophical conceptions of the self: implications for cognitive science. *Trends Cogn. Sci.* **4:** 14–21.
22. Dennett, D. 1991. *Consciousness Explained*. Little, Brown and Co. Boston.
23. Gazzaniga, M. 1998. *The Mind's Past*. University of California Press. Berkeley.
24. Gillihan, S.J. & M.J. Farah. 2005. Is self special? A critical review of evidence from experimental psychology and cognitive neuroscience. *Psychol. Bull.* **131:** 76–97.
25. Legrand, D. & P. Ruby. 2009. What is self specific? A theoretical investigation and a critical review of neuroimaging results. *Psychol. Rev.* **116:** 252–282.
26. Vogeley, K. & S. Gallagher. 2011. Self in the brain. In *Oxford Handbook of the Self*. S. Gallagher, Ed.: 111–136. Oxford University Press. Oxford.
27. James, W. 1890. *The Principles of Psychology*. Dover, 1950. New York.
28. Neisser, U. 1988. Five kinds of self-knowledge. *Philos. Psychol.* **1:** 35–59.
29. Strawson, G. 1999b. The self and the SESMET. In *Models of the Self*. S. Gallagher & J. Shear, Eds.: 483–518. Imprint Academic. Exeter.
30. Metzinger, T. 2005. Precis: being no-one. *Psyche* 11. http://www.philosophie.uni-mainz.de/metzinger/publikationen/precis.pdf.
31. Gallagher, S. 2005. Metzinger's matrix: Living the virtual life with a real body. *Psyche* 11. www.theassc.org/files/assc/2614.pdf.

Ann. N.Y. Acad. Sci. ISSN 0077-8923

ANNALS OF THE NEW YORK ACADEMY OF SCIENCES
Issue: *Perspectives on the Self*

A self-fulfilling prophecy: linking belief to behavior

Varadaraja V. Raman

Rochester Institute of Technology, Rochester, New York

Address for correspondence: Varadaraja V. Raman, Departments of Physics and Humanities (Emeritus), Rochester Institute of Technology, Rochester, NY 14623-5603. vvrsps@rit.edu

The following contemplates the historical and evolving ideas of freewill and determinism in relation to the self. The role and utility of experiential freewill in the self-fulfilling prophecy of the self is suggested.

What is the self?

We recall St. Augustine's famous quip to the effect that he knows what time is, but that he could not explain it if someone were to ask him what it is. This is equally true of the self. We all seem to know what we are, what our self is, but if we have to explain it to others, we are hard put to do it. All we know is that one consequence of biological evolution is that we have inherited extraordinarily complex brains. One aspect of this complexity is an intangible structure in the brain that we call the mind.[a] We take the mind to be the source of all our thoughts.

The mind imprints in each of us an experiential uniqueness that we cannot share with any one else. This is what we refer to as our self. Thus, no matter what the self ultimately is, there is in each one of us this "I"-ness that is impenetrably insular. It is a separateness from which we simply cannot escape, and into which no other person can gate crash, as it were. The totality of our thoughts and feelings, urges and inhibitions, opinions and convictions, ideals and aspirations, likes and dislikes all come to form what we recognize as our individuality.

One of the remarkable aspects of human evolution is the range and richness in the expressions of individuality. In all the long history of humankind, there have hardly been two individuals identical in all respects, not just in facial features and fingerprints, but in the complexity that marks them as individuals. This unrepeated variety probably arises because the human brain is made up of billions of neurons, and it is their networking and link with the external world that, in some as yet ill-understood way, causes the particularities we observe. Each of us is like a book written with randomly constructed sentences using a billion word dictionary. Imagine the number and variety of books that can be thus authored. It is unlikely that any two shuffles will result in the same stories and sonnets.

Approaches to the self

The self can be and has been approached in quite different ways. Meditators and mystics explore the deepest recesses of the self; philosophers reflect and write profusely on it; neuroscientists probe its origins in neuron firings; psychologists analyze its roots and track down at least the self-image of people; metaphysicians paint poetic pictures of its essence; physiologists trace it to heartbeat and lung function; physicists may seek its origins in hadrons and leptons with field bosons thrown in the mix; cognitive scientists synthesize all this with our knowledge of artificial intelligence—some of them even fantasize about building robots with self-awareness. Someday, perhaps, we will arrive at an understanding of the true nature of the self. As of now, however, we are not unlike the six blind men who wanted to know the elephant by touching its different parts. So, although each may be partly in the right, all seem to be missing something or other.[b] The self still remains inscrutable to our collective grasp. And we certainly have not been able to reduce it to the molecules

---

[a]Needless to say, many other processes that occur in the brain, such as emotion, imagination, will, and memory, are also regarded as functions of the mind.

[b]In John Godfrey Saxe's poem *Blind Men and the Elephant*, we read

doi: 10.1111/j.1749-6632.2011.06143.x

and atoms that make up our physical bodies, nor to microtubules in the brain.

What this means is that Socrates' injunction "know thyself"[c] still remains an unfinished project for most people. The mystery of the self is safe and secure from all our efforts to break into its secret citadel and unveil its stark essence.

Not surprisingly, maybe wisely, the vast majority of normal people go through the chores and charms of life without raising their eyebrows, let alone profound questions, about the ultimate nature of the self. They just do not see any relevance to the knowledge of the self in the context of food or fun, politics, or their problems. There is no need to know about the roots of the self in applying for a job or filing tax returns.

Diversity and older view

We all make decisions of major and minor significance during our lives, on the assumption that it is *we* as individuals who make the decisions. We are inclined to think that we are in full command, although if really pushed, some may admit that it is spouses or partners who are in charge. In any case, there is a happy diversity in our thoughts and opinions of people in society, and this is healthy because it is conducive to what we call democracy.

Before we understood of neurons and genes, it was believed that the self alone was at the root of all that we think and do. The self[d] was regarded as an immaterial appendage of every living person. It was believed to have been endowed with many capacities, most importantly the power to think and the will to act independently of external factors. This, it was capable of doing, though it did not always do so, in accordance with the religious and moral guidance that it was forced or fortunate to receive. What this implied was that we were morally free as human beings, having received the blessing of freedom from our Creator.

Free will

The assumption of this innate capacity led to the notion of free will, to distinguish it from the *que sera*

sera rigidity of predestination in which all that happens now and will happen in the future has been etched in the past. Religion accepted this to have been done by the omnipotent hand of a divinity. As the Persian poet Omar Khayyám so succinctly put it, "The first dawn of creation wrote the last day of reckoning shall read."[e] From the perspective of 19th-century physics, articulated by Pierre Simon Laplace, the evolution of every aspect of the universe was determined by the initial conditions of the differential questions that encapsulate the basic laws of physics.[f]

On the other hand, free will refers to an ability that every individual is supposed to have to accept or reject something, and act differently from what one is inclined to do. It means that we can act in accordance with or willfully against a canonical code. Most importantly, free will has an inherent moral dimension. It is not just the freedom to choose between hot chocolate and cold coffee, between vanilla and strawberry, but the willful choice between helping and hurting, between doing homework and lazily lying in bed, between casting one's vote in favor of or against a candidate.

Free will as illusion

Many modern scientists and philosophers repudiate free will: that is to say, they do not accept the idea of total independence of individual mental processes. As we understand the matter today, our thoughts and behavior arise from many intractable forces over which we have little control. These forces are constantly conspiring to direct our thoughts

---

Though each was partly in the right,
    And all were in the wrong!
[c]The Indian mystic Ramana Maharished posed this as a question in his Tamil language: *naan yaar*? Who am I?
[d]The terms *soul* and *spirit* are used for this when referring to other people; *self* refers to one's own.

---

[e]In the Rubaiyat of the 11th-century Persian poet Omar Khayyám, we read (54):

> With Earth's first Clay They did the Last Man knead,
> And then of the Last Harvest sow'd the Seed:
> Yea, the first Morning of Creation wrote
> What the Last Dawn of Reckoning shall read.

[f]In his classic *A Philosophical Essay on Probabilities* (p. 4),[1] Laplace wrote, "An intellect which at a certain moment would know all forces that set nature in motion, and all positions of all items of which nature is composed, if this intellect were also vast enough to submit these data to analysis, it would embrace in a single formula the movements of the greatest bodies of the universe and those of the tiniest atom; for such an intellect nothing would be uncertain and the future just like the past would be present before its eyes."

and deeds. These subtle causes are normally not discernable. They remain hidden from the cognitive plane, with the result that we enjoy the impression that we make decisions and choices without external coercion, except perhaps when a youngster is urged to take spinach with dinner and similar obvious situations where the control is overt.

The first decisive factor over which we have no control whatever is the genetic coding that was etched at the moment of the fusion of egg and sperm in the Fallopian tubes of our mothers, causing the formation of our pristine physical self. As of now we can do very little to alter the genetic constraints that were thus imposed on us. Perhaps at some future date its alteration might become possible.

Thus, for example, for our opinions on political matters, the media gets a large share of credit or blame. We are molded, for instance, by the *New York Times,* the *Wall Street Journal*, National Public Radio, or Fox News, and not so much on our own as we tend to imagine. It is important to recognize, in this context especially, the destructive and distorting influence of commercials and op-ed pieces that influence our attitudes and opinions in significant and often uncontrollable ways. The net result is that each of us functions in a framework of values and beliefs: a framework that has a well-defined pattern, yet one that is in a constant creative and created flux.

Roots of the misperception

One may wonder why we are deluded into believing that we alone decide what to do and what to eschew. It may well be that we have been led to the conviction of an illusory free will by evolution because it gives us a more satisfying feeling of being human. Imagine knowing that in our thoughts and words and deeds we are simply being tossed up and down, right and left, like passengers in a boat on the turbulent sea. We would then see ourselves as routine robots or marines permanently in drill, or abject yes-men under a dictator, perpetually helpless, moronic, and mechanical in our actions. So it could well be that conviction of free will is an evolutionarily healthy impression in human personhood, just as attraction to the opposite sex is a device imprinted to perpetuate the species.

It is to be noted that whether real or illusory, free will has an advantage. In a society based on laws and collectively agreed-upon acceptable behavior,

without granting free will, muggers and mischief makers would have an easy excuse for antisocial behavior: their actions were determined entirely by external causes over which they had no control.

Levels of determinism

The physical universe is governed by immutable laws. However, the impact of these laws is different at different levels of reality. At the macrocosmic level, their rigidity enables determinism and predictability. In systems involving extraordinarily large components, as in gases, they cause statistical outcomes. In the quantum world probability laws reign. In chaotic and complex systems involving nonlinearity, there can be entirely unpredictable outcomes. At the hypercomplex level of human thoughts and interactions, there is virtually no telling what will lead to where or when.[g] The course of human events is, for all practical purpose, a clean slate on which anything can be written.

Some of this may seem contrary to the law-like behavior of the natural world. But this need not necessarily be so. We note that the indeterministic principles governing quantum systems give rise to the precisely predictable motions of planets and comets. This too is a law of nature. The reverse could well be true in the context of brain and behavior. The goings on in cerebral chemistry may be perfectly deterministic, yet their impact at the emergent mental level may be subject to an elastic nonrigidity. This may well be another law of nature.

What this means is that we should distinguish between a *submerged determinism* that pulls the strings like a puppeteer and *experiential free will* that makes us consciously unaware of it. This inability to observe how our own neurons are firing away in our own brains could well be at the root of experiential free will. Even the most eloquent philosopher or psychologist who argues that there is no such thing as free will still probably chooses his friends and playmates, let alone lasagna or ravioli from the menu in a restaurant, with the feeling that he is the one who does the choosing. Benjamin Libet *et al.* have established beyond a doubt that there is a conscious mental field that arises in the brain as an emergent phenomenon where processes occur prior to conscious decisions.[h] However, for all

---

[g]For details on the hypercomplex level, see V.V. Raman.[2]
[h]For technical details, see Benjamin Libet.[3]

practical purposes, when we base ourselves on this finding and say that at every tick and turn of our lives we are just instigated by unseen forces, we are essentially embracing the ancient excuse for naughtiness that it was the "devil that made us do it." Such explanations are not acceptable in courts of law in the context of, say, a bank robbery or vandalizing your neighbor's house with graffiti without his knowledge. In extreme instances of such adamant denial of free will, the individual deserves either psychiatric care or safe haven in solitary confinement.

Relevance and recognition

Thus, we see that the question of free will is not merely of academic interest. It has real-world relevance. It is one of those quandaries associated with the human condition. We may compare it to the following: can we go to the moon? Of course, we can, in principle. But in practice we are constrained by earth's gravity. But though we are bound thus, we still can move from place to place. This ability to walk and run, to swim and sail, to fly and jump, does not mean that we are not bound by the gravitational grasp.

How we walk or run, and where or why, is always determined in the sense that we are influenced by external factors. The reference to physical, neuronal, and genetic factors to explain human behavior is certainly revealing in the scientific context. However, sometimes the explanatory framework tends to underestimate the practical human context where child rearing and ethical injunctions are more important than scientific explanation and philosophical debate. They could also reduce the respect and recognition that must be given to the inculcation of values and the positive dimensions of religious conditioning.

Self-fulfilling prophesy

Ultimately, what we do and how we behave hinges largely upon our conviction about what we are and what we can do. Knowing that we are formed by external influences is important, in that this knowledge will enable us to expose ourselves to sources that enlighten, enhance, and broaden our outlook on life and humanity. It can keep us away from corrupting, narrow, and hateful factors. In other words we can voluntarily censor messages in the formative periods of lives. Indeed, this is what sound education is all about: the instilling not only of knowledge and skills but also of the values of, for example, self-discipline, caring, compassion, and tolerance.

Then again, if we reconcile ourselves to the notion that we are but puppets that dance to the tune of unseen strings, we may not have the inner strength to act in meaningful ways. Sensing full freedom is often the key to doing the best we can. Even when we are consciously aware of the fetters that bind us, belief, and confidence in our will can goad us to worthwhile undertakings. In this sense, subscribing to the tenet of experiential free will is more productive than succumbing to the idea that we are like dogs on leashes.

In the *Upanishadic* view of the Hindu tradition, every separate self is a fragment of a cosmic self.[i] Whether this is really so or is only a poetic vision, no one can affirm with certainty. However, this idea can enable a person to more heartily empathize with, and to better appreciate, even the bitterest of our opponents, if we only internalize it, for we will see in one and all embodiments of the cosmic self. When we recognize our individual selves as little pots of water from an oceanic whole, and regard others likewise, we are apt to see fellow humans as our own self encased in another frame. Such a view not only enriches our vision, it also enhances our respect for fellow human beings. Our view of the self can thus incite us to positive modes in the experience of life. In these examples we see how belief and behavior are interlinked.

Conflicts of interest

The author declares no conflicts of interest.

References

1. Laplace, P.S. 1951. *A Philosophical Essay on Probabilities.* Dover Publications, Inc. New York.
2. Raman, V.V. 2009. *Truth and Tension in Science and Religion.* Beech River Books. Center Ossipee, New Hampshire.
3. Libet, B. 2004. *Mind Time: The Temporal Factor in Consciousness.* Harvard University Press. Boston.

---

[i]A great saying (*mahávákya*) in the Chandogya Upanishad (VI:8.3) is *tat tvam aśi:* thou art that, meaning you are the same as the cosmic whole. This is a central theme in Upanishadic wisdom.

Ann. N.Y. Acad. Sci. ISSN 0077-8923

ANNALS OF THE NEW YORK ACADEMY OF SCIENCES
Issue: *Perspectives on the Self*

Me, myself, and I: the rise of the modern self

Robert Hanna, Gerald Izenberg, Raymond Martin, Norbert Wiley, and Jerrold Seigel

Moderated by Robert Hanna (University of Colorado), historians Gerald Izenberg (Washington University, St. Louis) and Jerrold Seigel (New York University), philosopher Raymond Martin (University of Maryland and Union College), and sociologist Norbert Wiley (University of Illinois) trace the evolution of the meaning of self from antiquity to the present and consider how the self described by classical philosophers matches the reality of what we know about ourselves from human experience and research.

Hanna: I will start by briefly introducing our four panelists. First, Norbert Wiley is a professor emeritus in sociology at the University of Illinois at Urbana-Champaign. He has a master's degree in philosophy from Notre Dame and a PhD in sociology from Michigan State University. He's written several books, including *The Semiotic Self*, and he's now working on books called *Inner Speech and the Reflexive Self* and *On Structure and Agency*. He's also written with two other coauthors a book called *Uprising at Bowling Green: How the Quiet Fifties Became the Political Sixties*. And his particular interest is pragmatic conceptions of the self.

Next is Raymond Martin, who was professor of philosophy and distinguished scholar-teacher at the University of Maryland, College Park, and subsequently professor at Union College in Schenectady, New York. He's published widely on the self and personal identity theory, including the book *Self-Concern*, and with coauthor John Barresi, the books, *The Rise and Fall of Soul and Self* and *Naturalization of the Soul: Self and Personal Identity in the Eighteenth Century*.

Third from my left is Jerrold Seigel of New York University, the William R. Kenan Professor of History at NYU. Jerrold taught at Princeton for 25 years. His first field of historical specialization was the Italian Renaissance, but since the 1970s, he has concentrated chiefly on more recent topics, beginning with *Marx's Fate: The Shape of a Life*. His next book, *Bohemian Paris: Culture, Politics and the Boundaries of Bourgeois Life*, was a finalist for the National Book Critics Circle Award in criticism. More recently, he's written *The Private Worlds of Marcel Duchamp: Desire, Liberation and the Self in Modern Culture* and *The Idea of the Self: Thought and Experience in Western Europe since the Seventeenth Century*. His current project is called *Modernity and Bourgeois Life*.

Finally, Gerald Izenberg is professor emeritus of history at Washington University in St. Louis, where he has taught modern European intellectual and cultural history for 35 years. He's also a practicing psychoanalyst, a faculty member of the St. Louis Psychoanalytic Institute, and former president of the St. Louis Psychoanalytic Society. He's written a number of books on the concept of the self and European thought since the French Revolution, including *The Existentialist Critique of Freud: The Crisis of Autonomy*, *Impossible Individuality: Romanticism, Revolution, and the Origins of Modern Selfhood*, and *Modernism and Masculinity: Mann, Wedekind, Kandinsky through World War I*.

So, each one of you listening to me now hears the words "me," "myself," and "I," and when you think those words to yourself with meaning they seem to refer to something, or to something familiar to you. So it seems clear that each one of us, in some sense, *has* a self or *is* a self. But of

doi: 10.1111/j.1749-6632.2011.06185.x

course the question of precisely what the self is—what its explanation is, and what its endurance and permanence are—are philosophical, cultural, and historical questions of great pitch and moment.

I am a philosopher of eighteenth century German philosophy, particularly the philosophy of Immanuel Kant, and I also do work in contemporary metaphysics and philosophy of mind. Philosophers will ask quite general questions about the nature of the self, including two different kinds of questions, each of which will show up in the many issues that arise tonight. The first is the question, What is the self? In other words, what is the *nature* of the self?, which is a large metaphysical question. And the second one of particular concern to philosophers is, Who am I?, or What is the identity of the self?, which is a question about the conditions under which there are individuals. And from the first-person standpoint of me, myself, or I, the question arises Who am I precisely as a self?

Tonight we're going to address those questions, as have other panelists in the "Perspectives on the Self" series. But we will address those questions from a specifically historical and cultural standpoint, tracing various conceptions of the self from the premodern period up through the modern period.

Before we start, I want to mention several general concepts of the self that we might have in the background, particularly in the modern period. I won't explain them in detail, but just mention them to you, and then mention some of the philosophers who would be associated with these notions. We will come back to these different conceptions of the self.

For instance, from the seventeenth century European tradition forward we might think of the self as a *thinking substance*, which is an idea associated with the philosophy of René Descartes. Or we might think of the self as a mere *psychological bundle*—not a unitary or immortal self in any way—which is associated with the philosophy of David Hume. We could think of the self as a *rational, moral agent*, for instance with respect to the philosophy of Immanuel Kant. We could think of the self as a *social agent*—as belonging to communities and larger historical movements—which is associated with the philosophy of G. W. F. Hegel; the self as a *rational egoist*, associated with the work of Ayn Rand; the self as an *alienated animal*, associated with Sigmund Freud; the self as an *existential agent*, from John Paul Sartre; or the self as *embodied*, from Maurice Merleau-Ponty. These are names I'm sure you've encountered before.

Before the seventeenth century, there was a long tradition of formulating conceptions of the self. My first question is for you Raymond. In your books particularly, you've critically analyzed the history of the concept of the self from ancient Greece right up to the contemporary period.

If you would, please, tell us something about that premodern period, to get the ball rolling.

Martin: I'm told that I have five minutes to talk about classical conception of the self (*participants laughing*).

Hanna: Precisely... (*participants laughing*).

Martin: In classical times there were three theories of the self that are especially worth mentioning. By far the most consequential of these was the theory advanced by Plato in his dialogue *Phaedo*, which is about the jail cell conversation that took place between Socrates and a few of his students on the day that Socrates was put to death. Plato's concern in that dialogue is with two issues: the causes of generation and corruption (how things come to be and pass away) and with the question of whether a person can survive his bodily death. In this dialogue Socrates makes the case that a person can survive his bodily death. He does this by arguing that humans are composite beings who have a material part and an immaterial part. The immaterial part, our souls, is what we essentially are. Since this part is a simple part, that is, one that has no parts, it can't cease to exist.

In fact, it can't even begin to exist. According to Plato only composite beings can either begin to exist or cease to exist. So the soul, in virtue of being a simple immaterial substance, is immortal. The reason this view turned out to be so consequential is that in the third century the Christian church ultimately adopted it as its official view.

The second classical view that was very consequential, but not quite so much in modern times as Plato's view, was the view of Aristotle. Aristotle, unlike Plato, didn't stress that natural objects were divided into material and immaterial parts. For the most part Aristotle's review was monistic. And he was not as interested as Plato was in whether humans can survive their bodily deaths. Rather, Aristotle was primarily interested in the question of what makes something a living thing. His idea was that all living things, vegetables, nonhuman animals, and humans, are composites of form and matter, and the kind of form that a thing has determines its status as a living thing. In Aristotle's view, the human soul is a formal property of material human beings. Matter individuates us from one another, but all of us are humans and we all have that same form, that is, the same character or nature as a human being, which accounts for why we're alive and have the essential characteristics that we have.

The final view from classical times that's worth mentioning, and I think I'm probably pressing on my five minute limit here, is that of the materialistic atomists. Leucippus and Democritus were the originators of this view. It is the idea that all of reality is made out of indivisible material atoms, and that the various things we see when we look around are composites of these atoms in various arrangements. When the atoms come together in such a way as to make an individual like you or me who stays around long enough to deserve a name, then that person is a living human being and has a material soul, a psyche, that accompanies or is part of his being a living human being. Once we die and the atoms come apart and that's the end of us.

Maybe that's enough for classical conceptions of the self. However, I should also mention the patristic period, which began in the first century when the church fathers got together and tried to come up with the theology for Christianity. The original church fathers were Stoics, and thus held a version of materialistic atomism. Subsequently, Plato's views entered the fray. In the third century, the neoplatonist Church fathers began to win the day. Ultimately the church fathers who were most influential, starting with Origen in the third century and ending with Augustine in the fifth century, endorsed a platonic view of the self according to which we have an immaterial part and a material part, and that view turned out to be the influential one for European philosophy.

Hanna: Thank you, Raymond.

So I'm going to follow up on that one with Gerald. You've done work on seventeenth century conceptions of the self, self and the liberal tradition, and the concept of individuality. I wonder if you could say something to connect what Raymond was saying about the premodern period.

Izenberg: It's really concerned with the post-French Revolutionary period. And it does, in some important ways, take off from classical philosophy because some of the people that I've been concerned with, in one of my projects, were contrasting what they saw as the modern sense of the self with what they saw as the classically ancient sense of the self, not in terms of problems of soul and immortality but in terms of what the ideal aesthetic and ethical person was. For example, one of the thinkers I'm most concerned with, Wilhem von Humbolt, based his idea of individuality on the classical notion of weaving together all of the aspects of the human being—the aesthetic, the moral, the economic, the political—into a well-rounded personality, developing all aspects of the self and integrating them into a unique personality. And Humbolt saw this as based in the classical idea of the *citizen*.

However, Humbolt saw limitations in the classical idea of the citizen. For him, the citizen was only one model, one identity, and it made uniqueness—individuality—impossible. His argument essentially was that it was *modernity* that made possible the full flowering of the human personality—of individuality.

For Humbolt, also, this ideal was pitched against another notion of the self and modern times, one quite different from the classical notion of the citizen, and that is the notion of the individual motivated by *material self-interest*. One of the things we see in the period just before, the Revolution in the century and a half before, is the validating of self-interest, which was valid neither in classical nor in Christian thought.

And so the idea of individualism underlies a good deal of modern ideas of rights, for example. For people like Humboldt, and after him John Stuart Mill, individualism was an important and valid idea, but they saw it as a very limited notion of personality. And they wanted to bring in the classical and aristocratic heritage of individuality and pitch that against individualism.

So, both of these notions were considered to be valid as ethical strivings for human beings. But at the same time these notions also demanded very different kinds of societies. On the one hand, a society of modernity, of commerce, of individualism, of openness, which was quite different from the closed polis of Athens in republican Rome. At the same time they saw this kind of society as favoring only one model of the human being, the materially self-interested model. And so out of the classical heritage, they tried to modernize a notion of individuality that would include all of the faculties, and would also not be limited to one model of *the person*, which instead would be allowed to develop. But they did see modern commercial society, modern capitalist society, as not a favorable ground for the development of individuality.

Hanna: Thank you. Norbert, I wanted to follow up on that with you. You've worked on pragmatic and American, specifically, conceptions of the self. And so could you say something that links to what Gerald was just saying about the individualist conception of the self?

Wiley: Okay. The American view of the self is really a break with the past; it's a brand new idea. So, let me fill it in.

The United States starts with this extremely wonderful Declaration of Independence where everybody's equal, a morally powerful statement that comes from Jefferson. And unfortunately The Declaration of Independence was followed up very quickly by a racist Constitution in which Americans were divided into white males, white females, African-Americans, and American Indians in rank. We had legal ranks. So, the wonderful Declaration of Independence, which was made for war—you know, when you are going to fight a war, you want everybody to be equal; after the war is over, that's when the reality sets in and you get your ranks—was followed by the Constitution, which was a ghastly thing that took a long time for us to get rid of. It's a long story, how the minorities got equality in this country, and they're still not quite there.

It's a long story but a key move occurs right after the Civil War: the American pragmatist Charles Sanders Peirce defines human beings *as signs*—signs, symbols, semiotic entities. That definition of the self has no reference to the body. The human body is not involved, it's just cultural. Once you define human beings as cultural, you open the door to complete egalitarianism, which is back to the Declaration of Independence. Peirce did not know that at first, but the other pragmatists, William James, Dewey, Mead, gradually teased out an extremely egalitarian notion of what a human being is. The idea of the self as semiotic or a sign is very close to culture too. The notion by Franz Boas, which was a very egalitarian idea in the social sciences, was that all cultures are morally of equal value. So, there are a number of social sciences, and they were all drifting in the same direction.

The way the pragmatist view of the self as a sign worked out was that it was a sign in a somewhat special sense of a mirror, a representative phenomenon, a sign in that sense. So a potential sign or a universal sign. And from that point of view, the way the idea was developed, it became not just one mirror but two mirrors: human beings are one mirror in that we can represent the world around us, but we also have self-awareness or what's called reflexivity. Self-awareness is a distinct human characteristic, and that's the second mirror, which is looking at the first mirror. You're always watching yourself; that's what a self is: a thing that always watches a self, that's aware of itself, that's got a kind of back-onto-itself loop.

The idea that humans are two mirrors, which became the semiotic self, was gradually developed to deal with the problem of the Constitution and the minorities. The minorities had to amend the Constitution but also amend the social structure, and women were the first ones who got to vote. They gradually were able to equalize, but then slowly so were African-Americans and other ethnic groups, and then gays and lesbians. That whole process of minorities fighting against the thing that the Constitution left us with is the story of the American self: the American self *becoming* an egalitarian entity.

So, the pragmatist view of the self, as I see it, is extremely democratic. This is the most democratic view of the self there is: we're all the same because we're all made out of just abstract symbols, that's what we are to begin with. There's no difference among us; none of us are better than anyone else. That also meant that we're all equal in a moral and a legal sense; each of us has exactly the same rights. And, really, this is true not just for Americans. All people, from the beginning to the end, have the same rights. That's what pragmatist view implies. This is a very egalitarian idea of the self.

But always against this idea is the actual material inequality among human beings. This is a separate idea of the self—resulting from economic differences. And this economic inequality, which today is increasing in the United States, fights against the moral equality of the pragmatist. The moral equality demands equal material prosperity, while material prosperity seems to mean—at least in our society—that people aren't equal. This is a historical thing about wealth. People with the wealth have a strong tendency toward racism, that is, to say the people who don't have the wealth are that way because they deserve it, because they were born that way. So there is a dialectic in American history between the egalitarian notion of the self, which was gradually won back from the Constitution, and material inequality, which we now know creates recessions and depressions. That struggle, which is going on right now in New York and elsewhere, is the story of the American self.

Hanna: Thank you, Norbert. Probably you're already deeply confused because there are many different conceptions of the self we've already covered. One of the reasons I wanted to ask Jerrold Seigel the last question in this round of questions is that he's attempted to combine different dimensions of the self and to try to get a more unified conception of the self. And so Jerrold, could you tell us something about that?

Seigel: I'm not sure it's quite the case that mine is a more unified conception of the self. But I do have a kind of theory that I use in my book. It's not a theory of the self, or at least it doesn't set out to be one; rather it is a theory about the history of *thinking about the self*. One reason I developed this theory was to defend the tradition of modern Western thinking about the self. I don't mean I would defend every person who has contributed to this tradition, but overall I think it deserves to be defended against a particular charge that is often made against it, namely that the modern Western theory of the self is overly focused on coherence, stability, and independence. Such a self is supposed to insist on its independence and coherence and to deny that it is subject to division or fluidity. Such an image of the modern Western self has been offered from a number of different points of view.

One of these is a Marxist perspective that sees the modern self as bourgeois, a self that sees itself as self-made, and therefore is independent from social life. Another one, both very different and remarkably similar, is the critique of the modern self mounted by the German philosopher Martin Heidegger, who argued that the basic and characteristic Western notion of the self was Cartesian. When Descartes says, "I think, therefore I am," he is claiming that the self constitutes itself through its independent mental activity, so that it has no dependence on anything outside itself. Heidegger then sees the later history of Western thinking about the self as in one way or another confirming this Carteisan position.

What I propose in my book is a different approach to modern thinking about the self. In my view, the Western tradition of thinking about the self, from the seventeenth century on down, proceeds by conceiving the self along one or more of three dimensions or axes. Of these, the first is *the body*, the second, what I call *relationality*, and the third, *reflection or reflectivity*. To emphasize the first dimension is to highlight the self's quality as embodied, to note that human beings are physical creatures, subject to passions and impulses and characterized by certain temperaments. To stress the second, relational dimension, is to insist that we belong to cultures or societies that give us certain characteristics that we share with other people around us; here the self is very much determined by social and cultural relations. To conceive the self along the third dimension is to point to the independence humans can acquire by reflecting on their being and thus establishing a distance from their bodily or social existence. This what Descartes does when he says, "*Cogito ergo sum*," saving himself from the doubt that his experience has bred in him about all the other elements of his existence. In my view, these three dimensions, in one configuration or another, have appeared over and over again in Western thinkers.

But the important question is, in what relationship are they put? How do people view or imagine the relations between them? The number of possibilities is extremely large, but within them a particular choice is especially significant, namely between what I call *multidimensional selves*, and *one-dimensional self*. A multidimensional self, in some way, combines two or three dimensions. By doing so it creates a self that is never wholly coherent because it will experience tensions between its constituents. If it has a dimension of reflectivity then it will have some degree of independence, but its freedom will be limited by the material and social conditions of its being. Thus multidimensional selves are complicated, they have both a degree of autonomy and a set of limitations to it. One-dimensional selves, however, are permeated by the qualities of the single dimension that constitutes them; they may be purely bodily, as some eighteenth-century materialists and some modern genetic biologists portray them, they may be dominated by their relational dimension, as Marx and in a different way the French sociologist Emile Durkheim had it, or they may be wholly reflective and thus essentially independent of both the physical and the social worlds, as for instance the German idealist Fichte held, at least in some moments of his thinking.

In the history of thinking about the self these dimensions have been put together in different patterns by different thinkers. There have been purely reflective selves, such as Fichte's and in some moods and moments Descartes's. Such selves do indeed seem to possess the kind of independence, coherence and stability that Marx, Heidegger, and others decry in Western views of the self. But these are rare cases and don't really obtain in the ones often said to show their prominence. If you read Descartes with any care, you'll discover that he never intended the formula of the cogito as a general theory of the self; sometimes he speaks of the body as the active subject and the mind as subject to its passions and ills. More important, a whole series of prominent Western thinkers who have been portrayed in the way I've mentioned had much more complex and interesting theories of the self.

For instance, a much more important figure than Descartes in the history of the modern self is actually John Locke. Locke, who, as you remember, believed that the mind was a *tabula rasa*, an empty slate, on which experience writes. If that's the case, and experience is subject to shifting winds, then, then the self is always changing, anything but stable and fixed; indeed a lot of people have seen in Locke's idea of the mind as the *tabula rasa* the origin of a postmodern notion of the self as completely fluid and without autonomy.

Even in the seventeenth century who complained about Locke's view for this very reason. But at the same time, Locke believed that human beings were rational. That is, that they could reflect on their being, and by reflecting on it, he said, they could put off the fulfillment of their desires, thus creating a certain amount of independence from passion and impulse.

In Locke's view we always have two kinds of identity. One is what he called our identity as *a man*—using the sexist language that everybody thought natural for a long time—which is simply the identity we have as a living creature, the persistence in any person of a certain vital impulse. This kind of self-identity is bodily. Alongside this we also have an identity as *a person*, and a person is a moral agent responsible for its actions. This self exists by virtue of its memory of itself over time, its sense of itself as including all the things that it has done or might do. Just what, at bottom, this self was, Locke insisted he did not know. He rejected any metaphysical notion of the self, any knowledge of its deep essence. What we do know about our selves is that they are sometimes stable and sometimes not, that we exist in relation to the people around us and to our deeds, that we have bodies, minds, and social relations. If I had time to speak about other figures, I would try to show that they followed Locke in his attempt to think about the self as some configuration of the various parts of our being. Such a self is stable and unstable, coherent and divided, autonomous and dependent on outside powers, all at the same time.

Hanna: I want to follow up on this notion of an *unstable* self and ask Raymond, who's done work with John Barresi on the—this is actually a term that came up earlier in Richard's remarks as well—notion of a fragmented self, and a specifically modern conception of the self. Raymond, could you say something about that?

Martin: I am not sure I'll directly speak to what you have in mind.

Hanna: Okay.

Martin: I'd like to tell a story going back to classical sources. There was a comic playwright from Syracuse, in Greece, named Epicharmus. In a fragment of a play of his that survived from the fifth century BC, a lender meets a debtor by accident at the market and the lender says, "OK, time's up, pay me back." The debtor replies, "Well, do you believe that an object, a pile of pebbles from which one pebble has been removed, is the same pile or a different pile?" And the lender says, "A different pile." The debtor then says, "And do you think that human beings are constantly changing or do they remain the same?" The lender answers, "Oh, no, human beings are constantly changing," to which the debtor responds, "Well, then, I don't owe you anything, because the person to whom you lent the money was not me" (*participants laughing*). Where upon the lender hits the debtor and knocks him to the ground. The debtor gets up bruised and says, "Why did you do that?" The lender replies, "Why did *who* do that?" (*Participants laughing.*)

The thing about this story that indirectly relates to what Robert tried to prompt me to talk about is that in this scene from Epicharmus' play both the lender and the debtor have a point. There's a sense in which if over time an object changes in any way, then it becomes a different object. So we can say, for instance, that we're not the same people that we were a year ago, or not the same people that we were even this morning, because we're different. We're always changing. Each time a person changes, that person ceases a new person comes into being in its place. We understand that notion; it's perfectly clear and it applies not just to humans but to any object that changes over time. That's a clear view of the limits of human persistence. The problem with it is not that it could not be true, but that for practical purposes it's utterly useless.

For *practical purposes* you have to have objects remain the same over time and through changes. In particular, people have to remain the same people over time and through changes. To account for ownership and responsibility, for instance, a human has to remain the same even though it undergoes various sorts of changes. For instance, if you get a divorce or have a mental breakdown, you aren't thereby relieved of having to pay your mortgage.

So if it's practical *utility* that we're after, then an object, like a human, will remain the same over time and through various changes provided that it's socially useful to think of those changes as compatible with his or her remaining the same person. And since there are lots of different purposes for which a notion of the self (or person) could be useful, you are going to end up with a plurality of different notions of the self. According to some of these notions, a self can persist through various sorts of changes, whereas according to others it cannot. There may be no absolute truth of the matter about whether we're the same people that we were several years ago or yesterday, or even this morning. We're accustomed to thinking of ourselves as remaining the same in some core way over time and through various changes. But this conceit may just be a kind of practical artifice. There may not be any truth of the matter about whether certain kinds of changes are better thought of as compatible with a person's continuing or as the cessation of one person and the beginning of a new person.

This question comes up in the patristic period, when church fathers were trying to clarify the dogma of the resurrection of the body. Critics said this dogma is philosophically problematic. An old body dies—a body gets eaten up by the lions in the Coliseum, let's say—and then according to the dogma of the resurrection on the Day of Judgment—which [joking] I understand is 21 May 2011, I found that out today (*participants laughing*)—the body is reassembled. But is the body that is reassembled the same body or a new body, which is merely a replica of the original? Is there a true answer to that question or, for different purposes, are there just more or less useful ways of thinking about whether the body that gets reassembled is the same body that earlier died? I would say the latter. And I think the point needs to be generalized: there are more or less useful ways of thinking about whether an object remains the same object through various kinds of changes and at any given time which ways of thinking about this are most favored is determined by social, cultural conditions that probably have their own dynamism over time.

Hanna: All right. Thank you.

I want to not necessarily talk about the fragmented self but come back to this question about whether the self is in some sense an illusion, and one of the audience members raised that question. So we're talking about different conceptions of the self. But it's possible that each one of these conceptions is false, and that there is no self, and certainly philosophers have raised skeptical questions. I think it would be nice for us to address the question, Is there a real self? Are we in error about the nature that there is a self?

Gerald, would you like to say something?

Izenberg: It really depends on what you mean by the self. I don't think anybody today would question the notion of subjectivity, that there is a core of self that is a core of subjective experience. The kinds of questions that have emerged in modernity about that core of subjectivity are about its continuity. In fact, John Locke first raised that problem precisely because the self is constantly changing—the self is a bundle of impressions that change moment to moment. What is it that links them? Locke's answer was memory. The thing that makes us unified people is our memories. And that answer was sufficient for a very long time, until the twentieth century; it stopped being sufficient for psychological reasons. Because in addition to continuity of memory there are questions like, Am I the same self if I've changed my values? Am I the same self if I've changed my body, or if I have had a sex change operation? Am I the same self if I've changed my nationality or my beliefs?

In the twentieth century, thinkers and writers raised a question of identity different from the one that Locke was asking. It's a question of whether there is a continuity of *self-definition*, of substantive self. Not in the sense of *essence*; Locke got rid of that forever. It's not enough to say, "I remember having done something." Marcel Proust was very interesting in this regard; he said, "Yes, because people can remember having made promises we can feel a sense of obligation, even though we're no longer the same people that we were, to fulfill those promises, because there's that continuity of memory." But the question of identity that truly bedeviled Proust concerned the continuity during states like passionate love—life-consuming love—that then dissipates to a point where you can't understand (recognize) the self that loved that other person. It's as if you are no longer self that—that love doesn't exist anymore. This is the fragmentation you were asking about—that we are capable of *losing* our identity.

The question of identity in that sense of self-definition first arose in the 1920s when people started to question all of the substantive identities that they had taken for granted before—bourgeois morality, nationalism, gender, and so on. And the odd thing about it is that the question of identity emerged through questioning the *possibility* of identity. This was followed by Eric Erikson, the psychoanalyst, who first put the question of identity on the agenda as a psychological issue. Erikson argued that people have to have a substantive sense of self-definition, *a core identity*, for them to be able to function psychologically and socially.

So now you have two opposite poles. You have writers and philosophers questioning the substantiality of identity, and you have psychologists who say we can't get along without it. And that debate goes on today between postmodernists, for example, on one hand, and people who argue, as Raymond suggested, that you can't get along socially without a set of identity roles, but you can't get along psychologically either without that.

Hanna: All right, thanks.

So Norbert, I wanted to ask you, this is a follow up on that line of thought that there may be ways of forming a conception of the self that is not substantialist in terms of social practices and in terms of social action of various kinds. And one of our audience members asked about a specifically American conception of the self. Is there a specifically American conception of the self? And, if so, does it answer the worry about whether the self can fall apart? Whether there's alienation?

Wiley: Well, here's where I put together the American pragmatist theory of the self. Human beings have three parts, the way I look at it. The most profound core part is composed of traits that I think are always there: that we think, that we choose, that we act—and maybe also that we talk to ourselves. Those characteristics aren't there in the same way at all times. Sometimes the individualism is more pronounced, sometimes your communal connections are more pronounced in some cultural and historical periods. Nevertheless, I see this as the continuing part of a self.

The middle level is what I call the identities. The identities are like the IBM card: age, sex, job, politics, sexual orientation, etc. those things. And the minorities are in with the identities, and all of the reform in the twentieth century for the minorities has changed the nature of the identities, kind of scattered them.

So, identities do change and one might say that they're kind of fragmented—mine aren't; I have similar identities to the ones I always had and I managed to adjust to history's changes. But we can say, and postmodernists say this, that the self is fragmented. That's the middle level, which is different from the core level.

Then there's a level that I call quotidian or everyday, these are the ordinary things: what you like to eat, what you do in the morning, etc., those kinds of things. These things are constantly changing.

So we have a core of traits that are always there if there's a self at all. And it started with when humans split off from the chimpanzees, and these core traits cease when the last one of us dies on the globe. Those are, I think, what we used to call essence and what we call definitional. Then there are these mediating identity things that do change, and that's what all of the discussion is about the identities. Very little is about what I call the core. Then the trivial quotidian things, of course they change.

So that's the way I look at it. Some things about the self change and some things don't change.

Hanna: Something that seems to me to be fundamental to the self, and this came up earlier, Jerrold, in your discussion of the three dimensions, is the body. Particularly in our case, the living human body. Suppose someone just said, "there's an obvious sense in which there is a self: there must be a self because, except for science fiction examples, we have the same body over time and we, therefore, must be the same self over time provided that our conscious experience continues to go on."

Do you think that might be an answer to the question?

Seigel: If you answer the question that way, you're answering it in a very narrow way, because you are specifically identifying the self with the body. And part of the problem with the body as a center of the self is that although it has a kind of continuity and coherence, it does change greatly over time. Of course a religious question arises, as Raymond was saying, about the whole problem of the relationship between soul and body. It's very important to have a lot of skepticism about the notion that the self is a *thing* or an object. The self is an *idea*, and as an idea, it's something we use as a vehicle for trying to make sense out of the different components of our lives.

Now, that may mean the different temporal components—for instance, Proust's notion that at one point he's defined completely by his love for, you know, Mme de Guermantes, and at another point he just can't remember what it was like to be like that. On the other hand, it's perfectly easy to say, as a lot of French people in Proust's time and earlier did, that the self is not either the person who loved Mme de Guermantes or did not, but the self is the person that is aware that it can have both these embodiments or emanations. In other words, that the very ability to ask the question is the source of the self.

I don't mean to offer that as a definitive comment about the self. Instead, I just want to say, again, that we use the notion of the self as a way of trying to make sense of the different components of our being, and we do that according to what sort of understanding of human existence we want to have.

Hanna: Right. I mean, sometimes philosophers will say, look it's one thing to have conceptions of the self and it's another thing to have a theory of the self as a fact of some kind, and so these philosophers might appeal to metaphysics or contemporary sciences, cognitive science and so on.

Raymond, do you think that there's a way of going beyond the way we described the self or concepts we have of the self to some sort of scientific approach to the self?

Martin: Well, there's been a huge change in the way the notion of the self has been proposed and received by theorists over time. From classical times until about World War II, the self was thought of by those thinkers who believed there was a self, which was almost everybody, as something that was unified and that did some explanatory work. For instance, it was thought that selves were unified and were needed in order to explain how other things are unified, most importantly, how humans have unity of consciousness. The change that occurred around World War II is that in the view of most theorists, the self ceased to be something that was thought to be unified and available to theorists in order to explain other things. Instead of this, people began to think of the self as something that itself required explanation.

So, theorists turned to the task of explaining not the self as a whole, but the different aspects of the self, such as self-awareness, self-reference, self-conception, and so on. In other words, theorists turned their attention away from the self itself and toward these hyphenated versions of the self, which they tried to explain that on the basis of other characteristics of the person.

So from classical times until, say, 1950, the self is thought to be "out there," more or less unified, and available to do some explanatory work, and then from 1950 to the present it's no longer thought to be unified or available to do explanatory work. Instead, it's thought to be fragmented into a large array of hyphenated self-behaviors, which themselves require to be explained. And these self-behaviors have not themselves been explained in a unified way.

So, the theoretical fragmentation of the self comes partly in that way. I personally do not think that's this aspect of theories of the self is going to change. I think that because science has no use for the self as a unitary explanatory postulate, the unified self is probably gone. If you pick up a psychology book and look in the index for the word "self," very likely, in a regular psychology book that you would use, say, in an introduction to psychology text, you may not find it. It's not an important scientific notion. Whereas hyphenated self properties, such as self-esteem, you will find. These hyphenated self notions are theoretically important. Scientific work is being done on them, but not in a unified way. Different theorists are devoted to different aspects of the self. They formulate their theories about these aspects often without even knowing what other theorists are saying about other fragmentary aspects of the self. And when these theorists are in different disciples, often there's no shared theoretical framework that they can appeal to to talk to each other. And that situation, I suspect, is likely to persist. I don't think it's going to go away.

Hanna: Yeah, I've wondered, though. In my own work on Kantian conceptions of the self, I've wondered whether there's a more fundamental notion of the self that's just built into the idea of moral responsibility or agency. For each of us, if we choose to make a movement of some sort, then this is something that we did ourselves—we weren't forced or compelled. If you reached over and you slapped someone beside you, you'd be doing something for which you could be blamed. It's not only that we can't do without a more fundamental notion of the self that's built into moral responsibility or agency, it seems to be built into our political and legal systems, and so they seem to be more basic in some way and something we can't really give up—and science won't compel us to give up. Gerald, do you have a comment here?

Izenberg: I think that then any rejection of the notion of self is incoherent, it's contradictory. Take the notion of self-esteem: what is that to which esteem is being directed? What are we saying is the subject or the object of esteem? We're saying a self. The moment you start talking about a center of agency, you're talking about a self. In contrast, I think it's the *essentialist* concept of self that's been questioned, as it was questioned a long time ago, certainly as long ago as the seventeenth century. And I think that the question of the unity of the self is both an ethical and a psychological question. It's also a social question, but I tend to look at it from these other points of view. I don't think we can get along *socially* without a concept of the self. I don't think we can get along *ethically* without a concept of the self, and I don't think we can get along *psychologically* without a concept of the self.

And I think the questions are not whether the self exists or not but what does the self want, how does it conceptualize itself. To go back to what Jerry was saying about the body, feminists have pointed out that it's not enough to say that the body is the self, because the body is interpreted. For example, the fact that we have certain sexual attributes doesn't tell us what we're supposed to do with them, because that's a matter of choice and decision. So you interpret the feminine; you interpret the masculine. And this was a reaction precisely against one notion in modernity: that anatomy is destiny; that the body is our identity. If that's not the case, then there is a subjective, in fact reflexive, consciousness aspect of the self. The self is something that is indeed interpreted. The questions are then, What does the self need to interpret itself? What problems does the self wrestle with as it interprets itself? At the very least, the unified self is the self that interprets itself.

Hanna: Here's another thought that I think is consistent with what you said, and this flows more from the existentialist tradition: that each one of us is a free agent of some sort, but we're in search of a self-conception that we can live by, and so our project is to become selves. Right? We're not yet selves, we're not yet the sort of being that counts as a self, and so that's our project.

Norbert, do you think that's something that the pragmatist could sign on to?

Wiley: Well, I think the idea of self being a process is more like what a pragmatist would see. The process is dialogue. Selves are internal dialogues. There are two, or maybe three, aspects: "I" and "me" is a pair of terms that are often used. The internal conversation is going on all the time. We're talking to ourselves or something like that, and that goes on throughout the day as a kind of flashlight. It's a self-regulatory device. We figure out what we're going to do today, from hour to hour with a person and so on, by talking it over with ourselves. The talking is not always real loud. It might almost be unconscious. But we're constantly talking to ourselves, even when we're talking to someone else.

So, inner dialogue is a highly noticeable feature of the self that we carry from year to year. This internal conversation can be unhealthy, for example, when you're psychologically disturbed; the internal conversation can go bad. For example, schizophrenics hear the internal conversation *as external*, and they say things like, "Officer, God told me to kill my children; that's why I did it." We have all heard awful stories about what happens when the internal conversation goes wrong for people who are disturbed. But if you're not disturbed, that's how you get through life, through internal conversation. Everybody has it and everybody uses it; it's our resource.

That would be the way a pragmatist would look at the self: not as a substance or something you're trying to obtain, but as something you're trying to use.

Hanna: But the thing I was talking about was, when people look at themselves over their lives and think about their conscious states and their various responses to things around them, they often think, Who am I? They ask themselves, What am I? and Who am I? and they're looking for unity, and not necessarily a unity that's fixed forever—a sort of permanence—but some sort of unity that is satisfactory in many dimensions.

This is a lead-up for Jerrod Seigel, too; you said there were three dimensions of the self and that you weren't sure whether there was some sort of overarching notion of the self. But here's a suggestion: the self is some sort of unity of all these various aspects—bodily aspects, reflective aspects, social aspects. And the self is just this guiding end we have as creatures trying to find out about ourselves. Does that make sense to you?

Seigel: I think there's no doubt that in some way we are all as human beings mixtures of these dimensions. I believe that any theory of the self that does not recognize that, whether it is which tries specifically to *exclude* one of the dimensions, is bound to be inadequate. And it's almost certain to have been created for some particular purpose, to argue something about human beings that allows a certain person to give them advice or claim that they are radically free or radically unfree. These are the uses to which the notion of the self is put.

Let me just stop there and point out to you what I've said. I think we ought to think about ourselves in a certain way. When I said that, was I saying that we ought to think about something about ourselves, which we call the self? That is, should we think about our selves [two words] in a certain way or should we think about ourselves [one word] in a certain way?

The notion of the self is, to begin with, a reflexive notion. It simply turns the object we are talking about back onto itself. In many languages, the idea of the self or the phrase "for the self" contains the notion of *sameness*, so that in French you say for "the self," *moi meme*, or in Italian you say, *io stesso*. Those are both words that mean *same*. Or in German, you can say *die sache selbst*, that is, "the very thing" or "the very notion." The self is a notion we use to emphasize our attention to something, whether it be our personal being or some other kind of thing. The whole question is in what way we want to make that emphasis.

Izenberg: I would say that's what's new about the modern idea of the self. That's what's modern. We can't take for granted that the self *is* anything. It was easy to take that for granted in the past.

So the notion that the self is a process, that it's self-making, raises all kinds of questions. It's both freedom on the one hand and vertigo on the other hand. Because although there are fixed dimensions, as Jerry says—reflexivity, the body, the social self—the questions of how we define these dimensions, how we relate them, what importance we give to each of them, these are questions for us. But they haven't always been questions for people because religion or metaphysics or nationalism or fixed gender theories provided definitive answers. Today these questions are no longer answered to our satisfaction. That's where the vertigo comes in.

Hanna: We're just about at the end of the time here. I agree with everything you've said and want to add, again, that it seems to me that the self is not a mere process just as if it were going *nowhere*. Rather, the self has to have some kind of goal-directed character to it, and the process by which we create ourselves *as* individuals, to whom we can say "I" or "me, myself, and I," whatever that comes out to be, seems to be the proper end.

Ann. N.Y. Acad. Sci. ISSN 0077-8923

ANNALS OF THE NEW YORK ACADEMY OF SCIENCES

Issue: *Perspectives on the Self*

What is the self?

Robert Hanna

University of Colorado at Boulder, Boulder, Colorado

Address for correspondence: Robert Hanna, Department of Philosophy, C.B. 231, Hellems 142, University of Colorado, Boulder, CO 80309-0232. rhanna@colorado.edu

In this paper I briefly sketch a theory that answers the question "what is the self?," where this question is understood in a scientific sense that includes both natural science and systematic fundamental metaphysics. As selves, we are essentially rational human minded animals or real persons in a fully natural and desperately non-ideal world—animals with meaningful lives, for better or worse.

It seems to me to be clearly and distinctly true that any creature who is capable of reading and understanding these words *is* a self, or *has* a self, that we also correctly call an "I" or "ego" or "first person."

In turn, it also seems to me to be correct to say that there are two fundamental questions that we can ask about selves or egos or first persons:

- What am I? That is, what kind of being is the self or ego or first person?

This is the question of the *nature* of the self or ego or first person.

- Who am I? That is, precisely *which* of all the beings that are or have selves or egos or first persons is the one that I myself am?

This is the question of what constitutes the *identity* of the self or ego or first person, both in relation to other selves, egos, or first persons, and also in relation to the changes that each of us undergoes over the time of our lives, from birth until death, and perhaps even beyond death.

Correctly answering one or both of these questions, it seems to me, would take us a significant distance toward answering some of the big and important questions about the meaning of life and about what it is to be human, that is, what it is to be a *real human person*.

In the conversation I moderated, "Me, myself, and I: the rise of the modern self," we raised these two questions: (1) the question of the nature of the human personal self, and (2) the question of human personal identity, in a specifically historical way. So we examined various conceptions of the self in the modern era. But suppose that a critical philosopher had said to us: "That's just anthropology, or the history of ideas, or sociology. You're just telling us what's been *believed or conceived* about the self. But why should we care about mere beliefs and concepts? Don't we want to know the actual facts about the self and the real truth about the self? And in order to do so, shouldn't we be looking to the natural sciences, and particularly to evolutionary biology and cognitive neuroscience, at the very least, and perhaps also to systematic fundamental metaphysics?"

It seems to me that this critical question has significant rational force, and that correspondingly we need to distinguish carefully between the *ideology* of the self, and the *science* of the self.

Both issues are of deep importance—in a very real sense, how I think about myself, what I believe and conceive about myself, and how I feel about myself, are all central to my own personal life and all my projects, fundamental or otherwise—but they are distinct issues.

In my own philosophical work, especially in my books *Rationality and Logic*,[1] and *Embodied Minds in Action* (coauthored with M. Maiese,[2] and in my current book in progress, *The Rational Human Condition*, I have directly addressed the scientific question about the self, although also not in such a way as to neglect the ideological question about the self, but rather only to situate that ideological question

doi: 10.1111/j.1749-6632.2011.06124.x

fully within the framework of what I regard as the more basic scientific question.

In a very small nutshell, here is my view about the nature of the self, where this question is understood in a scientific sense that includes both natural science and systematic fundamental metaphysics. I think that the self is a *rational human minded animal*.

First, however, before I say what I think a rational human minded animal is, I should briefly define my basic terms. By the notion of a *minded animal*, I mean any living organism with inherent capacities for:

(i) *consciousness*, that is, a capacity for embodied subjective experience;

(ii) *intentionality*, that is, a capacity for conscious mental representation and mental directedness to objects, events, facts, acts, other animals, or the subject herself (so, in general, a capacity for mental directedness to *intentional targets*); and

(iii) *caring*, a capacity for conscious affect, desiring, and emotion, whether directed to objects, events, facts, acts, other animals, or the subject herself.

Over and above consciousness, intentionality, and caring, in some minded animals, especially including ourselves, there is also a further inherent capacity for:

(iv) *rationality*, that is, a capacity for self-conscious thinking according to principles and with responsiveness to reasons, hence poised for justification, whether logical thinking (including inference and theory construction) or practical thinking (including deliberation and decision making).

Second, then, what is a rational human minded animal? Rational human minded animals are what we really are and who we really are. More precisely, according to my account, rational human minded animals are individual living organisms in the human species, and *also* unique real persons who are innately and irreducibly capable of consciousness, intentionality, and caring, including affect, desire, and emotion, sense perception and imagination, memory and thought, logical and mathematical cognition and inference, empirical knowledge, *a priori* knowledge, and above all, free agency

and moral responsibility. They consciously care intensely about themselves, about one another, and also about other things that affect themselves and one another. They effectively desire things, and they thereby intentionally move their bodies, sometimes spontaneously, sometimes habitually, and sometimes self-reflectively and deliberatively. They consciously perceive things through their senses, they make judgments and have beliefs about things, and they know some things. They formulate and recognize reasons. On the basis of these reasons, they establish normative principles for themselves, which they then attempt to follow consistently and with appropriate generalizability. They try to justify themselves, both theoretically and practically. They can also deceive themselves, and they are very good at making mere rationalizations. They can be insincere and lie. But even more importantly, and correspondingly, they can also be sincere and tell the truth.

Rational human minded animals or real human persons have complete, finite, unique lives, in the sense that every such life has a definite beginning with the emergence of conscious experience, a definite middle in which human personhood is fully actualized and sustained, and then a definite ending in the destruction of their essentially embodied real human personal lives at death. They can intensely enjoy themselves. They can be enthralled or enthused. They can be amused or bemused. They can be embarrassed, frustrated, bored stiff, or deeply depressed. Hence, they can also suffer intensely. They worry a great deal about dying. Sometimes, in despair, they deliberately take their own lives. And sometimes they are very wicked. They can torture others, and they can treat each other like mere garbage or offal. They can ignore each other, criticize each other, envy each other, betray each other, hate each other, and kill each other. They can also respect each other, trust each other, like each other, lust after each other, copulate with each other, love each other with all their hearts, jointly produce other rational human animals from inside their own bodies, live with each other as friends, partners, or families, and also look after each other compassionately until death finally parts them.

Rational human minded animals or real human persons are aware of reasons, and they try to be moved by the highest reasons, which in turn express the highest or supreme good. They also want to be *happy* in all the senses of that equally deeply ambiguous and deeply morally important term. This includes, at least,

(i) happiness as egoistic "lower" or "higher" pleasures (in John Stuart Mill's terminology) and/or the reduction of pain or suffering;

(ii) happiness as the egoistic or public satisfaction of desires and preferences;

(iii) happiness as privately virtuous self-perfection;

(iv) happiness as publicly virtuous flourishing; and

(v) happiness as wholehearted self-fulfillment, that is, psychic coherence and self-sufficiency, that is, *authenticity*, and perhaps other distinct forms of human happiness as well.

Rational human minded animals or real human persons can freely choose and act, and they can take responsibility for their choices and acts. They can also take responsibility for things over which they had no control. In this way, rational human animals or real human persons have both Kantian autonomy in the robustly potential, dispositional sense of an online capacity for rational self-legislation, and also authenticity in the robustly potential, dispositional sense of an online capacity for purity of heart, single-mindedness, or wholeheartedness. Together these online capacities make possible the fact of a free, self-legislating wholehearted adherence to one's moral principles, including some absolutely general moral principles, together with sometimes taking responsibility for brute contingent facts, which I call *principled authenticity*. Principled authenticity is morally better than happiness, although of course happiness is extremely good too, and also an intrinsic proper part of a completely good rational human animal's life. That rational human animals or real human persons really do have lives in which there is a highest or supreme good (principled authenticity) and a complete good (happiness guided by principled au-

thenticity), and also an at least partial achievement or realization, to some degree, of these highest goods in their lives, even if they never can fully attain these highest goods, is the same as to say that their lives have meaning. Only creatures whose lives really do have meaning would be capable of intense suffering because they can, falsely and tragically, come to believe and feel deep in their hearts that their lives do not have meaning.

In this way, as rational human minded animals or real human persons capable of principled authenticity, we are essentially the animals with meaningful lives. This is not to say, however, that we ever actually manage to live up adequately to our principles. We can screw things up, and very frequently we do screw things up, both colossally and trivially. That is where the evil and suffering part comes in. We can do horrendous, terrible things to one another, or to ourselves. Also, it can happen that either we are not what we want ourselves to be, or other people are not what we want them to be, or the world is not the way we want it to be. Any of these facts, or all of these facts together, can make us feel sick unto death. So we are also essentially the animals capable of evil and suffering. That is the tragic side of us. Nevertheless, as the necessary flip side of our tragic capacity for evil and suffering, we are also essentially the animals capable of principled authenticity and happiness.

Conflicts of interest

The author declares no conflicts of interest.

References

1. Hanna, R. 2006. *Rationality and Logic*. MIT Press. Cambridge.
2. Hanna, R. & M. Maiese. 2009. *Embodied Minds in Action*. Oxford University Press. Oxford.

Ann. N.Y. Acad. Sci. ISSN 0077-8923

ANNALS OF THE NEW YORK ACADEMY OF SCIENCES
Issue: *Perspectives on the Self*

The modern notion of self has reached its ultimate conclusion

Gerald Izenberg

Department of History, Washington University in St. Louis, St. Louis, Missouri

Address for correspondence: Gerald Izenberg, Ph.D. Washington University in St. Louis, Campus Box 1062, One Brookings Drive, St. Louis, MO 63130-4899. gnizenbe@wustl.edu

Keywords: self; individualism; individuality

It is a cliché—which is not to say that it is untrue—that the modern chapter in the Western history of the self is the story of the emergence of the autonomous individual, with his/her rights and desires, as both ultimate truth and value. Both religious and secular can agree on this, however differently they may find the value of the individual. But on the question of what exactly the individual self "is" there is less consensus. Furthermore, the issues involved have changed over time; the definition of the modern self has its own history.

If we agree that our current conception of universal individual rights first appeared in the Enlightenment, from their religiously founded political conception in John Locke to their metaphysical–ethical foundation in Kant, and if we see Adam Smith as the thinker who first broached the idea of the individual's material self-interest as the source of the wealth of nations, it is also true that it took the political revolutions of the eighteenth century to translate individual rights and interests into political goals and concrete institutions. It was with the American and especially the French revolutions that the modern argument about the nature of the self began.

Its most exalted version came quickly on the heels of the French Revolution. As government came to be seen not as an imposed alien externality but rather as the embodiment of the people's will and purpose, Romantic literature and philosophy claimed that this was but one manifestation of the essential nature of the self. The self strove to make the whole of creation its own by finding human use and meaning in everything. The essential thrust of human consciousness and will was to overcome the initial "otherness" of the cosmos through subjective appropriation, thus making it a recognizable home for humanity. Human freedom was an infinite reaching out, a creative striving like that ascribed to the divinity in traditional religion. By embracing all, it aspired to be the *All*.

Almost immediately, however, the grandiosity of the claims for the self seemed to the Romantics to turn into justification of murder and destruction during the revolution. Most first-generation Romantics retreated from what they now saw as dangerously false claims for the self's virtual divinity. Instead they arrived at a contradictory synthesis in which the infinite creativity of the self depended on its fusion with a totality other than and greater than the merely human, whether nature, the All, the state, or the eternal feminine. Where the infinite was figured as nation or empire, this move could and did have conservative political consequences, but truly consistent Romanticism remained a primarily literary movement because the self as the Romantics conceived it had to remain fictive or notional. As a striving for infinity or totality, the Romantic self was unrealizable in the world except in the imagination, as abstraction or allegory, or as a story of infinite longing that could never be fulfilled this side of dreams or death.

doi: 10.1111/j.1749-6632.2011.06188.x

On the ground, so to speak, on the matter of the practical social and political consequences of the emergence of the individual, the debate about what the individual was devolved into a confrontation between two different ideas of the self and their respective consequences for social mores and governing institutions. One was made famous (though not first named) by Alexis de Tocqueville in the wake of the revolutions as *individualism*. This was the specifically modern form of self-interest; in contrast to eternal human selfishness, individualism was a socially constructed and socially sanctioned ideal, the result of the rise of commerce and "democracy," that is, equality. A similar conception of individualism was also at the root of James Madison's ideas about the American Constitution of 1787 he had helped draft as expressed in the *Federalist Papers* promoting its adoption. The second concept of the individual, the ideal of individuality, was first fully defined by Wilhelm von Humboldt in the first years of the revolution but made famous in the English-speaking world by John Stuart Mill. Humboldt defined individuality as the development of all of the unique individual's abilities, interests, and talents to their fullest potential and their integration into a harmonious whole personality. Since each person embodies only a small portion of human possibilities, the ideal of individuality was best fostered by social interaction with others who could stimulate and supplement the self with their unique capacities.

The face-off between individualism and individuality has preoccupied political and social thinkers, especially within the liberal tradition, down to the present. Most liberal thinkers were in fact partisans of both ideas, but since each ideal seemed to demand quite different social institutions and values, it was a struggle to reconcile both in their theories. Self-interest demanded a free-market economic system with as little interference by government as possible and a legal and political focus on individual rights as protection of person and property against government encroachment. The promoters of individuality also saw the free market as necessary both for the prosperity that increased opportunities for self-development and as an arena of freedom, but they feared that the tyranny of life as self-interest would overwhelm any other value and constrict the personality to the pursuit of profit. Mill's advocacy of a *stationary state economy*, which would no longer single-mindedly pursue economic growth once it

reached a certain level of wealth, was a bid to leaven self-interest with the cultural mores of individuality, with social norms encouraging a much greater range of government action to promote culture, art, science, and learning. In the twentieth century, figures like John Maynard Keynes and Jürgen Habermas updated these recommendations to reconcile individualism and individuality under the vastly more threatening economic, social, and political conditions of the times.

During the nineteenth and into the twentieth centuries, the preeminence of the autonomous individual did not preclude thinking of the self as also part of a community—indeed, identified as a member of a range of communities. On the contrary, community became all the more important as individualism threatened to isolate the individual and shut him up within himself. It is no coincidence that modern nationalism developed in tandem with individualism in the nineteenth century; the modern nation, made up of free self-determining citizens was the form of community that superseded older organic conceptions in which the individual was subordinated to the whole. By the same token, moral probity took on new importance in an individualistic world; freedom depended on self-regulation if it were not to descend into anarchy. The free self was also the moral self.

The easy relationship between individual freedom and national identity, as well as belief in objective moral absolutes, was shattered for an avant-garde of European writers and thinkers by the catastrophe of World War I. Communal and moral identities were called into question because they had licensed hypocrisy and destruction. Identity, hitherto taken for granted as both real and consistent with freedom, suddenly became a self-conscious issue. Existential thinkers argued that identity itself was the ultimate abnegation of freedom because it imposed false limits on the self, trying to enclose it in objective roles freedom itself had created. Identity was escape from freedom. But once opened up, the question of identity became a matter of contestation. Psychologists and sociologists argued that psychological identity is indispensable to emotional health and role identity to smooth social functioning. In the wake of the social upheavals of the late 1960s women, blacks, gays, and former colonial peoples claimed recognition in terms of their collective identities—former badges of shame transformed into sources of pride. Against such demands, post-modernism, taking up the existential critique in the name of liberation, attacked identity as a set of social constructions historically used to define certain subject groups as *other*, different from and less than the norm of "humanity." Today even those who defend the idea of identity grant that in a fluid and mobile world in which traditional static identities have largely dissolved; individual identity must be a work in progress, constantly changing to meet new conditions, provisional and multiform. Whether or not such a concept of identity can furnish the emotional security for which it was originally seen as indispensable, it is at least consistent with the idea of the autonomous individual. Thus has the modern notion of self reached its ultimate conclusion.

Ann. N.Y. Acad. Sci. ISSN 0077-8923

ANNALS OF THE NEW YORK ACADEMY OF SCIENCES
Issue: *Perspectives on the Self*

The American self and the long march to legal equality

Norbert Wiley

Department of Sociology, University of Illinois, Urbana, Illinois

Address for correspondence: Norbert Wiley, 43300 Little River Airport Rd., #9 Fern Canyon, Little River, CA 94546. norbert@redshift.com

Legally, women, Native Americans, and African-Americans were defined by the American Constitution as inferior. The pragmatists gradually showed that all selves are equal. These ideas helped the minorities to attain nearly full legal status. But economic status is going in the other direction, toward inequality. It threatens to overcome the hard-won legal equality and make it meaningless.

Keywords: self; Declaration of Independence; Gettysburg Address; United States Constitution

Introduction

The nature of the American self has been a political issue since this country was founded in the late 18th century. This conflict is dramatically visible in the contrast between the Declaration of Independence and the Constitution. The Declaration defines the human being or self in a strikingly egalitarian manner:

> We hold these truths to be self-evident, that all men are created equal, that they are endowed by their Creator with certain unalienable rights, that among these are life, liberty, and the pursuit of happiness.

In contrast, the Constitution defines human beings in what must be called, by today's standards, a racist way. White males are at the top level; then come white females; then come the two racial minorities, African-Americans and Native Americans. These four strata differ in political rights, the bottom two having none. Overall, the Constitution contained several important political and legal innovations that promoted democracy in the world, and, in that respect, it is laudable, but it did so on a foundation of a legally unequal population.

The Declaration was a war document, formulated to motivate the population to fight for egalitarian goals. The Constitution was a postwar document, composed when the elite had more self-confidence and could speak its mind without fear of reprisal. The carrot turned into a stick.

The history of the United States has been in large part a fight between the generous Declaration and the discriminatory Constitution. The Civil War was fought, as Lincoln pointed out in his Gettysburg Address, over whether the ideals of the Declaration could prevail over the slavery of the Constitution. This war gave half a loaf to American blacks, for slavery was abolished. But after a brief period of freedom and what appeared to be an equalizing constitutional amendment, a highly restrictive system, including Jim Crow in the South, was put in its place.

The American reform tradition since the Civil War has centered on bringing minorities to full economic and legal status. These initiatives have had only modest economic success, but near-equal legal status has gradually been attained by women, African-Americans, other ethnic groups, the elderly, those with disabilities, and gays and lesbians. This movement for full civil status was an attempt to define the American self, contrary to the original Constitution, as a completely egalitarian community of citizens. This process was based largely on organization and protest, but it was also based on a set of ideas. These were the philosophical arguments for an equal self, and they were forged largely by the American pragmatist philosophers and the social scientists who were influenced by them.

Most of this paper will be about the process of reaching legal equality, with an emphasis on ideas rather than organizational struggle. But at the end I will touch on a second dialectic, between the legal

doi: 10.1111/j.1749-6632.2011.06191.x

and the economic, and briefly consider the prospects for this conflict.

Peirce and the pragmatists

From the Revolutionary War on, there was agitation, largely centering in New England, to end slavery. This agitation was based mostly on the ethical argument that slavery was morally wrong. There was little argument that blacks were psychologically equal to whites or that slavery was intellectually wrong. Jefferson and Lincoln had made a strong moral plea for equality, but they were not helpful on the "why" question. They did not explain how blacks were ontologically the same as whites, constituted by the same qualities of human nature. To explain how the American battle for the self became intellectualized or theorized, I will have to devote several pages to the presentation and analysis of ideas. After this I will return to the larger issue of the political fight for the self.

The first important intellectual move toward equality was made by the American philosopher Charles Saunders Peirce in 1868 (p. 233),[1] when he defined humans as *signs*. Peirce was creating a semiotic theory of knowledge in contrast to Descartes's "cogito ergo sum," which was an intuitive theory of knowledge. Semiotics says we know things, not directly and intuitively as Descartes thought, but indirectly as signs and symbols. A semiotic explanation is always incomplete and in process; it is subject to an indefinite amount of interpretation. When Peirce defined humans as signs, he used semiotics to initiate the turn against racism and toward an egalitarian view of human nature.

Semiotics resembles linguistics in being a study of meanings. Its most distinctive object though is not language but the nonlinguistic forms of meaning. The nonverbal conversation includes such features as gestures, tone of voice, clothing, hair style, eye messages, and loudness. In the sea of meanings, the nonlinguistic ones are just as important as the linguistic ones. In Peirce's view, human beings not only use but *are* nonlinguistic or semiotic forms of meaning (pp. 9–13).[2]

Another contribution of Peirce's semiotics is that it led to the anthropologists' notion of culture (pp. 332–337).[3] Culture is composed of signs and symbols. It was the theory of culture that smashed the various forms of racism in the intellectual, and gradually also the legal, world. The cultural anthropologists showed that there is equality among all cultures and that humans in preliterate societies think with the same logic as those in literate societies. Anthropology promoted a nonhierarchical view of cultures, societies, and human beings.

When Peirce defined humans as signs, he did not deliberately intend to create an egalitarian view of human nature. On the contrary, this was a classic case of unintended consequences. The effects of Peirce's definition went in a different direction than he had in mind. Only gradually and over several decades did the other pragmatists and social scientists take the semiotic view of human nature in an equalitarian direction.

The politically important feature of Peirce's definition of humans was that it made no reference to the body. This exclusion of the body is what allowed the pragmatic approach to the self to combat racism, for racism has meaning only in relation to the body. For the same reason sexism or male superiority was disallowed by Peirce's definition. Signs are not biological or material. They are nonmaterial, or to stretch the idea a bit, "spiritual." In other words, the distinctive feature of humans consists of cultural elements.

Of course Peirce did not mean humans do not have bodies. Rather the special feature of humans, that which makes them a unique species, is their symbolic component. The self, as I will return to later, is a property of the body. But it is such an important and powerful property that it can be defined independently of the body. The body itself may be born with various problems or limitations, but these do not correlate with ethnicity or race, and they are not, strictly speaking, part of the self. Peirce chanced upon the fact that human nature, in its most distinct and defining form, should be—or at least can be—defined in exclusion from the body.

The contemporary pragmatist theory of the self

The pragmatic theory of the self as it exists today is not neatly organized. There are a variety of pragmatist ideas on this topic, and there is more than one way of putting them together. The synthesis I will present is my interpretation.

Reflexivity and the mirror analogy

Peirce's notion that humans are signs was just a first step. It had to be developed by the other major pragmatists, William James, John Dewey, and George Herbert Mead. Gradually it became clear that humans were not signs in the sense of having some distinct meaning or signification, like a traffic sign. Instead they were potential signs or *signifiability*. They were plastic, and, like a piece of putty, they could take any shape. They had universal pliability. They also resembled mirrors in that they could represent or signify anything.

So, on the one hand we have the body, which has its distinct biological characteristics, and on the other, we have a property of the body, which we call the self. This property is distinctive in having no *significative* characteristics, somewhat like Sartre would later call the "self as nothingness." It can take on any characteristics, but in itself and to begin with, it is defined by the absence of signification.

The mirror analogy to the self is helpful, and there are many versions of this metaphor. The mirror suggests the way the self can reflect anything, but it does not capture the most distinctive feature of the self, namely, self-awareness or reflexivity. The self is an object to itself in that it can loop around and be aware of itself as though looking from the standpoint of another. Immanuel Kant thought self-awareness was always present when we were conscious at all.

This looping or reflexivity is not a simple mirroring relation. The mirror represents only linear cognition, but self-awareness is curvilinear. It is us looking at ourselves from an outside vantage point. George Herbert Mead referred to this process as *role taking*, which was his term for reflexivity. This is usually represented by a curving line of 360 degrees, which goes out from the self, takes a twist and comes back to its starting point, our self. It is not like us holding a mirror out to reality. Rather it is like us looking into a mirror at ourselves. In other words it is a second mirror analogy.[a]

What is needed here is a way of representing both mirroring functions, the one that pictures the outside world and the one that pictures our self, in the same metaphor. I would suggest the following idea, which I think is merely an extension of the thought

---

[a]Charles Horton Cooley's looking-glass self, by which we tend to internalize what others think of us, is still another mirror analogy. It should be added onto the one I am describing, but for purposes of this paper, it is in the background.

of Peirce and the pragmatists. Picture two mirrors in the self: one reflects the outer world, and the second reflects the first mirror. In other words, we watch ourselves as we watch the world. As we listen to the world, so to speak, we eavesdrop on our listening process. The first mirror has an implicit form of self-awareness, for we know it is us doing the watching. But the second mirror gives us a more express, explicit, and pronounced form of self-awareness.

The double mirror analogy also evades the awkwardness of the bent sightline. To look out and somehow loop back, 360 degrees, and see ourselves, is not how the eyes or sightlines work. But the two-mirror analogy respects the linearity of the sightline. To sum up, the first mirror gives us phenomenological consciousness and the second gives us self-consciousness.

The other animals have only the first mirror, phenomenological awareness, and even their first mirror is not as strong as ours. They do not have self-consciousness or the second mirror. Babies start with only the first mirror, and gradually, in ways that are not yet fully understood, they attain the second mirror or self-consciousness. It also appears that certain kinds of brain damage, as well as intrusive medications or chemicals, can weaken or remove the second mirror, leaving you unaware of who you are.

The pragmatist's semiotic selves are not only similar to each other in the way they mirror the world, they also have the democratic quality of being politically equal. All selves, as universal pliability, have a common nature. They are all the same, with none being any different from, let alone better than, any others. This universal uniformity also means all selves have the same rights, as stated in the Declaration of Independence and by Lincoln at Gettysburg. Unfortunately, the egalitarian clause was not present in the original Constitution. It took a good two centuries, and still counting, to bring legal equality to the entire population. It was the pragmatists who explained the "ontology of equality," that is, the psychological nature of human beings that makes them all equal.

The tripartite self

As I have argued, self-awareness is a core trait of the self, present whenever there is a self and giving it definition. This quality is part of Peirce's "self-as-sign." There are several other traits that seem to

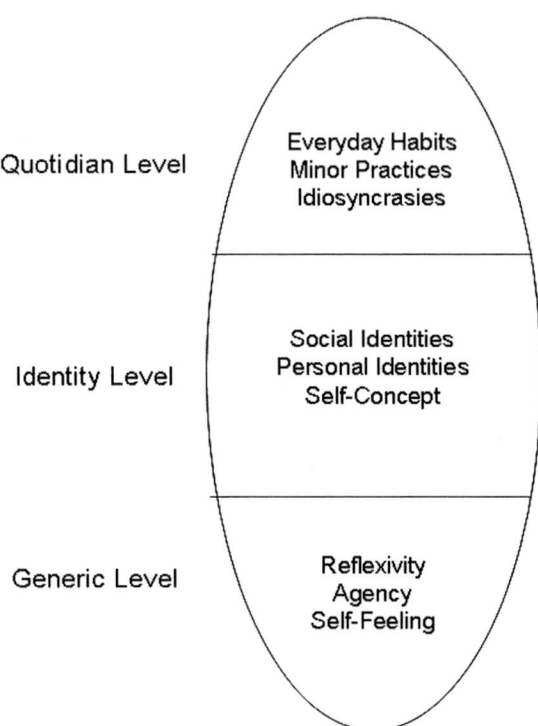

Figure 1. The tripartite self.

be universal or omnipresent in the self. There are also traits that, to differing degrees, are variable, meaning not omnipresent, to the self. These traits exist within a tripartite or three-level structure, as illustrated in Figure 1.

The bottom, most important level, contains the traits that are present in all selves, a level to which I refer as "generic." There are six traits that belong at this level, as I will explain, but for convenience I will list only the main three in Figure 1. The middle level has traits that are important and tend to remain in the self for an indefinite period of time. Yet they can still change, undergo transformation, or disappear. I refer to this level as that of "identities" and the self-concept, the latter being the way we internalize our identities. The top level is the least important and subject to the most change. This is the level of ordinary activities, practices, and habits. I call this the "quotidian" level since it consists of everyday elements.

I see the generic level as follows. We all think, choose, and act. We also are all self-aware or reflexive. And an extension of reflexivity is the internal conversation or interior dialogue. In addi-

tion to these five traits I would add William James's idea of "self-feeling." (p. 319).[4] This is our sense of "mineness" or self-possession. This feeling is directed toward anything that we think of as "mine:" our minds, bodies, family, friends, property, and actions. Here, James is drawing on the idea that "where your heart is, there you are." Self-feeling is also the basis for the self-related emotions, such as shame, guilt, pride, and embarrassment.[5,6]

Everyone might not agree that these six traits are universal to the self, that they were present when the first humans evolved from the primates, and will continue until the last of our species dies. Still it is difficult to imagine a self without these traits, and I have yet to see anyone describe one. In people with the normal human powers, including the absence of serious brain damage, they are always present.

Turning to the second part, the self at the identity level has to do with those chunks of meaning that humans use to explain who or what they are. The so-called demographic qualities are here: for example, age, sex, ethnicity, marital status, religion, occupation, social class, and sexual orientation. These are the traits that bind one to society and indicate in which social niches one belongs. Unlike the generic qualities, these features vary historically. Some thousands of years ago when all humans were in hunting and gathering bands, some of these traits were not present. People in these bands were all the same. There was age and gender, but there was no distinct ethnicity, religion, occupation, or social class. For most of human history then, or rather prehistory, there was a narrower batch of identities than in industrial society. But in the contemporary period the longer list is pretty much the one we use. It may also be that at some time in the future, the contemporary list of demographic traits will be replaced in some way.

Some people might not think of themselves in these terms, but rather in terms of their personal qualities. These are more diversified and often less stable than the social identities. Both batches of traits, the social and the personal, are relevant to the identity or self-concept level. But, in either case, the qualities of this level are not permanent or present for all humans. Nor are they transient and of minor importance, as is the case at the quotidian level. They mediate between the generic and the quotidian.

The third and least important level of the self is the everyday or quotidian level. Here, the habits that carry us through the day are located. Our diurnal routines and practices are, for the most part, quotidian. Similar is the way one performs one's work or occupation. One's inner speech is also a set of habits, for example, how one daydreams, plans, or solves problems. The everyday self is constantly changing, partly because the aging process brings new practices to fit the flow of time. It also appears there are borderline cases between the quotidian and identity levels, but it should be possible to clarify these eventually.

In the literature on the self, there is frequent discussion of self-fragmentation and loss of identity (for example, Gergen).[7] In my model, the things that do not change or get lost are the generic self-qualities. These might get modified in the way we exercise them; for example, we might become more assertive in our actions or introspective in our thought processes. We also might become more individualistic or more communal at times, which would affect the intensity of our self-awareness. But reflexivity would still be present, even with changes in nuance. In other words, the loss of self or identity, when it occurs, only applies to the nongeneric qualities of the self.

A similar category error is the one Foucault made when he announced the erasure of man or the demise of the subject (p. 387).[8] This was actually the death of a certain idea, which he called an *episteme*, about human nature. Ideas about things may come and go, but the things themselves may continue to exist. In my terms, Foucault's episteme belongs not at the generic level, but at the middle or identity level. Changes at the generic level could actually bring about some kind of death of the self or subject, but changes at the identity level merely modify the self in some way while continuing to allow it to exist. To sum up with an example, being able to speak a language is a generic property, speaking a particular language such as English is an identity, and speaking rapidly or slowly is quotidian. To put it another way, your generic qualities make you a human being, your identity traits make you yourself, and your quotidian qualities make you yourself on any given day.

I have now presented the three-part model of the self. The uniformity and egalitarian basis of the self is at the generic level. These traits are both universal and uniform from one person to another. It is these qualities that anchor the rights of human beings, as the Declaration of Independence suggested. Changes of the self, at least up to the present time, are at the other two levels. They do not alter the fundamental universality and egalitarianism of human beings. In addition, if there were no abiding or omnipresent traits in humans, the argument for egalitarianism and rights would lose its force.

The dialogical self

Another major idea of the pragmatists is that the self is dialogical and constantly engaged in internal communication. For Mead, this was a conversation between what he called the *I* (the present self) and the *me* (the past self).[9] Peirce, by contrast, thought the conversation was between the I and what he called the *you* (the "self that is just coming into life in the flow of time") (p. 258).[10] I prefer to combine these two approaches by saying the I talks to the you about the me, that is, the present self talks to the future self about the past self. This occurs on a timeline where the future is constantly becoming the present, and the present, the past. In other words the internal dialogue is ensconced in William James's stream of consciousness, which is, in turn, riding the flow of time.

The inner dialogue is the main way we use thought to solve problems. More specifically it is our means of self-regulation. Our agency or actions are also largely steered by inner speech. If humans have any free will, it seems to be exercised in the inner conversation, as when we say to ourselves, however furtively or impulsively, "I'll do that."

Returning to the I-you-me triad, how can the three temporal points coexist at the same time? They can do this because the self exists, not just in clock time but also in psychological or felt time. In this latter temporal realm, the present is not a pinpoint but rather a chunk or swatch of time. Our felt present includes a bit of the past and a smidgen of the future. This is how we can exist at three points in psychological time, while existing at only one point in physical or clock time.

These ideas suggest the following definition of the self—the self is a reflexive relation among three temporal stages of consciousness: the present (the *I*). the immediate future (the *you*), and the past (the *me*). This means the self is a property of a property. Consciousness is a property of the brain and reflexivity is a property of consciousness.

The self is not a free-standing substance, although it sometimes seems like one. A relation is a property of a substance, and it is not in itself free standing and autonomous. For a long time, from classical Greece to modern philosophy, philosophers thought the self (or the soul as it was then called) was a substance. This was partly because the idea of the soul was so grounded in the religious cultures of the times, but also because the self feels to us like a substance. Its psychological, as opposed to its ontological, reality is like a substance. It is so independent of and unlike the body it seems like a totally different entity. In terms of Hans Vaihinger's "as if" philosophy, the self seems "as if" it were a solid, permanent thing (pp, 36–38).[11] But despite the highly substantial power of the self, it is nevertheless, in the strict sense, a relation.

The two warring inequalities

In this paper I have thus far concentrated on the civil or legal self, showing how the United States began with a highly unequal civil self and gradually worked its way to near equality. I also went into some detail about the pragmatist theory of the self. But there is another issue of inequality of the self, as mentioned earlier, and this has to do with wealth and income. These two selves, the civil and the economic, and their inequalities are distinct, at least conceptually. But they are connected to some extent empirically.

This is because the two distributions or inequalities are connected by a rubber band, so to speak. By that I mean they pull on each other. A legally equal community of selves tends to pull the economic distribution in the direction of equality. The pull may be slight but it is there. And an economically unequal population tends to pull the legal self in an unequal direction, that is, toward civil inequality. If the poor are equal to the rich legally, they may want a broader share of the prosperity to make the two distributions more alike. And if the rich feel uncomfortable being legally equal to the poor, they may want to believe the poor are biologically inferior, thus justifying the wealth of the rich. As the historical sociologist Max Weber pointed out, those of high status have a tendency to explain their success as a superiority of "blood," that is, as a racist superiority (p. 276).[12] To put it another way, there is intense cognitive dissonance when a community that is equal in a legal or civic sense is sharply unequal in an economic sense. A small amount of income inequality may be useful as an investment incentive, a point that has not been completely proved. But this inequality does not need to be anywhere near as large as it is now.

The long fight for civic equality is only half the job. If economic inequality is allowed to proceed unchecked, as it is now, it will not only continue to cause business downturns and a weakened democracy, it will also exert a continuous pull back toward legal inequality. Unless prosperity itself becomes more democratic, the democracy of citizens may gradually be replaced by oligarchy.

Conclusion

This paper was primarily about how, in the battle of ideas, the American legal self was established in an egalitarian way. This required the minorities of race, gender, ethnicity, and sexual orientation, among others, to organize and struggle in the political arena. But organization and agendas were only part of the fight. There also had to be a solid, logical argument that equality was the correct path, both scientifically and morally. This paper was concerned with how the pragmatist philosophers and the social scientists put together that argument. In doing so, they not only explained the underlying meaning of American democracy, they also pointed the way for the rest of the world. The pragmatists took the two great American beacons—the Declaration of Independence and the Gettysburg Address—and showed their implications for bringing justice to the American community.

Acknowledgments

For advice on earlier drafts, thanks are due to Randall Collins, Zeke Hecker, John Heil, Jack Martin, E. Doyle McCarthy, Robert Perinbanayagam, Michele M. Thompson, Steven J. Wagner, and Vincent Wiley.

Conflicts of interest

The author declares no conflicts of interest.

References

1. Peirce, C.S. 1955. *Philosophical Writings of Peirce*. Dover Publications, Inc. New York.
2. Perinbanayagam, R. 1991. *Discursive Acts*. Aldine De Gruyter. New York.
3. Wiley, N. 2006. Peirce and the founding of American sociology. *J. Classical Sociology* **6:** 23–50.
4. James, W. 1950 (c.1890). *Principles of Psychology, Vol. 1.* Dover Publications, Inc. New York.

5. Denzin, N.K. 1984. *On Understanding Emotion.* Jossey-Bass Publishers. San Francisco.

6. Scheff, Jr. T.J. 2006. *Goffman Unbound: A New Paradigm for the Social Sciences.* Paradigm Publishers. Boulder.

7. Gergen, K.J. 1991. *The Saturated Self: Dilemmas of Identity in Contemporary Life.* Basic Books. New York.

8. Foucault, M. 1970. *The Order of Things.* Vintage Books. New York.

9. Mead, G.H. 1964. *Selected Writings.* The Bobbs-Merrill Company. Indiana.

10. Peirce, C.S. 1955. *Philosophical Writings of Peirce.* Dover Publications, Inc. New York.

11. Vaihinger, H. 1924. *The Philosophy of "As If."* Kegan Paul, Trench, Trubner & Co. Ltd. London.

12. Weber, M. 1946 (c1922–1923). *From Max Weber.* Oxford University Press. New York.

Ann. N.Y. Acad. Sci. ISSN 0077-8923

ANNALS OF THE NEW YORK ACADEMY OF SCIENCES
Issue: *Perspectives on the Self*

Who am I? Beyond "I think, therefore I am"

Alex Voorhoeve, Elie During, David Jopling, Timothy Wilson, and Frances Kamm

Can we ever truly answer the question, "Who am I?" Moderated by Alex Voorhoeve (London School of Economics), neuro-philosopher Elie During (University of Paris, Ouest Nanterre), cognitive scientist David Jopling (York University, Canada), social psychologist Timothy Wilson (University of Virginia), and ethicist Frances Kamm (Harvard University) examine the difficulty of achieving genuine self-knowledge and how the pursuit of self-knowledge plays a role in shaping the self.

Voorhoeve: Many thanks to both the Nour Foundation and the New York Academy of Sciences for organizing this event. In a moment, I'll introduce the speakers to you.

But first, I'd like to reflect on today's theme, "Beyond 'I think, therefore I am.'" Of course, it comes from René Descartes. Descartes has become a bit of a whipping boy in discussions of the self, for two reasons. The first is his claim that the mind and the body are two completely distinct substances, which of course leads us to wonder how the two could ever interact. And Descartes was frank about the fact that he hadn't really figured that one out. We won't belabor this problem with his substance dualism tonight.

The second error attributed to Descartes, which is closer to the heart of what we're interested in today, is mentioned by Tim Wilson at the beginning of his book, *Strangers to Ourselves*. The purported error is that our thinking and our sensing are always *transparent* to us. That is to say: we are conscious of what we think and sense. We know what's going on in ourselves, insofar as we're thinking. And you might think that seems pretty plausible. In a moment, we'll get to the bottom of why Tim thinks this is nonetheless mistaken. But first, I want to stress that it doesn't follow that Descartes thought that we were *entirely* transparent to ourselves. Indeed, he believed some of our motives were unconscious.

We know this, because Queen Christina of Sweden wrote to Descartes to ask what "causes...often incite us to love one person rather than another before we know their merit." Descartes replied that when we experience a strong sensation, this causes the brain to crease like a piece of paper. And when the stimulus stops, the brain uncreases, but it stays ready to be creased again in the same way. And when a similar stimulus is presented, then we get the same response, because the brain is ready to crease again.

And what did he mean by all this? Well, he gave an example. He said that all his life he had had a fetish for cross-eyed women. Whenever he came across a cross-eyed woman, desire would enflame him. And he figured out, he said, after introspection, that this was because his brain had been strongly creased by his first childhood love, who was cross-eyed. Now what's interesting there is that he says there was this unconscious desire moving him quite strongly, of which he became

doi: 10.1111/j.1749-6632.2011.06186.x

conscious through introspection. And he adds that once he became conscious of it, he stopped immediately falling in love with cross-eyed women.[a]

There are three interesting things in this example, I think. First, we have unconscious desires. To some extent, according to Descartes, we are strangers to ourselves. Second, we can, at least in this case, through introspection become aware of these desires. Third, by bringing them to awareness we can extinguish these desires, insofar as we don't want to be moved by them. The example is a story of success in that respect. Now, tonight, we're going to look at challenges to the latter two ideas: that we can come to know our unconscious desires through introspection and can eliminate them when they are undesirable. In addition, we'll look into the aforementioned question of whether our thoughts, at least, are transparent to ourselves because we are conscious of everything we *think*.

And some of these challenges involve the following questions. First, what is the nature of the unconscious? Is it like the Freudian unconscious that we've all heard about, or is it something different? Second, how can we come to know ourselves, our hidden motives, our hidden thoughts? Is introspection, the thing that Descartes engages in this snippet of a conversation with Queen Christina, a good, reliable way? (Many of our panelists have challenged introspection.). And the third question is, if we try to gain this knowledge of our unconscious self, what is it good for? In Descartes' case it was useful, but it might not be so good in every case. Maybe, as Jack Nicholson's character says at the end of *A Few Good Men*, when he is pressed by a lawyer to confess the whole truth: "You can't handle the truth!" After all, we all can think of aspects of ourselves that we'd rather not have brought to our consciousness.

Let me briefly introduce the people we have here to discuss this. First, Timothy Wilson, professor of psychology at the University of Virginia, author of the book *Strangers to Ourselves*, which focuses on the three themes I just outlined. This is a fascinating book, with the subtitle *Discovering the Adaptive Unconscious*. I'll be asking him some questions about that.

Then we have a philosopher who's deeply interested in psychology, David Jopling, professor of philosophy at York University in Canada. He has written a beautiful book, *Self-knowledge and the Self*, in which he explores, among other things, how we come to know ourselves. He argues that introspection and the therapeutic sessions you've all been paying so much for are of pretty dubious value, and that instead, to know ourselves, we should engage in a different form of dialogue. So I'll be asking him some questions about that.

And then there's Elie During, associate professor at the University of Paris-Ouest Nanterre. In one word, Elie is an omnivore in philosophy, because he's written on questions in the philosophy of science, on questions of self-knowledge, and on ethics. One of the key things I want to question

---

[a]Here is the relevant passage:

...The objects that touch our senses move, by the intermediary of the nerves, certain parts of our brain, and make there, as it were, certain creases that undo themselves when the object ceases to act; however, the part where they were made remains afterward disposed to being creased again in the same manner by another object resembling the first in some aspect....
For example, when I was a child, I loved a girl of my age who had a slight squint. Because of that, the impression made upon my brain by the sight of her crossed eyes so closely joined itself to that made there to rouse in me the passion of love, that for a long time afterward, in seeing cross-eyed persons, I felt myself more inclined to love them than others, only because they had this defect. Nevertheless, I did not know that was the reason. On the contrary, since I have reflected upon it, and recognized it was a defect, I have no longer been affected by it.

From *Descartes: His Moral Philosophy and Psychology,* translated by John J. Blom, New York University Press, 1978. Quoted on http://sites.google.com/site/psychiatryfootnotes/case-histories-from-the-history-of-psychiatry/descartes-self-analysis

him on tonight is his claim that "ethics is a self-transformative process." That's to say, you come to know yourself in order to make something of yourself, to change yourself.

Our fourth panelist is Frances Kamm, professor of philosophy at Harvard and one of the world's leading ethicists. [Jokingly:] I would *almost* say I could recommend—but you have to have the stomach for it!—her two-volume *Morality, Mortality*, and following that, *Intricate Ethics*, and, most recently, *Ethics for Enemies: Terror, Torture, and War*. Frances is known for a distinctive method of doing ethics, which is, if I could sum it up rather roughly, introspective. She imagines herself in a particular situation, a moral case, and asks herself, "How would I respond in this case?," and then tries to uncover the reasons why she would respond to it in that way. Now, that's an interesting method, but it seems that some of the other speakers here tonight challenge it in their work—which I hope will make for interesting debate.

But let us return to that second purported error of Descartes I mentioned at the outset. Tim, maybe you could start us off by helping us to understand what unconscious *thought* is?

Wilson: Well, as with most things, it depends how we define it. If we mean by thought the self-talk that we're all used to doing and engaging in, then almost by definition that is conscious. But research psychologists over the past few decades have expanded their views of the extent to which our minds operate unconsciously. The kinds of cognitive operations we can perform outside of awareness, such as learning new material, detecting patterns, filtering information as it comes in, is vast. Even such higher-order processes as setting goals for ourselves and combining information to reach decisions can occur unconsciously. There is gathering evidence that all of these things, which we used to think were performed only by our conscious minds, can occur unconsciously as well.

Voorhoeve: And you conceptualize this unconscious as the *adaptive unconscious*. What does that mean?

Wilson: Well, partly it's to contrast with the Freudian unconscious. I'm not denying that there may well be a Freudian unconscious, a repository of instinctual urges that we do our best to keep hidden in the basement of our minds. The point I want to make is that there may be a much different kind of unconscious that probably evolved earlier in our development as a species than consciousness did; an example of what I have in mind is the ability to transform information and to think in ways that further our survival—hence the term *adaptive*. I think this kind of quick sizing up of the world, interpreting information, and deciding how to act can happen very quickly and outside of conscious view; it is not something that's buried because we don't want to know it. It's part of the architecture of the brain that is unknowable.

Voorhoeve: So, unknowable. That seems to say that what Descartes was engaged in, trying to figure out the reason why he had this fetish for cross-eyed girls, is an impossible exercise.

Wilson: There are various metaphors for introspection and I think the Descartes example is an interesting one. One metaphor for introspection is that it's like a flashlight that we're shining in the dark; and we flash it in the corner and discover that crease in the brain that we just hadn't bothered to see before.

Another metaphor that Freud was fond of is *introspection as archeology*. We're digging up things that were buried deep down in our minds. If we dig deeply enough we'll find them.

The metaphor I prefer is introspection as *narrative building*. We're constructing stories about ourselves based on some access to desires, but not as much. This process is similar to how we would construct a narrative about somebody else, such as observing what they do and bringing our vast cultural knowledge to bear. I'm not so sure that isn't what Descartes did. He deduced almost as another person might have: "Ah, this is the tenth cross-eyed girl I'm attracted to and I remember that first one, so maybe there is a pattern here. . ." So it may not have been by shining a flashlight or digging deeply, rather he may have simply inferred his liking for cross-eyed women based on self-observation.

Voorhoeve: So you're saying we figure out things about our unconscious by imagining how someone else would look at us?

Wilson: In part. I think that's actually not a bad way to try to do it, to see ourselves through the eyes of others. That's a difficult thing to do, to get outside of our own heads. But I think that is one interesting path to self-knowledge.

Voorhoeve: One of the things that struck me when you said that what we're trying to do is create a narrative about ourselves is that a narrative brings to mind the thought that we're just storytelling. And you mention some cases to illustrate this narrative capacity. For example, psychologists hypnotize people and then get them to do absolutely crazy things—I think, in one case, to put a lamp shade on the head of someone else who is in the room and kneel in front of this person. (Quite interesting, by the way, why one would choose that to suggest to one's experimental subject!) But when the subjects in this situation were asked, "Why did you just put the lamp shade on the head of the other guy in the room?" they would come up with a story, such as, "Oh, I just thought we should lighten the mood here a little bit." But that's *confabulation*.

Wilson: Yes. There are very striking examples of brain-damaged patients and others who can't know exactly why they did what they just did but are very fluent in inventing reasons that they seem to truly believe are the reasons they did it. It seems to be very important to us to have a narrative of why we are doing what we are doing. And we're very skilled at constructing such narratives.

Voorhoeve: David, I thought I might bring you in on this point. You claim that this construction of an unreliable narrative is what happens in a lot of therapeutic sessions, right? But you don't seem to be so sanguine about the idea that such a narrative will do.

Jopling: No. I have some reservations about the so-called *talking cures* or the exploratory psychotherapies, where the goal is insight or self-knowledge. If you look closely at the interpersonal dynamics in a psychotherapeutic or clinical psychological situation, there's a huge amount of pressure on patients, or clients, to produce the sorts of insights that are expected of them by their therapists or psychiatrists. There is also a very strong expectation for them to comply with the doctrine. It's called *doctrinal compliance*: comply with the doctrine or the theoretical orientation of the therapist. If they don't, they're not good patients. There are a lot of subtle cues and pressures, leading questions, and suggestions to get patients to see things as their therapists want them to see them.

And certain turning points in the talking cures—such as psychodynamic psychotherapy, Freudian analysis, and narrative psychotherapy, for which insight is one of the highest goals—the therapists offer interpretations to the clients about what their problems are, or about what their Freudian unconscious looks like, or about the various pathologies from which they're suffering. And these interpretations are generated from hours and hours of clinical material that have been collected by the therapist. But they're very powerful frameworks for patients to use to think about themselves and their problems. It is expected, then, that the patients develop insights that more or less conform to these and confirm these interpretations. The insights that clients thus acquire are vivid, they are intense, and the clients often have very high levels of conviction about them. But my question is, are they true? I don't know.

Voorhoeve: Does it matter?

Jopling: Sometimes it does not matter because these insights trigger therapeutic improvement. They generate more clinical material, they can be adaptive, very helpful; clients feel good about them. And yet in my interpretation, some of these insights are placebos. They are the psychological equivalent of a sugar pill. They're missing some vital ingredient; that's the nature of placebos. They're missing active, medicinal ingredients; they're empty pharmacologically. The psychological equivalent is what is missing. And I would venture that in some cases, not all cases, these so-called insights are placebos because they're not truth-tracking. They're not true. They're false but adaptive; they work and they bring about some degree of therapeutic improvement.

Wilson: If I could just jump in. I agree with most of what you said except perhaps the idea that truth is the ultimate goal. There are many versions of truth about one's life and many narratives that might make sense to a person. In fact, the data on psychotherapy of which I'm aware show that psychotherapy does work for many problems. What's interesting and not inconsistent with what you're saying is the theoretical discipline doesn't matter much; very different kinds of psychological therapies work, and the key predictor of whether they work is whether the client buys into the belief system of that therapy.

   The only place we may differ is whether that means that therapy is somehow false or not helpful or placebic. Instead, perhaps we all crave a narrative that we believe in and can help us make sense of our lives and move beyond our problems. I tend to think the latter.

Voorhoeve: Elie, you and I were discussing this before and you said, "if it works, it must be true in some sense," no?

During: Well, the intuition is that if it works somehow then it means that you've hit upon something.

   But to come back to the general question, the one you raised earlier, which is why should we care at all about knowing ourselves?

   My first answer would be, it's not very clear what we mean by *knowing*. The self is one thing, and although we decided not to raise the general question of what is the self, I'd like to raise the question, What do we mean by *knowing*, by knowledge? And from the various examples we just had, it's clear that it can mean a wide variety of different practices, actions, and operations, from locating in your memory one particular event—Descartes and the cross-eyed girl and kind of weirdly relating that to a crease in your brain, or today we would speak of a synaptic path rather than crease—to the therapeutic relationship. And it also could mean the kind of self-modeling process, unconscious mostly, that's going on in any learning activity. These are very different ways of relating to oneself and very different ways of trying to know something about oneself. And I don't see how you could be interested in knowing yourself in general, if self-knowledge covers all these very different activities. I don't see what it means really.

   So what I'm interested in, when I grapple with the problem of self-knowledge, is what do I get personally? And my intuition is that if we are interested, in the first place, in knowing ourselves, it's because we want to change something about ourselves—that there's something in ourselves that is not very satisfying—something that must be transformed. In my view, the proper reference frame or context we need to make sense of self-knowledge is *ethics*. That would be my answer.

Voorhoeve: I can imagine wanting to know myself not merely in order to change myself, but in order to make a big life decision. To take an imaginary case, I might ask, "Should I stay with my girlfriend, and do I really love her?" That's not necessarily about my wanting to change myself, but just really wanting to know, is this the person for me?

And what struck me in some of Tim's and David's work is that they claim that sitting in a room thinking deeply about whether this is the person for me is probably one of the *worst* ways I can go about it. Why is that?

Wilson: Well, I think there's only so much that gazing at our navels can accomplish, and I think being acute observers of our behavior can be very helpful. There is increasing evidence in psychology that our friends often pick up on things about us that we don't see. But I think, as in the Descartes example, we can be very good observers of how we're reacting and what the circumstances are, of what seems to trigger joy and love and what doesn't.

Kamm: But surely you ask yourself, besides how do I feel about this, you look at certain objective factors, such as do we enjoy being together, do I feel satisfied after having spoken with this person, do we share the same interests? And these are more objective things than simply how do I feel. Will there be conflicts because I want one thing and this other person wants another thing? Surely. But if you're not looking at those things, you're looking at the wrong navel. I mean, there are lots of holes in the body—right? There are these more objective factors we refer to that will tell us or help us decide whether we're in an appropriate relationship or doing the right thing in our own lives.

Voorhoeve: That's true. And the example might move us to some of your cases in ethics. One of the things that Tim claims is that there are a lot of things that I *want*, *think*, and *believe* that I can't articulate. No matter how hard I think about it and try to introspect, I can't figure them out. One way of figuring them out is to place myself imaginatively in a situation and imagine how I would respond. And that's a way of gaining indirect access to my subconscious desires and thoughts.

In my imagined case, the question might be, "Does my heart leap up if I imagine spending the next ten years with this person?' But here's how I thought it linked to some of your cases, Frances. For those of you who aren't yet familiar with much of Frances' work, her methodology involves placing yourself in a given case, seeing what your intuitive response would be when you really imagine yourself in that case, and then trying to figure out, through introspection, what the reasons are that drive this response—I see you shaking your head! Am I mischaracterizing?

Kamm: That's right.

Voorhoeve: Well, how about you take over then.

Kamm: Well, I was reading the writings you helpfully gave me of Tim Wilson's things, and I thought, there's a lot here that I agree with. So, let me tell you the sort of cases that I imagine, that I'm discussing. They're thought experiments. They're like scientific experiments done in a laboratory, where you can hold all factors constant and alter a variable, just one variable at a time, to see the effect. Scientists still do that, I assume, right? However, of course, in thought experiments, you're just imagining.

Philosophers of my type, analytic moral philosophers, spend a lot of time discussing this one case that has been made famous called the trolley problem. There's a trolley headed toward five people that's going to kill them, and a bystander could turn the trolley onto another track away from the five. But unfortunately there's one person on the other track who will get hit and be killed. And the question is, is it permissible to do that, to turn the trolley? So that's an imaginary case. It's not like I'm there, standing there.

There are thousands of variations of such imaginary cases and each one is a little thought experiments. This is what Alex means by saying that I think of myself in a case.

So, the trolley's headed toward the five in another variant: there's someone standing on a bridge over the trolley tracks. If you push that one person in front of the trolley, it will stop the trolley and save the five people from it; may you do that? Now, many people say no, though I haven't done surveys. And that is another part of the method: you think about something rather than do surveys.

So, I think it's permissible to turn the trolley away from the five people, though it will hit the one person. But I do *not* think it's permissible to push the one person over a bridge in front of the trolley even though, again, one person will die and five people will be saved.

So what's the difference? Why do I have these intuitive judgments? I make a judgment about right and wrong. And this is supposed to be an objectively true judgment; it's the sort of judgment I think you all should agree with. It's not something that's just expressing my own personal point of view any more than Professor Wilson's views that you've come to hear are just a way of reaching into his soul and understanding himself. He claims to be talking about the truth about the adaptive conscious.

Voorhoeve: He's not just giving us a narrative—he's aiming at the truth.

Kamm: That's the thing. We're not just interested in ourselves—you know, what am I thinking? We want to know whether we're latching on to the truth about the subject matter we're thinking about. And that's the same in ethics.

Where I agree with Professor Wilson is that I think, first of all, that a lot of people tell themselves stories. He calls it confabulation; I would call it conjectures that are not correct. For example, some psychologists have thought that the only distinction between these two trolley problems I've introduced you to is that in one, I'm up close and personal to the person I push over the bridge, but not to the person that I turn the trolley to. The way you deal with a hypothesis like that is you think, suppose instead of pushing the person over the bridge, I had a machine that I could use to press a button from a distance, and this would push the person over the bridge. Do I think *that* makes it permissible to push him over the bridge? Intuitively, my judgment is no. So when I remove the factor that is presented as the crucial variable between permissible and impermissible, I do not get a change in my judgment about impermissibility, which suggests that this factor is not accounting for my judgment. This is a way of teasing out whether a particular factor or conjecture is correct or incorrect.

Similarly, you could do it by taking this factor that people say makes the action impermissible, construct another case where it is present, and find it doesn't make the action impermissible, which I've done also, which is why I have so many cases.

I think that this is like the method that Tim Wilson says gives access to the adaptive unconscious, which is called *inference*. It doesn't mean that I have privileged access to myself that I couldn't have with someone else. Because I'm constantly trying out and testing hypotheses about why I have made that judgment. And Professor Wilson grants that you can have access to yourself of that sort, inferential. That's one of the reasons I agree with something else he says, namely that I could have as good knowledge about why someone else makes a certain judgment as about why I do. Because when I see all the people who say, "Yes, you may turn the trolley this way but you may not push the man over," if I have explained by this method of inference, considering all different cases, what the crucial factor is, I would understand that they would respond to that factor. That's why I think that there is some degree of agreement here. But it doesn't mean that this adaptive unconscious is completely inaccessible. That isn't what he's claiming.

The interesting other thing that I found was that very often the so-called confabulations that people give, they tend to be quite simple, like this one: well, you're up close and personal, you're pushing the guy over. My explanation of the difference among all these cases, and not only these two, but many others—you've got to get a theory that accounts for all of them—it can be quite complex or at least unexpected. One's response can be something like, "What? I would never have thought of that."

I was very struck in Professor Wilson's book by what he called *implicit learning*. Experimenters flashed certain lights or "x's" in various quadrants of a screen or grid according to a very complicated formula. Implicitly, subjects learned to adapt to that flashing of light, so that eventually they came to predict where the next "x" would be. If you asked them to verbalize this complicated formula, what made them do that, they said other things, simple-minded things that didn't correlate at all with the way they behaved.

The actual truth was complicated, and so when the theory that explains people's intuitions is discovered, if it's complicated or not, that really may be what's going on, that's really what is causing people to behave in certain ways or respond in certain ways. I take that as consistent with something that Professor Wilson had said about implicit learnings.

I want to emphasize that we're not just looking into our navels when we do this as philosophers. When I claim that this is a factor that accounts for why it's permissible to do something in one case and impermissible to do it in another, I'm claiming that that's the *moral truth*. This is a step beyond investigating grounds for intuitions. And that means that it's supposed to be *universalizable*. That is, everybody, no matter how much they differ from me in their likes or dislikes, their upbringing, their interests in life, should agree that this is the way they ought to behave—that it's permissible for them to do this and impermissible to do the other thing. So there is this claim to objectivity and universality about permissibility. And that's not just self-knowledge. And my sense is that's what's *really* important—to find that out.

During: It's definitely important, and I find it highly interesting to, as you do, experiment on our intuitions to dig out the invariant structures of moral judgment. In what sense is this self-knowledge at all in the sense of how myself, this particular self that I am, is concerned by this? If it's a universal structure of moral judgment, I would say the real question, the ethical question, is how is it that I'm not always ready to agree with this universal truth that you unearth?

Kamm: Agree?

During: How is it that I don't always act upon this kind of intuition? What prevents me from seeing the moral truth behind these very sophisticated scenarios? And at this point I think we're touching on an actual problem of self-knowledge. It's why me, as this particular individual that I am, why am I having an issue with these general questions?

Kamm: I agree with you. You come back to the question of the self when you see, for example, that some people may disagree about the principle. A member of the Nazi party may say, "There's nothing wrong with burning these people; those people it's impermissible to burn, but *these* people it's right to". And then you would want to see by considering their views whether you could find fault in their reasoning, and who has the correct moral view. But you're right, they may say, "I don't see your point of view." And then you may just say, "Well, that doesn't mean it's not correct; you may have reasoned incorrectly." But you will have people who will say, "I see that it's wrong to take the drugs, but I want them so much, I'm going to give in."

So we have personal qualities, weakness of will or habitual behavior, that can interfere with doing the objectively right thing. And that's the point at which we have to consider what philosopher Harry Frankfurt has considered, the meta-judgmental self. This self may stand and see that you have this desire to ignore the distinction between permissible and impermissible: you want the money, you're going to take it, you know it's wrong. But if there is this meta-judgment, some people will have a part of themselves that says, "I don't want to be this way; I do not endorse my desires; I do not endorse my predilections." And then the question is, can they be put in control? Can that part of the self that judges the other part be put in control? The trouble is that this process may go on to the next level. Because when you're thinking about truth, you may say, "Is the perspective from which I do or do not endorse my desires, is that the correct perspective?" You've got to check on that first meta-judgment, whether that's true as well.

Voorhoeve: The thing that you bring up there, Frances, this question of our endorsing our desires, I think, is of crucial importance. If I were to answer the question you put to us earlier, namely, "Why do we care about figuring out ourselves, including our subconscious selves and desires?", then my answer would be: to gain self-control, to become more autonomous. Because I think one of the most unsettling things is when we don't know why we do what we do, or we don't endorse the desires on which we act. And one of the reasons we turn in on ourselves, or try to figure out by inferential methods what we are like, is to get past the point of lacking this control over ourselves. Either because we don't know what's driving us, or because we *do* know what's driving us but we don't want that to lead us. And Elie, at some point in our correspondence, you quoted Bergson to the effect that one *becomes* a person only with great effort, rather than, as we ordinarily would say, simply becomes a person once one has reached the age of reason.

During: Yeah. That's if you're a psychologist. If you're a philosopher, you'd say you are a person when you're a moral agent and you're responsible.

Bergson had this theory about the fact that it's a strenuous effort to be a person, to maintain this continuous attention; attending to oneself is something that costs a lot. But I was thinking also of another thinker whom Richard referred to, Ostad Elahi, who had this very sophisticated notion of the *imperious self*, which echoes what you were just saying. I think the issue of self-knowledge really becomes ethically significant and important when you start differentiating within yourself between different layers or levels of the self. A deep level—I wouldn't say authentic, because I don't know what that means—but a deep level and a superficial level, which is the superficial ego and the one that projects a social image to other, this social self that William James referred to. And as I said, there is a spiritual self or deep self.

And Ostad Elahi had this notion of the spiritual self, or self modeling itself, self modeling its personality, as attention between an imperious self, which is a bundle of drives or urges or desires that basically come down to animal nature, and a higher self, call it the second-order self, which is present not so much to establish control (well, yes, of course, the ultimate goal is to maintain some control over this and transform yourself accordingly) but to get something from the knowledge of this imperious self. It's not about crushing your desires or just getting rid of these very annoying urges. It's about getting something from them and building virtues upon them. We use these very old-fashioned terms ("virtues") that Aristotle reflected upon.

Virtues are basically about transforming your passions and desires into something that's constructive and will make you flourish as a spiritual self. But I think it's very important to have this self-model and this dynamic tension between two levels of ourselves. And the notion of imperious self developed by Ostad Elahi is a case in point. It's a very interesting way of self-modeling without having any perspective of gaining an absolute objective knowledge of yourself, as an embodied person or as an unconscious psyche. These are all elements that can be useful in the ethical process of self transformations, knowing about unconscious drives or aspirations. But the ultimate goal is not to map your personality in every detail. That doesn't make sense. Again, the idea is to come up with an effective model of your ethical self. And this involves, at some point, a tension between two levels, call them first-order and second-order selves, or a superficial self and something that you identify with.

Voorhoeve: Tim's been shifting uncomfortably . . . Would you like to come in on this point?

Wilson: To go back to something that Frances was saying. I actually resonated a lot with the idea of thought experiments. It's something we psychologists do a lot too. But I think there are somewhat different goals. We do sit in our offices doing these thought experiments, but then we go and do the actual experiments. Because the goal, for us, is to predict what people actually do. Your goal is, I think, somewhat different: to specify what people ought to do.

And the trolley example was very interesting, because I've always wished I could do a real experiment with that. Obviously I can't for ethical reasons (*participants laughing*). But I'm not sure that any of the analyses of people's intuitions about it would match what they would actually do in that situation, faced with a split-second decision of "I can save five lives or one" and "I can do it this way or that way." I'm not sure that the kind of hypotheses we come up with through thought experiments would do a great job of predicting people's actual behavior.

My friend and colleague Dan Gilbert and I have done a lot of research on what we call affective forecasting, which is people's ability to predict their future emotional reactions to future events. And although we're not terrible at it, we do make systematic errors in knowing exactly how we will feel, for example, whether it really would be horrible to push one person to save five. These are predictions that aren't always correct.

Kamm: But suppose you could put someone in this situation, as you say, if it were ethical to do so, and they pushed the person over the bridge. The question, as you said, is not resolved of whether they ought to have done that. They may have done it, and they may have done the wrong thing. They may have not done the right thing in the split second. So as you say, your question is different from mine. Similarly, I know about some of these experiments, but please correct me if I'm wrong, about predicting your future affective state.

Many people say that it would be horrible for them to be paralyzed. They think about the future. They wouldn't want that—very bad. But if you ask people who have actually become paralyzed they say, "I have a fine life." What we have to be careful about is thinking that all that is at issue is your feeling of well-being—and you said, "Would I feel horrible if I pushed the man over the bridge?" That's not the important issue. The question is whether you've done the wrong thing, and that's not always a matter of how you feel. Similarly, the paralyzed person cannot walk. The fact that he adapts in a certain way or tells himself certain stories about how it's not important to walk—you can do lots of other things, you don't need to walk—does not show that it isn't bad not to be able to walk.

The fact that we can perhaps delude ourselves in a certain situation is not an indication that, for example, if people come into the emergency room and some people have severe headaches and another person will have spinal damage, that I should say, "Well, treat the person with the headache because he's really in pain. The other guy, he'll be paralyzed but he won't be in pain, and psychologically he'll adapt very quickly." I think that is absolutely the wrong decision to make, because there are more objective criteria. There's something else besides how you *feel* that is relevant to whether you're living a good life.

Wilson: Well, let me give what I think might be a fairer example. Suppose you're the physician who has to decide how much to treat someone who's going to become paralyzed or someone with another severe disorder that's more difficult to adapt to. I think certain digestive problems or urinary problems that have to be dealt with daily are much more difficult to adapt to than other disorders. And I think that's relevant information. And although there may be some self-deception and delusion in a paralyzed person, I think that what we can't predict is how much we will adapt and come to terms with something. I'm not sure I would use the term *delusion* as much as *adaptation*. But I think that's precisely what we find hard to imagine in advance.

Kamm: Okay.

Voorhoeve: David, it seemed that you had some objections to Elie's earlier remarks.

Jopling: No, I just wanted to follow up on something that Elie was saying about this, these different levels of self. Talking about the self this way goes back to William James, who talked about many different kinds of selves, and asked whether there was a self of selves that he could know, and he had a lot of trouble; all he came up with were some movements in his throat.

But this notion of reflective self-evaluation, which is directed to answering the question who am I, what am I like, who do I want to be? This is a theme that Frankfurt picks up. It's a very interesting process: you look at the desires that you actually have and you ask yourself, "Do I want these desires, do I want these desires to motivate me and to constitute my will?" And you can do this with a number of de facto desires and beliefs that you find in yourself. Persons are not simply given static entities, but they have an ability to shape themselves to a certain extent. But I wonder about who was there at the second-order level asking do I want these desires? And I wonder if it gets you into a kind of regress and into a third level and a fourth level and so on.

Kamm: Yes, that's what I mentioned before, that the meta-judgment can go on to the next level. You can have an evaluation of the values that you have right now.

Jopling: Where does it stop and where is the self that you finally want to stick with and say, "That's me. This is the self I want to be or I am"?

During: There's a very simple solution practically: desires never muddle themselves. There are particular instances where you frame yourself and picture yourself as having the kind of personality traits that you want to get rid of at some point. I don't know where that comes from, but that's what I'm interested in. But would that be a problem if this wasn't the monitoring superself that philosophers imagined—if it were different, if it were a bundle of different powers or instances within myself, that would be OK.

The important thing is that we have this tension between two levels.

Kamm: One level has authority. It's not just a conflict between different desires. The whole idea is there's an authority that one level has that the other one doesn't. The question is, where does that come from?

Jopling: And where does it go? How far up does it go?

Kamm: Yes, right, right.

Voorhoeve: No, I don't think this necessarily involves an infinite regress. Just take questions like: "Do I love my children?" and "Do I *want* to love my children?" Now, "Do I love them?" That's the first-order question. And the answer is: "Yes." The second-order question is: "Do I want to be the type of person who loves my children?" If I answer "Yes", then that's an affirmation of my first-order desire. Now, David's saying, "Well, you could go on forever, asking questions of an even higher order, such as "Do I want to want to be the type of person who loves my children?" But it seems to me that when I am satisfied with myself, with my constellation of desires, I can realize that no matter how much I would think about it, and how many orders I add to the question, I will always answer in the affirmative.

Kamm: But someone like Peter Singer, who thinks we should take a more impersonal point of view on ourselves versus others, will say, "I do now think that it's right to care for my children, but should I care for them more than for the other children in the world, given that, objectively, their status is equal?" And he thinks—I don't want to attribute to this to Peter Singer exactly so let's just call this a Peter Singer–like fantasy person—all right, someone who takes the impersonal point of view will say "You ought *not* to want to be the person who loves your child more than someone else." Now, that may be the wrong moral conclusion, but at that point you can't just say, "I find myself wanting to be this sort of a person." Instead, you've got to give yourself a *reason* for wanting to be one sort of person rather than another. So you've got to start reasoning about these things.

Voorhoeve: I'm going to bring in the audience here, because I think you all deserved a chance to ask questions of the speakers. Here's the first question: "Is knowledge of the self an introspective process, or more of what other people say we are? If so, then should we weigh what people say against what we believe about ourselves?" Do you want to start, Tim?

Wilson: Well, as I mentioned before, I think there is increasing evidence that if you ask people close to us to rate our personalities, they have a somewhat different view than we do of ourselves. There's overlap of course. But both of those views are good predictors of our behavior. So it seems that there's some element of truth in how we view ourselves and some element of truth in how others view us. And so I think paying attention to how others think of us is important. But I don't think it's terribly easy. We tend to think others see us the way we see ourselves, for example.

I've often wondered if there should be a new Hallmark holiday called Friendly Feedback Day, (*participants laughing*) when our friends send us cards with helpful hints of things that we don't seem to know about ourselves. There might be some benefit to that. You heard it here first (*participants laughing*).

Jopling: Could I just add to that?

Voorhoeve: Yes, please.

Jopling: I think we can learn a lot from Socrates, who mastered the art of dialogue. Getting people to learn about themselves by coming up against Socrates' way of questioning—he was brusque and arrogant and tough-minded and really put people through the wringer—is one particularly difficult form of self-examination with another person. And I think we've inherited a tradition, going at least back to Descartes, possibly to Augustine, where self-knowledge is thought of as an activity that's pursued by the self, for the self, and, ultimately, with the self's own resources. And other people, their biases, their influences, they're kept at the side, because they are contaminating influences. So the best way to know about yourself is to retreat, or to suspend the influence of society and other people.

I think there are a lot of problems with that. I would say you learn about yourself in dialogue with other people; at least this is one of the ways to learn about yourself. Not every kind of dialogue is conducive to self-knowing, but there are some dialogs where the other person is a presence that evokes honesty or truthfulness from you that you might not otherwise have been amenable to. The Other is possibly a moral witness, to your accounting, to your owning up. You're owning up to an Other and learning about yourself this way. So I think there's a role for dialogue, and not just interjecting what other people say about you, but other people serving as foils and challenges to your explorations.

Kamm: I think you might have to be careful, though, especially if you are a member of a group that has been subordinated or for whom there has been a stereotype for certain behavior. That what you may get back from others is the expectation of a continuation of that position. So you should always question. And again, think about the reasons. Ask the other person, "Well, why do you think I should change in that direction? Give me a reason." Because otherwise you open yourself up to the possibility of self-diminishment.

Voorhoeve: That's the point about the nature of the ideal partner in dialogue. Socrates wasn't a friend to the people he was investigating, right? Tim was talking about friends, but you don't put your friends to death for being really annoying, which is what the Athenians did to Socrates. Then again, telling your friends what you really think of them might end rather badly (*participants laughing*).

David, if I could ask, how is the type of dialogue you propose different from other types? It's not the dialogue of therapist and patient, according to you; it's not necessarily a friendly dialogue. It's not a dialogue with someone who has preconceptions about you. So what type of dialogue is it?

Jopling: Well, I think perhaps there are psychotherapeutic or psychiatric dialogues that strive toward this, but they get trapped up in technique, technology, manipulation, and goals that are foreign to the person. I think some dialogues—probably quite rare—are spontaneous, unpredictable and from which you have no idea where it's going to end up and how you're going to be changed, but you are changed. A blind spot that has been preventing you from seeing yourself— some really basic dimension about yourself—has been removed by the challenge of the presence of the other person.

Voorhoeve: So, in part, it's about the dialogue being open ended?

Jopling: Yes. Very much an open-ended dialogue, and it's being open to another person.

During: Another point is that most of the insights we get from the feedback of other people come through problems of ethics, such as "you're behaving in a certain way, it infringes upon my rights." Most often they are not worded like this, but it comes down to "what you're doing to me or to us is a problem." So it's really ethical feedback. It's not an insight or inner psyche. You have a privileged access to whatever happens in your mind, I'm convinced of this, and the feedback you can expect is directly moral or ethical feedback. So it directly contributes to this ethical self-modeling. It's interesting in that particular way. I'm not expecting very deep, insightful feedback on my inner personality from people. I'm really mapping out my relationship with others in terms of rights and what am I doing wrong to you.

Kamm: I wanted to ask the psychologists here. There are certain techniques that are used, mostly in the Eastern traditions, for example, mantra meditation, which has been studied by Western scientists; sometimes it's called the relaxation response, sometimes it's more sophisticated. And people who practice these techniques find that a lot of the inner chatter, the conflict about "what should I do, should I go this way or that way," tends to go away and there is a confident sense of what one really wants to do or what one really should do. Not as a result of dialogue, not as a result of introspection or inference, but simply as a result of using a very mechanical technique that seems to affect a certain part of the brain. Do you think that if someone were to have a difficulty in life figuring out what he should do, if the reports of these effects of the mantra, for example, are true, that this would be a way to discover what he really wanted to do?

Wilson: Very interesting question, and while I'm no expert on the research on this, my reading from somewhat of a distance is that meditation of these sorts can be very useful for turning off the chatter and for achieving at least temporary peace of mind. Whether it actually gets us more in touch with our so-called true desires, I'm not so sure. If it's turning off the bad introspection that's confusing us and misleading us, then perhaps. But I don't think it gives us a direct pipeline into something that's true.

Kamm: Okay. Thank you.

Voorhoeve: I have another question here from the audience. "What are the principal obstacles to gaining self-knowledge?" Who wants to tackle that one?

During: Jack Nicholson answered this question. . . (*participants laughing*).

Voorhoeve: You mean Nicholson saying, "You can't handle the truth"? Now we've quoted the great Jack Nicholson in the same breath as Descartes (*participants laughing*)! Can you elaborate on Jack Nicholson?

During: Not really. The interesting paradox is that, to come back to this notion of imperious self, the more we gain knowledge of this personality within us, which we want to get rid of, the more difficult it becomes, in a way. Because this personality in us is also what prevents us from facing the truth. It's all the self-justifications, the rationalization that we give ourselves, in order to avoid framing problems in ethical terms. But as the process unfolds and we get to know ourselves more, this impediment, this obstacle, fades out. It can become a very interesting process. You can really get some taste of self-knowledge as a very interesting, passionate activity at some point. That would be the natural solution: that the obstacles just, at some point, disappear.

Voorhoeve: Is the obstacle that we don't desire the truth, or is it that some part of us knows it would be frustrated if it were made conscious?

During: Yes, this egoistic surface level of the self, which is driven by self-interest, has no particular interest in knowing what it is acting for. But the problem is solved in a natural way as soon as you start practicing, that is, modeling yourself in those terms and experimenting on what you're able to transform—the parameters you can alter, which is the process of ethical self-transformation. There's no principal *a priori* obstacle to self-knowledge. I think it's merely a matter of getting the process.

Wilson: I will mention one that Frances alluded to and agree with, which is that our culture gives us lots of expectations and stereotypes about who we ought to be, and it can be difficult to see through that smoke screen sometimes. It can be hard to see that that's not who we are, or that we have certain traits or desires that don't conform to those cultural expectations. That can be very difficult to sort out sometimes. And it takes a lot of good self-observation to do so.

Jopling: Here's another obstacle, a very simple observation; it's as close to a truism as I can get: reality is richer and more complex than we can ever figure out, and that includes ourselves. I think the self is enormously complex—its causal history, its developmental history, various components of the self and their interrelations with one another—it's really complex, and it's hard to figure out. There is one other obstacle that comes to mind, which is this: in some respects, it's easier to remain self-ignorant or self-deceived.

Tim you know this research on creative self-deception and depressive realism. The research seems to be showing that people who maintain creative self-deceptions about their abilities, their looks, their talents, their future, and also positive illusions about themselves, tend to be more well-adjusted, have better health, and be better off than people who have sober, realistic, truth-tracking accurate self-knowledge. I don't know how the research stands up methodologically, but it's a very interesting idea. And so the authors of this work, Shelley Taylor being one of the main ones, actually defend the virtues of creative self-deception over accurate self-knowledge (*participants laughing*). So, that's yet another obstacle: it's perhaps just easier and more conducive to well-being to be self-deceived!

Kamm: What I wanted to say was somewhat in the same line, though a little bit different. If you are succeeding at the things that you value and you are interacting successfully with others, it will seem that that is an obstacle to your investigating yourself. I don't think it's a bad thing. Because ultimately, your investigation of yourself—if you're not just a scientist who wants to give an adequate diagnosis of yourself—is for another purpose; it's for succeeding in what's important and successfully dealing with other people and living up to values. And if you're doing that, then you're doing the most important thing. And it seems that you needn't investigate this other part, this other aspect.

But I want to bring it back to the investigation that the philosopher of my sort uses in dealing with these hypothetical cases, in finding out why exactly do I have that intuitive judgment—forget about the truth of it, the objective side of it—there is the rush to judgment. People are always thinking, "Oh, it's this factor and I finally found it." And tomorrow a counterexample comes up. So one of the obstacles is that it takes a long time and it can be hard, and the tendency is to want to say, "I found it."

Voorhoeve: You and others mentioned that self-knowledge is really an effortful enterprise. We have to make inferences; we have to try to see ourselves the way others see us; we have to engage in a difficult dialogue with an unpleasant Socrates. So why do it? Well, you all answer: "Do it only if it'll make you more successful at your projects or will help you figure out the right projects to pursue." But one audience member has an opposing view, writing: "Knowing yourself in order to make a change or decision seems less important to me than doing so simply in order to fully know yourself for the sake of doing so." How would you respond?

During: There are so many things we can know about the universe.

Kamm: Yeah. I'd rather know the cure to cancer than know everything about myself, I think. So, you have a choice to make about what you know.

Voorhoeve: That's a very instrumentalist view about the pursuit of self-knowledge! I'm shocked (*participants laughing*).

Kamm: The important thing is to be a good self. And if someone were a really good self—like one of Dostoevsky's characters in *The Idiot*—he might not realize he's good or be very self-reflective, but act from the best motives and respond to others correctly. To *be* a certain sort of person rather than to *know* that you are that sort of person is important. Bernard Williams has this phrase "One thought too many" that may apply here. To *be* a Tristan could be more important than to *know* that one is a Tristan. Too much reflecting on what one is may be unnecessary.

But someone may be intrigued by the whole idea of human personality. That we can reflect on ourselves; that we have consciences. Then it's not so much an interest in oneself but in the possibility of self-knowledge. So when Professor Wilson said he thought self-knowledge was such an important topic, he didn't immediately consider himself, he just thought about the topic, you see? And those are different issues.

Wilson: Yes, I would second that, and I think there's some recent research of which I'm fond that shows that if the goal is to be happy, then helping others and doing volunteer work is a better path than sitting around navel-gazing. So, it depends what your goal is. But if it's to be happy, then an outward focus is often a better path.

Voorhoeve: Well, on this surprisingly instrumentalist note about knowledge of the self, I think it's a good time to end, especially since we've just been instructed not to navel-gaze too much. Before ending, I want to thank all our panelists for their contributions.

Ann. N.Y. Acad. Sci. ISSN 0077-8923

ANNALS OF THE NEW YORK ACADEMY OF SCIENCES
Issue: *Perspectives on the Self*

Self-knowledge and the practice of ethics: Ostad Elahi's concept of the "imperious self"

Elie During

Department of Philosophy, University of Paris Ouest—Nanterre La Défense, Paris, France

Address for correspondence: Elie During, Department of Philosophy, University of Paris Ouest—Nanterre La Défense, Paris, France. during@ens.fr.

When approaching the perplexing issue of self-knowledge, two questions should be kept in mind: What type of knowledge do we expect? and, more importantly, Why does this knowledge matter for us? Among the motivations behind such an endeavor, the ethical project of self-transformation is of particular interest, for it sheds light on the inherently constructive nature of self-knowledge. Psychologists dealing with the issue of self-realization and identity formation, however, generally tend to overlook the resources offered by ethics considered as a genuine self-transformative practice (in contrast to morality as a set of rules or principles to be applied in specific contexts). The tradition of "spiritual exercises" is considered from this self-transformative perspective, as well as Plato's conception of self-knowledge ("know thyself"). Finally, Ostad Elahi's concept of the "imperious self" is examined in detail: beyond the particular context to which it belongs (spiritual ethics), the "imperious self" appears as a valuable tool for understanding the active part played by self-modeling in the process of self-transformation.

Keywords: self-knowledge; spirituality; ethics; self-realization

Self-knowledge: a philosophical conundrum

Philosophers have had difficulties with the question of self-knowledge for two main reasons. The first concerns the target itself: we do not seem to be very clear about what kind of thing it is that we are supposed to gain knowledge about. The elusive nature of the self has given rise to heated exchanges of arguments between philosophers: Locke, Hume, Kant, James, to name but a few. One aspect of these discussions is of particular interest here. It is generally acknowledged that morality would not be possible if human beings were incapable of referring to themselves as "selves" in a specific way—namely, as the proper subjects of actions, and more generally, the bearers of intentions. Whether that falls under experience is still an unsettled matter, but in the philosophical tradition inherited from Locke and further elaborated by Kant, the concept of a person has proved quite useful. In spite of its rather abstract character it reflects the very basic sense that the self is the locus of responsibility, that it can be held accountable for a number of things, and be rewarded or blamed accordingly. Granted, knowing *a priori* that someone is a person—an agent endowed with deliberative capacities, self-reflection, and self-determination—does not tell us much about who that person is, or whether she is reliable. But when it comes to trying to be a person ourselves and acting upon the concept of a responsible human being, we realize we are touching on something that certainly constitutes the core of our moral identity, albeit something that we can only strive to, an ideal to be achieved rather than a given state of affairs waiting to be registered.

The second reason why philosophers have argued over self-knowledge is directly linked to the first: it concerns the form of knowledge appropriate to such an object as the self. Should we expect some kind of direct acquaintance with ourselves, by virtue of a privileged access? Is the self even an empirical concept, or rather does it lie beyond the realm of perceptual experience? Among the many difficulties surrounding self-knowledge, one may consider the distortions induced by introspection, or the more

doi: 10.1111/j.1749-6632.2011.06203.x

general problem of self-deception. The fact remains, however, that we seem quite comfortable with the idea that we can gain knowledge about ourselves, or that some people seem to know themselves very poorly, at least judging by their behavior. A web of beliefs and representations, including psychological concepts and theories about the self, identity, and personality, help us to make sense of certain "cues" and gain indirect, inductive knowledge, not only about the self in general, but about our individual self as well.

Why does it matter?

But why should self-knowledge matter in the first place? Why should we even care about knowing ourselves better than we already do through the kind of intimate familiarity we naturally enjoy in our own company? I believe much energy would be saved if, before embarking on philosophical discussions concerning the pitfalls of self-knowledge considered in general, we first clarified the concrete motivations behind particular attempts at gaining insights about ourselves. One does not seek self-knowledge in the abstract. As David Jopling emphasizes in *Self-knowledge and the Self*, self-inquiry is by necessity perspectival and interested. Simply put, we *care* about our self, and in many different ways. The representations through which I aim at this particular object—or process, or dimension of experience—called my "self" critically depend on why it matters for me to know who I am. As Jopling aptly shows, even the incomplete, distorted, fictional self-representations I happen to use in order to reach some degree of understanding concerning myself may prove extremely useful in capturing certain salient dimensions or properties that otherwise would have escaped me. But this points to a deeper issue that the so-called fallacy of introspection expresses in its own way. Self-knowledge is a form of knowledge that is constitutive of its object: it is an integral part of the process that makes us who we are. And since self-knowledge is not disinterested, since it expresses a fundamental concern not only for what we are but for what we may become, it is only natural that it should include moments of self-identification and projection as well as self-avowal and revelation.[1,2]

The intrinsic motivation behind self-knowledge points in many directions, all of which involve to one degree or another the three dimensions of person-ality distinguished by William James: the physical self, the social self, and the spiritual self.[3] One may be concerned primarily with the socially adaptive advantage of knowing oneself well in order to conform one's expectations to one's actual capabilities. One may wish to address specific troubles ("target disorders") or release certain psychological tensions by achieving a better grasp of one's own patterns of reaction to environmental factors. More positively, one may want to achieve a certain level of self-realization—and thus happiness—by discovering the set of potentialities that constitute one's "true self" or *daimon*.[4] Finally, one may simply want to become a different person by engaging in an active process of self-transformation or self-modeling, aiming at an ideal self—more likable, more worthy of self-esteem—or striving to reach a more perfect—or at least, more desirable—state that is expected to give meaning and direction to one's life. Such an endeavor is more akin to self-construction than self-discovery, although it may still rely on the idea that the self to be achieved is the natural expression or actualization of one's true potentialities. It implies self-knowledge in an essential way because the "old self" one seeks to get rid of must first be identified, along with the levers that will foster the required transformation.

Ethics as self-realization

It would seem that ethics, aiming as it does at the flourishing of the individual by the cultivation of virtues, is of central importance if one wants to grasp the underlying mechanism of self-transformation. However, among contemporary perspectives on self-knowledge and identity formation, those that present themselves as eudaimonistic—that is, those that are concerned with achieving a better, more perfect and happy self—do not limit the scope of psychological inquiry to models of self-realization that explicitly rely on ethical considerations. They try to be as inclusive as possible without losing sight of the distinctly normative dimension implicit in the very notion of self-realization.

Granted, a theory about normativity need not itself be normative, but such a neutral stance regarding the ethical dimension of self-transformative practices is rather problematic if one considers, as does Alan S. Waterman, that "both ethical and unethical activities may be experienced as personally expressive," that is, as expressive of one's true potentials (see Waterman,[4] p. 361). "Under such circumstances, self-realization is not, and cannot be, used as a guide for determining what is ethical. Conversely, it would seem that ethics is not a privileged guide to self-realization considered in its full extent." But is it truly possible to live an unethical life while achieving a high degree of self-realization? Is it not the very purpose of ethics, understood in the most general sense as an eudaimonistic endeavor distinct from merely formal or regulative concepts of morality, to suggest that certain lifestyles or models of self-realization are inherently destructive, and thus self-defeating?

This problem has already been addressed by personality theorists such as Erich Fromm, Rollo May, or Abraham Maslow. Allow self-actualization to be defined "as an ongoing actualization of potentials, capacities, and talents, as fulfillment of mission (or call, fate, destiny, or vocation), as a fuller knowledge of, and acceptance of, the person's intrinsic nature, as an increasing trend toward unity, integration, or synergy within the person" (see Maslow,[5] p. 25). Yet isn't ethics precisely about achieving this "unity, integration, or synergy within the person," while linking the actualization of personal potentials with meaning and purpose? Or to quote from May, referring to Aristotle: "Happiness—or eudaimonism—is to live happily with one's *daimon*. Nowadays we would relate eudaimonism to the state of integration of potentialities and other aspects of one's being with behavior" (May,[6] p. 126). Again, isn't ethics precisely about conjugating the highest level of "integration" and consistency with the most inclusive array of human activities? Aristotle's doctrine of virtues, his views on the governance of the passions, may not be the only path toward self-realization, but what about the more general ideas of self-control and self-determination? Can we imagine any form of lasting self-fulfillment that would do away with these two levers altogether? If, according to May, there are other ways than "taming" the *daimon*, isn't there always something to be tamed, whatever we like to call it?

Ethics as practice

Psychologists may well want to avoid such questions and leave them to philosophers. Their position of scientific neutrality leads them to consider that ethics—which itself is by no means a unified field—is only one model of self-realization among others. Yet it is difficult to fight the impression that normative ethical views eventually resurface in such seemingly innocuous notions as "integration," "consistency," or "centeredness." Identity theories are valuable because the issue of self-knowledge can be raised in concrete, pragmatic terms in connection with the actual making of the self considered as a dynamic process. Nevertheless, I believe that much would be gained from a more direct confrontation with the eudaimonistic approaches that explicitly present themselves in terms of actual practice, rather than life project or identity formation. The word *ethics* naturally conveys this concern. Self-identifications and projections, beliefs, aspirations, and resolutions are one thing; the enactment of a self-transformative strategy in one's daily life is quite another. Even therapeutic trainings, coaching programs, and the like do not compare with the lifelong exercise in self-governance that Aristotle had in mind when writing about the virtues. As he says in the *Nicomachean Ethics*, it takes more than one sparrow for spring to come.

The advantage of focusing on the actual practice of ethics, rather than on moral principles (about right and wrong) and their application ("applied ethics"), is that it gives us concrete access to the concepts of moral agency and responsibility, in a way that inquiries about so-called "moral exemplars" or "altruistic personalities" cannot parallel. If moral identity is defined as the convergence or unity of the moral and self systems, then moral exemplars are people whose own personal interests and desires coincide with their sense of what is morally right. In other words, moral exemplars "seamlessly integrate their commitments with their personal concerns, so that the fulfillment of one implies the fulfillment of the other."[7] Such persons, however, correspond quite literally to what Kant would have called moral "saints." To speak the language of identity theorists, for such persons moral commitment is "expressive" of their "true selves." But if there is no contradiction, no struggle, no sacrifice or self-denial, not even a feeling of resistance or tension, the issue of "self-realization" does not even arise. On that count at least, it is as if the "ideal self" had merged with the "actual self." My point is that relying on such examples is not really helpful if we want to assess the part played by moral commitment in achieving self-knowledge: the dynamic is lost in favor of a personality type. At the other extreme, identity theorists interested in the stages of identity formation have tended to focus on moments of crises identified by the radical restructuring or reorientation of one's goals and motivations (the so-called midlife crisis being one example among others). My suggestion is that we should focus neither on conversion crises nor on the assumed saintliness of moral exemplars: as far as self-knowledge is concerned, the most revealing episodes are to be found in the details of the ordinary challenges of moral life considered as a training ground, a continued apprenticeship of virtue.

The question of course is, who actually relates to morality in that way? Everyone has experienced to some degree the mix of emotions and reasoning surrounding a moral dilemma or the commitment to become a "better" person by giving up certain habits, but who actually *practices* ethics? The term itself leaves room for interpretation. Ignatius of Loyola's "spiritual exercises" or Benjamin Franklin's "art of virtue" are extreme examples of the systematic way in which one can approach ethical matters (the development of virtues) by devising concrete methods and protocols to sustain a steady, long-term self-transformative practice.[a] I suspect most of us do not conceive of morality in such a rigid, codified way. One may observe, however, that even in these instances, ethics is no more codified than any training activity (think, for instance, of piano playing or the practice of a martial art). In any case, it is a matter of degree, and there are many more familiar "spiritual exercises" one can think of: restraining from what one perceives as a "bad habit" (smoking or backbiting), enhancing our compassion for others by focusing our attention on certain details we would normally overlook, or surveying one's thoughts and emotions, to name a few. The point is that the dynamics of such ethical practices, their experimental character, is more likely to lead to genuine insights in the process of self-knowledge than any consideration based on behavioral or motivational patterns ("moral schemas") considered as end results or goal states. As my aim is slightly different from that of a psychologist, however, I think it is best to focus on practices that present themselves in the clearest and most explicit way

as instances of self-knowledge and moral expertise gained through the deliberate implementation of global self-transformative strategies. Ostad Elahi's understanding of "natural spirituality" is the best example I can think of.[8] Not only did he devise a general metaphysical scheme for his account of the process of perfection, but his work as a whole—which unfortunately remains largely inaccessible to the English public—displays a very acute sense of the phenomenological and experiential dimensions of ethics considered as a genuinely spiritual practice.[b] In his case, "knowing" and "self-knowledge" take on their full significance. As explained by James Morris, the translator of *Knowing the Spirit*, the word knowing (*marefat*) refers not only to the kind of knowledge communicated through rational argument—although this is an essential aspect of Ostad's approach to spiritual matters—but also to "the necessarily individual, active awareness that is the accomplished fruit of direct, personal spiritual experience and contemplation."[9]

Spirituality and ethics

One may legitimately wonder, however, why spirituality should concern us at this point. The connection is provided by the very notion of self-knowledge as self-transformation. A short detour may be in order here. "Know thyself," the Delphic prescription popularized by Socrates, was never meant to suggest that we should set about scrutinizing our individual selves through psychological introspection. Its purpose, as the Platonic dialogues make clear, was to bring us to realize that one's true self reaches beyond the particular traits that make up character or personality, and to act accordingly. To know ourselves is to realize that we are basically souls, rather than extraordinarily gifted animals, living organisms endowed with speech, reflective capacities, and the like. When I speak to someone I care about, I have no doubt that I'm dealing with something

---

[a]See http://www.e-ostadelahi.com/eoe-en/wp-content/uploads/benjamin_franklin.pdf.

[b]Ostad Elahi (1895–1974) was a jurist by profession and a renowned musician. Much of his philosophical and spiritual research was made public only in his later years, or in a posthumous way. For further biographical and bibliographical references, see http://www.ostadelahi.com/. On the subject of Ostad Elahi's "natural spirituality," its metaphysical background, and ethical implications, see During.[10]

more than a bundle of physical and psychological traits: I'm directing my attention to what I take to be the core of the person, its active principle. In Platonic parlance, "soul" is the word that captures this dimension common to every being.

Yet, more than a metaphysical insight into what constitutes the true nature of the self, the Socratic prescription was meant to foster a new awareness and concern. As Michel Foucault rightly emphasized, in the platonic tradition the process of knowing oneself is incomplete if one does not act upon that knowledge by attending to oneself in a very special way.[11] Thus, "know thyself" naturally connects with another crucial message taken from Socrate's lessons: "take care of your self." The "care of the self" (*epimeleia heautou*) is a central theme in the ancient Greek tradition. It can be understood as a way of respecting oneself, of attending to oneself. The movement of conversion or introversion—detaching one's attention from the outside and turning it instead to the inside, withdrawing within oneself—is essential, but it is only the beginning. The care of the self involves a whole new attitude not only toward oneself, but more generally toward others and the world. Eventually, it may have less to do with knowledge of a particular kind—of a particular spiritual object, the self or the soul— than with a new form of activity. In the perspective opened by Socrates, self-knowledge indeed appears inseparable from the self-transformative action exercised on the self by the self. "Know thyself" asks us to take active responsibility for ourselves; it commits us to a new form of life, a life of self-realization dedicated to the flourishing of the self. Foucault stresses the concrete and practical dimension of the issue by observing that the care of the self was in fact intimately linked with a series of "spiritual exercises," such as self-examination and surveying, the checking of one's thoughts, along with practices of memorization and meditation. "Spirituality," from this perspective, can be defined in a very broad sense as the practice and experience through which the subject carries out the transformations required to have access to the truth—a truth that, in turn, can lead to a transformation of the subject's very being. The idea is that, in order to gain access to the truth, the subject must be changed, transformed, and altered accordingly. This requires some work: an elaboration of the self by the self, a labor of self-transformation that enables the self to reach, through an ascending

movement, a higher, more universal perspective on itself and the world as a whole, perceived as meaningful.[12] Thus, devoting oneself to oneself, properly understood, is the expression of a profound desire for radical ethical change; it must not be confused with a form of narcissistic self-absorption.

One does not need to subscribe to Plato's metaphysics of the soul—its relation to eternal, immutable ideas—in order to make sense of the proposition encapsulated in the Delphic formula. Self-knowledge is intimately linked with the prospect of self-realization, and hence self-transformation. What the various spiritual exercises have in common, precisely because they are exercises, is that the way they reveal the core self—or "personality," as some philosophers would prefer to say—is nothing but a continuous effort to shape itself by confronting the various forces or tendencies that seem to work against it. It is a constant effort of vigilance, a tension of every minute. Leaving Plato behind for the modern philosophical context, we can say that the "soul" is akin to a creative force, transforming itself unceasingly by increasing and directing the intensity of a continuous impulse forward[13]—that is, when it is not thwarted by all kinds of distracting, diffusive forces. It is through the resistance encountered on its way that the notion of agency, which we found to be at the root of our moral identity, becomes more palpable. Agency is not an abstract capacity to act on one's own. It is first and foremost a capacity to act upon oneself, to reorient one's motivation, to reprioritize one's objectives, and finally to act against certain urges, drives, or imperious tendencies that somehow threaten to overtake the will and confine the self to being the passive witness of its own experience. At this point it seems necessary to make room for a distinct representation of that counterforce that seems determined to actively prevent us from achieving ethical goals or taking the steps required to develop moral habits. Striving to be a person involves, sooner or later, a confrontation with this antiethical power within us.

Ostad Elahi's model of the "imperious self"

Ostad Elahi's thought has developed on the soil of Greek philosophy, as mediated by the rich tradition of Arab and Persian commentators. Yet, in his model of the self, the dimension that was traditionally conceptualized—from Plato and Aristotle up to Aquinas—in terms of the appetitive or concupiscent part of the soul, the seat of unruly passions and desires, falls under the concept of the "imperious self" (*nafs-e amârre* in Persian). This concept, which as we shall see must *not* be confused with the sensible or terrestrial soul, nor with any proper "part" of the soul, is by no means peripheral in his work, as shown by the following quote: "The path of perfection can be summarized in two points: constant attention to the Source and fighting against the imperious self" (quoted in Elahi,[14] p. 203).

At the conscious level, the imperious self manifests itself in an impulsive way through capricious, harmful, and potentially disintegrative desires. Just like the *id* of psychoanalysis, it seeks immediate gratification and systematically opposes the orientation given by the rational part of our personality. (For more details on the mechanisms of the imperious self, see Elahi[14]). This may sound a little too much like the personification of something that only manifests itself through its potentially destabilizing effects—to the extent that we're aware of them—something that exists as a functional—or rather dysfunctional—entity supervening on the overall structure of the self, rather than as a substantial entity. However, the personification is part of the game here; it is a pragmatic function. Picturing this aspect of the self as an agent in is own right serves the necessary purpose of self-objectification, which is in turn essential to the process of self-transformation, provided that the underlying mechanisms are properly understood. In order to grasp the practical as well as theoretical significance of the imperious self, it is important to view it as an active dimension of the *actual* self, rather than a mere representation of a potential or possible self. In that respect, and despite possible overlaps, it cannot be equated with what certain psychologists describe as the "dreaded self"—the kind of person one wants to avoid becoming.[15,16] The imperious self is not a feared possible identity: it is not substantially distinct from our actual self. Nor does it correspond to what is sometimes described as the "noisy," "inflated," or "wild ego."[17,18] These expressions refer to specific personality structures, while what is at stake here is a dimension fully active in every person, albeit in different ways and with varying degrees of intensity. If the struggle against the imperious self has something to do with taming or quieting the ego, it is in the very specific sense distinguished by Bauer and Wayment when they refer to "an ego that too readily capitulates to the id,

resulting in self-seeking motivation, egotism, and conceit (as connoted by a big ego)" (see Bauer & Wayment,[17] p. 9). Yet again, if the imperious self embodies a principle of egoistic self-interest, that can be counterbalanced to a certain extent by developing virtues, such as humility, compassion, or mindfulness, it remains a defining component of the human psyche as such. It should concern even people whose personality has developed along directions that make them more interdependent and less individualistic than others. Indeed, Ostad Elahi stresses the fact that the "excesses" of the imperious self can manifest themselves negatively, through the insufficiency of this or that quality. Thus a lack of commitment may develop into a state of pathological irresolution. There are such things as apathetic drives: they contribute to an unbalanced character just as much as the bursts of the "wild ego."

The truth is that only an active engagement with the practice of ethics—and this includes, of course, countering one's spontaneously selfish inclinations—is capable of revealing the full extent and many facets of the imperious self beyond its most obvious manifestations. "It is in the daily tests of life that fighting against the imperious self takes on meaning," Bahram Elahi writes[14] (p. 205). One has to watch the imperious self in action, as it actually operates, in order to understand the logic that binds together a host of sometimes indiscernible dysfunctional behavioral schemas, flawed beliefs, and deviant thought patterns. This can only be achieved by probing the self in a way that is not very different from what goes on in any experimental research. The self reacts to particular situations as a sounding board by producing more or less controlled responses (emotions, thoughts, and behaviors), which in turn bring about positive or negative results. The first step consists of collecting these cues and feedbacks, varying the situations, and trying new moves in order to identify dysfunctional patterns that may be indicative of a more general problem. The implementation of counterstrategies is the next step, provided that one finds the intrinsic motivation to change things. The working hypothesis underlying the very idea of the imperious self is that its reactions do not play out in a random fashion but conform to a certain logic. As whimsical as it may be, the imperious self abides by the rule of egoistic self-interest: there is logic to its madness, and to the way it interacts with our personality as a whole. That is why it is reasonable to work upon a genuine model of its action, based on the hands-on information gathered through the attentive practice of ethics. It goes without saying that such operational self-knowledge requires a little more than the convenient image of the little devil within us.

As Ostad Elahi explains through many concrete examples, the main problem remains that the imperious self is so shrewd and deceitful that most of its work goes unnoticed if we do not commit ourselves to fighting it actively, especially as its moves are accompanied with pseudo-justifications that make them seem innocuous or even ethically commendable. The "flesh" is not at issue here. Desires by themselves are not to be blamed. They are not a problem as long as they do not directly harm us and others. They represent a threat when, acclimated by thought patterns developed by the imperious self, they tend to infringe upon the rights of others without our being aware of it. More generally, the mechanism of self-deception illustrates a notable difference between the operations of the imperious self and the crude desires traditionally assembled under the heading "appetitive part:" the imperious self is as intelligent as it is imperious. Left to itself, it can colonize our entire reason. And therein lies the main difficulty, for it is through reason alone that one can actually come to detect and identify the imperious self's relentless assaults. More precisely, it is the rational sense of justice, the perception of the rights attached to the various beings we interact with—objects, plants, and animals included—that serves to gauge our intentions and motivations and contributes to giving shape to the imperious self.

At root, the imperious self is indiscernible from the desires emanating from the impulsive nature of our lower, animal self. And it gradually takes shape by resisting the ethical project of reforming oneself. Ultimately, the pragmatic definition of the imperious self seems to be whatever diverts us from our duty, and whatever runs counter to an ethical stance. Synthesizing all the actual and potential antiethical manifestations of our self (active vices or with mere weak points), it may be compared to a photographic negative of the moral self, which alone is in a position to discern its existence by viewing it "from above," so to speak. Not so much a wild animal to be tamed, nor a raw material upon which reason

strives to impose its form, the imperious self is rather like a virus that must be isolated and whose *modus operandi* must be analyzed with great scrutiny. Paradoxically enough, it is something to be cultivated and worked upon, rather than subtracted.

This brings us to the second main difference with the traditional conceptions of the governance of the passions by reason. The imperious self is indispensable in its own right, for it contains basic psychological ingredients that are necessary to the formation of the virtues themselves. These ingredients, which generally manifest themselves through unbalanced character traits, can only be assimilated through a steady confrontation aimed at establishing the right balance. For instance, the virtue of *courage* cannot be developed unless one has actually been confronted in a very concrete fashion with the overwhelming power of fear, as well as with its most subtle manifestations. Being courageous is not ignoring fear, as Plato acknowledges; it is about overcoming it by a resolute decision to keep it at bay. The same is true of *benevolence*, which supposes that one feels the sting of stinginess and strives to counter it by deliberate acts of generosity. Then again, there are many ways of being cheap or petty minded. This may all sound familiar to those who have read Aquinas: the Stoic view according to which passions must be obliterated and extirpated in order for moral virtue to exist, cannot be sustained. In general, there is an intrinsic relationship between virtues of character and the active passions. Not only can moral virtues be accompanied by passions but in a certain sense they cannot do without them. Thus, the perfection of such powers as *fortitude* and *temperance* cannot be attained without the corresponding passions: "It is plain that the moral virtues which are about the passions as about their proper matter cannot exist without passions" (*Summa Theologica*, I, II, 59, art. 5). In the same way, Ostad Elahi strongly opposes the idea that the "appetitive part" be weakened, deactivated and left unemployed. The business of the process of perfection is precisely to enable the self to grow by assimilating the indispensable characteristic psychological ingredients present in excess in human nature. But the underlying scheme is much more dynamic than what can be found in Aristotle (the "golden mean") or Aquinas (passions as the proper matter of virtues), who both rely on a fundamentally static form–matter scheme. The spiritual principle that underlies the whole discussion is in fact the exact equivalent of the biological concept of immunity. Even the character traits and tendencies on which the imperious self capitalizes should not be repressed or annihilated; they must be decreased to a minimum in order to be assimilated in homeopathic or vaccinal doses, so to speak. Bahram Elahi writes: "The desires of the imperious self are analogous to bacterial toxins; if the toxins are strong and in large quantities, they will be harmful and perhaps even fatal for the celestial soul, but if they are weakened and in small doses they help vaccinate the soul against the imperious self and enable it to gradually control the impulses of the imperious self"[14] (p. 205).

Clearly, such a notion of self-control involves a radical departure from the conception of asceticism as a systematic weakening of the animal side of human nature. On the contrary, Ostad Elahi insists that one should aim at strengthening this nature, while simultaneously strengthening one's willpower. In other words, the imperious self must not be crushed; it must be held under tension in order to serve the purpose of self-transformation in the best way possible. Reorganized around the axial struggle between "sound" reason (or moral self[c]) and the imperious self, the "psycho-spiritual organism," as Bahram Elahi calls it, appears as a dynamic structure that must itself be mapped, charted, and constructed as a reflective object as we go along. The basic recipe is to systematically aim at the opposite of what the imperious self seems to want. The imperious self appears in finer resolution as we become more aware of the points of resistance. The impediment, the antagonist forces, are absolutely necessary here, and it is crucial that we develop an attentive familiarity with the inner-antiethical personality nested within our self. The first and most important task is to devise a proper model of the imperious self, one that grants it enough visibility to be properly operated,

---

[c] "Sound" here also means educated by appropriate moral principles. What are those moral principles is another matter that cannot be dealt with here. The answer lies in Ostad Elahi's metaphysics of human nature, which he conceives in relation to a divine element. Suffice it to say that the education of thought is a fundamental dimension of the process of spiritual self-realization. The moral self that engages in the activity of self-modeling must itself be cultivated and strengthened in order to even detect the manifestations of the imperious self.

controlled, and regulated. Blaming our fallen nature will not be of much help.

The active task of self-modeling, of consolidating and sharpening an ever more adequate model of an evolving imperious self, is monitored by our core self, the seat of sound reason and moral conscience. Yet in order to achieve this, the deep self must itself be extracted from the surface ego where it ordinarily lives a shallow, barely conscious, and residual life. The problem, of course, is that our spontaneous identifications tend to consolidate a self-image that is generally "flat," even when it seems complex or contradictory. The multilayered texture of the self, its vertical organization in terms of surface and depth, does not clearly appear to us except in the rare moments of crisis where alternative selves seem to emerge, and a deep restructuring of our overall personality may take place. Yet the truth, as William James abruptly puts it, is that "by the age of thirty, the character has set like plaster, and will never soften again"[3] (p. 121). In terms of self-transformation, this means that the best we can expect from the practice of ethics is not a radical, spectacular shift but the slow and progressive awakening of a heightened level of awareness, achieved as a result of relentlessly pitching our moral intuitions against the moving, slippery texture of the imperious self. Thus, ethical practice comes down to a continuous experiment with oneself, whose natural reward consists in the expansion of our mental field of perception, together with the satisfaction gained from an increased sense of understanding and self-mastery.

Contrary to a prevailing tendency in psychological inquiries about self and identity, I would suggest that the role of ethics as a practice is to sustain the tension and even intensify it in order to prevent the self from collapsing into a single level of superficial self-identification. In that respect, the function of ethics—in contrast to the unifying scope of moral values and principles considered in themselves—is primarily disruptive rather than integrative. The whole point of practicing ethics rather than adopting a comfortable moral stance that suits one's individual potentials or is "expressive" of one's "true self," is to realize that there is no way we can fully identify ourselves with what we are, that there is something in us with which we shall never want to identify, as long as we are vigilant. The repelling self—Pascal's "despicable" ego—is not the body, nor our sensible nature; it is our all too human self left to its ordinary, semiautomated routine. Against it, something in us protests—call it the "soul," if you like. If this feeling of uneasiness is backed by a strong moral commitment, it need not be a source of psychological dissonance, much less a cause of guilt. Ostad Elahi has invented ethics without culpability.

Conflicts of interest

The author declares no conflicts of interest.

References

1. Jopling, D. 2000. *Self-knowledge and the Self*. Routledge. Oxford, United Kingdom.
2. Larmore, C. 2010. *The Practices of the Self*. The University of Chicago Press. Chicago, Illinois. Chapter 3.
3. James, W. 1950. *The Principles of Psychology* [1890], Vol. 1. Dover, Mineola, New York.
4. Waterman, A.S. 2011. "Eudaimonic Identity Theory: Identity as Self-Discovery." In *Handbook of Identity Theory and Research*, 2 vols. S.J. Schwartz *et al*., Eds.: Springer. New York.
5. Maslow, A.H. 1968. *Toward a Psychology of Being*. Van Nostrand. New York.
6. May, R. 1969. *Love and Will*. Norton. New York.
7. Colby, A. & W. Damon. 1992. *Some Do Care: Contemporary Lives of Moral Commitment*. Free Press. New York. 300 pp.
8. Elahi, B. *Foundations of Natural Spirituality: A Scientific Approach to the Nature of the Spiritual Self*, Element, 1998.
9. Elahi, O. 2007. *Knowing the Spirit*. SUNY Press. Albany, New York. 2 pp.
10. During, E. 2011. "Qu'est-ce qu'une spiritualité naturelle?" In *Spirituel et Rationnel: les alliances paradoxales*. L'Harmattan.
11. Foucault, M. 2006. *The Hermeneutics of the Subject*. Picador. New York. 1–19 pp.
12. Hadot, P. 1995. *Philosophy as a Way of Life*. Wiley-Blackwell. 211 pp.
13. Bergson, H. 1972. "The Problem of Personality" (Gifford Lectures, 1914). In *Mélanges*. Presses Universitaires de France. Paris, France. 1051–1071 pp.
14. Elahi, B. 2005. *The Path of Perfection*. Paraview. New York.
15. Oyserman, D. & L. James. 2011. "Possible Identities." In *Handbook of Identity Theory and Research*, 2 vols. S.J. Schwartz *et. al.*, Eds.: Springer. New York.
16. Hardy, S. & G. Carlo. 2011. "Moral Identity." In *Handbook of Identity Theory and Research*. 2 vols. S.J. Schwartz *et al.*, Eds.: 499. Springer. New York.
17. Bauer, J. & H.A. Wayment. 2008. The Psychology of the Quite Ego. In *Transcending Self-interest: Psychological Explorations of the Quiet Ego*. J. Bauer & H.A. Wayment, Eds.: American Psychological Association. Washington, DC.
18. Exline, J.J. 2008. Taming the Wild Ego: The Challenge of Humility. In *Transcending Self-interest: Psychological Explorations of the Quiet Ego*. J. Bauer & H. Wayment, Eds.: American Psychological Association. Washington, DC.

Ann. N.Y. Acad. Sci. ISSN 0077-8923

ANNALS OF THE NEW YORK ACADEMY OF SCIENCES

Issue: *Perspectives on the Self*

"Much ado to know myself. . .": Insight in the talking cures

David A. Jopling

Department of Philosophy, York University, Toronto, Ontario, Canada

Address for correspondence: David A. Jopling, Department of Philosophy, York University, Toronto, Ontario, Canada M3J 1P3. jopling@yorku.ca

Psychoanalysis, psychodynamic psychotherapy, and the other talking cures claim to help clients acquire insight into their selves. With insight, the unruly forces that govern lives and that make people strangers to themselves finally come to be understood and rendered subject to conscious control. These insights, it is claimed, are true, and fit the facts like a key fits a lock; they are not merely coherent fictions or confabulated cause-and-effect stories designed to please clients. But is this credible? The argument developed here is that some of the therapeutic changes in the talking cures are functions of placebos that rally the mind's native healing powers in much the same way that placebo pills rally the body's native healing powers and that some of these placebos are insight placebos. The talking cures rightfully claim that it is only talking with others that unlocks the soul and opens it up to ways of self-knowing and to caring for self that would otherwise be unavailable, but they fail to acknowledge the presence of placebo effects, and they operate with restrictive models of dialogue that may unintentionally encourage placebo effects and cognitive suggestibility.

Keywords: talking cures; placebo effect

In sooth, I know not why I am so sad:
It wearies me; you say it wearies you;
But how I caught it, found it, or came by it,
What stuff 'tis made of, whereof it is born,
I am to learn;
And such a want-wit sadness makes of me,
That I have much ado to know myself.

SHAKESPEARE
Merchant of Venice, I,I,1

I begin with a claim that is as close to an axiom as there is: reality is always richer and more complex that what we know of it and *can* know of it. This is as true of the reality that we call ourselves as it is true of the objects, events, and processes that are outside of ourselves. Self-knowledge—the sort of knowledge that answers the question "Who am I?"—is much more difficult to acquire than is commonly assumed and much rarer than is commonly claimed. Not only are there more obstacles in the way of answering the question than we are aware of, there are more obstacles than we *can* be aware of. The ways in which we can be wrong, confused, ignorant, or deceived about phenomena that are as complexly configured and causally opaque as our own behaviors, psychological make-up, desires, emotions, and deeply held values, are countless. Even a simple case of sadness makes a "want-wit" of us. Suffice to say that there are, and always will be, many *more* of these ways than there are ways to be knowledgeable. Self-ignorance is a given baseline condition against which our comparatively limited efforts of self-knowing take place. And yet despite this, self-knowledge is one of the goods of human life.[1]

We see the forces of self-ignorance playing out on the large stage and the small. Across human history, explanations of psychology and behavior that are false, empty, or incoherent have been the norm rather than the exception: explanations, for instance, that appeal to entities, such as humors, demons, astrological forces, or magnetic fields. And the list continues to grow, with newly debunked or retired explanatory systems being added every generation. On the smaller stage, we see forces of ignorance playing themselves out on the field of causal self-attributions, false inferences, skewed self-concepts, false memories, and biased self-perceptions; and also in more complex and

doi: 10.1111/j.1749-6632.2011.06189.x

 Ann. N.Y. Acad. Sci. 1234 (2011) 158–167 © 2011 New York Academy of Sciences.

insidious form as self-deception, self-blindness, willful neglect, and weakness of will.

There are too many of these forces of ignorance to list. Here I will focus on only one—but one that is more rather than less philosophically interesting, if only because it is a quirky and not so minor character in the drama that unfolds daily in the psychiatrist's or psychotherapist's office: pseudo-insight. I pick on insight because it is considered one of the high points of the talking cures, at once cathartic, deep, and healing; and I pick on the talking cures because, among their other aspirations, they often lay claim to helping people answer the question, "Who am I?"[2] (They are also part of a multimillion-dollar industry that is ripe for epistemic and logical examination, and a well-targeted application of Ockham's razor). With insight, it is claimed, the unruly and unseen forces that govern lives and derail relationships, that make us strangers to ourselves, finally come to be named, understood, and rendered subject to conscious control. Insight in the talking cures is generally supposed to be truth tracking: it is the key that fits snugly into the lock that is the psyche, revealing its secrets, making it speak. Or so it is claimed: the talking cures, after all, are not supposed to trade in fiction, illusion, or confabulation.

But is this credible? Do the talking cures *really* help clients deal with the question, "Who am I?" Is this the simplest and most parsimonious way of making sense of what they do? When clients emerge from psychoanalysis, psychodynamic psychotherapy, or any one of the many forms of so-called insight-oriented psychotherapy, are they *really* more insightful and more in touch with themselves? Are they any the less "want-wits" when trying to make sense of their sadness? On the face of it, it seems that they are. The talking cures can rightfully claim their fair share of satisfied clients, many of whom are convinced that they have acquired a level of insight into themselves that is far greater than what they had before they entered treatment. Many of the talking cures also conduct what seem to be scientifically rigorous outcome studies to determine their level of therapeutic effectiveness, with results that range from middling to astonishing. (Not surprisingly, however, the logical and methodological dimensions of these studies have also come under intense critical scrutiny, also with mixed results). And the talking cures are typically supported by robust theoretical frameworks that, to varying degrees,

seem to be open to testing and clinical validation. Given these considerations, why call the claims of the talking cures into question? What else could the talking cures possibly be doing *with* and *to* clients, if not putting them more in touch with themselves and helping them move toward insight and self-knowledge?

Insights in the talking cures (as well as the interpretations that psychotherapists provide to clients at certain well-timed stages along the therapeutic path) are said to be the keys that unlock the psyche. There are two assumptions here: that insights and interpretations actually fit at all, and that only one insight and one interpretation will fit properly. But just as some keys are poorly fitted to their locks, and others are force fitted, and yet others are underfitted, so there are insights and interpretations that fit poorly, or not at all, to the selves they are ostensibly about. These are pseudo-insights: explanations that clients in therapy come to acquire about their own psychology, behavior, and personality that appear to them to be plausible and accurate, but in fact are false, fictional, or confabulated. And that is not all. One of pseudo-insight's more curious cousins is the placebo insight: that is, pseudo-insights that are the psychological equivalent of sugar pills. What makes them placebos, or at least placebo-like? Like placebos in clinical medicine and in controlled clinical trials, placebo insights lack vital active ingredients; like placebos in clinical medicine, which mimic at least the outward appearance of active medications, placebo insights bear close outward resemblances to genuine insights; like placebos in clinical medicine, the people for whom they are therapeutically effective believe, mistakenly, that what has been administered to them are genuine treatments with active ingredients; and like placebos in clinical medicine, the therapeutic benefits of placebo insights can be quite significant, often to the point where they outperform conventional treatments.

But an *insight placebo*? An insight into self that is *also a placebo*—in what should be (and is claimed to be) one of the most carefully controlled environments that could be devised for the pursuit of insight? How is this possible? How could an insight *be* a mere placebo? How could the lofty ethical and psychological ideal of self-knowledge have fallen into such an apparently disreputable state?

Placebos have been called many things, none very salutary: the nothing cure, a treatment calculated to amuse for a time, a sham treatment, a nuisance variable, a pill given more to please than to benefit the patient, a humble humbug, a make-believe medication, something from nothing, and even much ado about nothing.

All of these pejorative characterizations, and with them the myths and misconceptions about placebos and their effects, are ready for retirement. Much more is known about placebo effects today than was known 100, and even 50, years ago. Their mysteries are yielding to fields as diverse as psychoneuroimmunology, cognitive psychology, medical anthropology, behavioral psychology, and the neurosciences. Placebo effects are found at play in almost all branches of clinical medicine and in a huge array of medical conditions; they pose daunting interpretive challenges to the gold standard of medical evidence—the controlled double-blind trial of new medications; they have enviable analgesic powers; they display objectively measurable physiological outcomes; they come in a multitude of shapes and forms; they are strangely sensitive to cultural variation; and they are yielding to increasingly fine-grained neuroimaging techniques. One thing is certain: placebo effects are not merely in the minds of patients, mere subjective phenomena that float on the surface of physiology like oil on water;[3] nor are they merely phony interventions devised to placate difficult patients, a merely "pious fraud," in the words of Thomas Jefferson. The slowly emerging view in the medical, behavioral, and neurosciences is that placebo effects are a function of the human organism's evolved and immensely powerful innate capacity to heal itself, to restore itself to equilibrium, and to repair damage.[4–8] What is remarkable about this capacity for self-repair is the sheer diversity of the endogenous and exogenous triggers that can activate it and thereby "uncork the internal pharmacopeia that all humans possess as a biologically programmed tool for self-healing;"[9] not only pharmaceutical and surgical interventions, such as sugar pills and sham surgeries, but widely divergent symbolic, cultural, and interpersonal interventions— including interventions such as the talking cures. Placebo-triggered self-repair, in other words, is a psychological as well as a biological phenomenon— and, some might add, a semiotic, symbolic, and information-theoretic phenomenon. Just as complex biological systems will rally together to repair physical damage, so complex cognitive and emotional systems will rally together to repair psychological damage. The talking cures owe much of their effectiveness to their capacity to trigger this innate capacity for self-healing, although credit is not typically given where it is due.

Despite the vast cultural differences in the types of available placebos, the manner of placebo administration, and the assorted medical conditions that have proven to be receptive to placebo intervention, what all placebos have in common is two things: they are treatments that are lacking the vital or characteristic ingredients that are theorized to be remedial for the specified disorder, and they are therapeutically effective because of the noncharacteristic—that is, the incidental or surrounding—factors of the treatment.[10]

To illustrate this definition, take the case of saline injection placebos for the treatment of pain. When administered to patients who believe they are receiving an active painkiller, saline injections are often surprisingly effective. But how? They have no active chemical ingredients (the vital or characteristic ingredients) other than salt, which has no known painkilling properties. Somehow, then, their effectiveness must derive from the incidental factors of the treatment. These range from small and apparently insignificant therapeutic building blocks, such as the use of needles rather than pills, the physician's level of confidence and authority, and the *materia medica*, to large therapeutic building blocks, such as the elaborate healing ritual, the socially sanctioned treatment methods, the physician's use of esoteric medical terminology and symbolism, and the physician's rationale or explanation of the treatment. Precisely *how* these incidental factors work—the mechanisms behind placebo effects—is currently the subject of intense scientific inquiry: competing theories identify as the relevant mechanisms of change the expectancy effect,[11,12] classical conditioning,[13,14] the meaning response,[15] neurochemistry and neuroanatomy,[5,6] interpersonal healing,[16] and psychosocial learning, among others.

Like saline injections, insight placebos also lack the vital or characteristic ingredients that are considered by the talking cures to be central for treating certain psychological disorders: namely, a good fit to the relevant psychological, historical, and behavioral facts about the self that they putatively target and explain. While they might *seem* to target these facts, and thereby *seem* to uncover hidden depths of the self, in fact they fall short, and sometimes far afield, of their mark. And yet hitting the mark is precisely what insights in the talking cures are supposed to do: the talking cures are not in the business of treating clients by instilling in them confabulations, fictions, illusions, or myths. Indeed, these are among the very obstacles that they are supposed to uproot and remove, in the name of the laudable goal of seeing things as they are.

If insight placebos are therapeutically effective, it is because of factors that have little or nothing to do with fit to the facts, or accuracy, or explanatory power. As with placebos in clinical medicine, these factors range from the small and apparently insignificant—the psychotherapist's confidence and authority, and the physical characteristics of the treatment environment—to the very large—the elaborate healing ritual, the socially sanctioned treatment methods, the use of an esoteric psychological terminology, and the rationale or explanation offered to clients. Few psychotherapists or psychiatrists would concede, however, that their treatments are effective because of the confidence and authority they exude when promoting their treatments.

Consider the therapeutic potency of just one of these building blocks: the psychotherapist's use of an esoteric theoretical terminology. In the psychodynamic and psychoanalytic psychotherapies, it is not uncommon for clients to acquire insights into what they have come to believe (at least during the treatment) are the dynamic unconscious forces that govern their lives. They come to think of their behaviors, personality, and feelings as subject to, or as expressions of, deeply buried forces of resistance, repression, denial, or regression; or as the playthings of transferences, reaction formations, displacements, reversals, sublimations, or splitting. It is also not uncommon for clients to acquire insights into what they have come to believe must be long-lost childhood events involving infantile and childhood sexual experiences. Since many of these are events for which there is little current or past evidence, the events are *inferred* to have taken place, and the evidentiary criteria and reasoning styles used to make these inferences diverge widely from those deployed in extraclinical contexts. What this way of looking at things gives clients is the feeling that they are engaged in dramatic struggles with mysterious and violent forces that threaten to destroy them. They

feel that they are much more interesting than what they had once believed.

Insights such as these may strike clients as entirely plausible and coherent, but neither plausibility nor coherence are, in themselves, a guarantee that the insights are true and that they fit the facts: an explanation or a narrative framed in psychodynamic terms and appealing to explanatory entities such as displacement or sublimation could be plausible but nonetheless false, just as it could be coherent but false. The insights might also be subjectively satisfying, even to the point of evincing high levels of conviction. In acquiring them, clients might have suffered a great deal of psychic pain, and so might feel strongly attached to them. But again, feelings of conviction are no guarantee that the insights are true: strongly held beliefs have turned out to be false or more occasions than not. Again, the insights might be endorsed by the psychotherapist, who regards them as confirmation for the interpretations, but authoritative endorsement is no guarantee that the insights are true. Finally, even if insights are followed by beneficial therapeutic change, the mere fact that change has occurred does not prove that it was *caused* by the acquisition of insight. This would be a case of falling victim to the *post hoc ergo propter hoc* fallacy (after it therefore because of it). Before concluding that the insight *itself* had caused the change, the other viable explanations of therapeutic change would first have to be ruled out. Therapeutic change in both somatic and psychological medicine could, after all, be caused by spontaneous remission of symptoms, the natural fluctuation of symptoms, self-limiting disorders, suggestion or expectancy effects, or the placebo effect.

Consider the following example of insight, reported by the psychiatrist Jerome Frank in his classic work *Persuasion and Healing*.[17] The client, a married woman and young mother, was diagnosed by Frank as suffering from depression, and was treated with brief psychodynamic psychotherapy over a period of several weeks. Early in the treatment process Frank learned that his client had had a difficult childhood, and was now confronting significant changes in her life, including marriage and motherhood. She confided in him that when she was a young child, her mother had committed suicide, soon after which her father had remarried and had been posted overseas. At an early stage in the treatment, at a point when Frank had had little time to assemble a sufficient amount of clinical material to develop a clear picture of his client's history and personality, Frank offered her a tentative psychodynamic interpretation. The main theme of the interpretation was that abandonment by her mother and father at such an early age had led her to fear putting trust in other people, including her husband. This, Frank told her, explained her depressive episodes, as well as the distrust she displayed during the therapeutic hour. Despite its simplicity and lack of detail, the interpretation, in the client's words, "went off like a gong." Not only did it trigger in her a number of insights that (she felt) confirmed the interpretation, it was also followed by positive changes in her behavior and mood, and it advanced the progress of the treatment.

But did the interpretation fit the facts? Did it really explain anything, or did it merely offer a re-description of the facts that were in need of explanation? Did it help her to see things in herself as they really were? And did it accurately hook up effects with their causes, as causal explanations are supposed to do? The problem with the interpretation, and the insights that followed from it, was that it was missing the characteristic factors that are typically associated with genuine interpretations: namely, a close fit to the historical, behavioral, and psychological facts. The interpretation was one-size-fits-all and so loose-fitting and inexact that it could have referred to a wide range of other clients in very different circumstances, and with very different problems. With such a questionable connection to the facts, its power to explain anything adequately was doubtful. And yet despite these flaws, the interpretation seemed, at least to the client—who by then was quite suggestible owing to the covert and overt effects of the therapeutic building blocks—to be plausible and coherent. It enabled her to re-label her feelings as normal, and allowed her "to construct a more optimistic apologia."[17] Frank observed that it enhanced her sense of mastery and helped to counteract the feelings of hopelessness that are one of the primary symptoms of depression. Frank also acknowledged the interpretation's loose fit and inexactness, and by implication the fact that a number of alternative loose-fitting interpretations would also have "gone off like a gong;" he did not, however, take the further step of characterizing the interpretation as a placebo. Nor did he tell her that it might have been a placebo. "The healing power of my interpreta-

tions seemed to lie more in the general attitude they conveyed than in their precise content."[17] His conclusion is guarded: "Therapists . . . who believe that only 'correct' interpretations will lead patients to change, find it hard to accept that the attitude their words convey may contribute more to therapy than the words' precise content."[17]

Frank's client did not suspect that the interpretation, and the insights that followed it, were placebos. Not only did she experience them as deep discoveries; she also believed that they fitted the facts, and that they adequately explained things. This is one of the curious features of placebos in both somatic and psychological treatments—a feature that has generated a great deal of controversy in medical ethics: in general, to be effective, patients have to believe that the treatments they are receiving are genuine treatments rather than placebo treatments. The administration of placebos, in other words, often involves deception, or the deliberate cultivation of intentional ignorance, or the use of misinformation. Sometimes it even involves deliberately letting patients fall prey to *self*-deception or willful ignorance.[2] Actions such as these are considered by some medical ethicists to be ethically impermissible, because, it is claimed, they violate the patient's autonomy.[18,19]

As a *general* rule, if placebo treatments are to be effective, patients have to believe that they are receiving genuine treatments rather than sham or dummy treatments. Placebos, in other words, have to go undetected *as* placebos. This is as true of placebos in psychotherapy as it is in somatic medicine. Clients in the talking cures do not normally experience their insights as unreal, fake, fictitious, or confabulated; they cannot think, "I now have these insights about myself, but I also know they are just fictions or confabulations." They believe that their insights fit the contours of their selves and help to answer the question, "Who am I?" (As with all general rules, however, there are exceptions, some of which are curiously counterintuitive. There is limited evidence to suggest that so-called open-label placebos can be therapeutically beneficial with certain conditions, as long as they are presented to patients in the right way).[2,20,21]

Insight placebos, then, do not come with the label *placebo* attached to them, just as the placebo pills that are given to unsuspecting patients in clinical medicine do not come with the label *placebo*. They are well disguised. Moreover, they display a psychological robustness that the simple-minded explanatory fictions populating psychobabble idioms do not. Their robustness is typically a reflection of the psychotherapist's theoretical orientation and sophisticated explanatory terminology, prolonged exposure to which tends to bias already suggestible clients to the importance of a narrow range of psychological and behavioral themes that excludes alternative ways of framing the psychological problems at hand. This in turn predisposes clients to expect that those themes can be addressed *only* by the treatment methods and exploratory styles to which they are currently exposed.

A number of experimental findings from the cognitive sciences about the vicissitudes of introspection, self-attribution, and self-reflection lend weight to the idea that the talking cures trade in placebos, and, by implication, to Frank's comments about the therapeutic benefits of one-size-fits-all interpretations and insights. Some of the more colorful of these findings—and there are many more that cannot be addressed here—include Barnum effects, causal self-*mis*attributions, and positive illusions.

The Barnum effect (also known as the Forer effect) makes its official appearance in the arena of personality psychology experiments, but it is likely a much more pervasive phenomenon than is currently acknowledged, and likely has been around long before the scientific study of personality even took root. Named after the showman P.T. Barnum ("we've got something for everyone"), it is a quirk of human psychology that is almost certainly pressed into service on a daily basis in everything from serious pursuits, such as business and personnel psychology, to questionably serious pursuits, such as astrology and fortune-telling. The experiments show that people have a strong tendency to accept bogus personality profiles (based on descriptions of hypothetical persons) as containing accurate and revealing insights about themselves just as readily as they accept bona fide personality profiles.[22–25] A smaller subset of these experiments shows that people even tend to accept *bogus* personality descriptions as *more* accurate than bona fide personality descriptions.[26,27] Typically the personality profiles in question are vague and short on detail. Like Frank's interpretation, they consist of one-size-fits-all statements that could be true of a wide range of people with very different personalities, while nevertheless displaying a minimal level of psychological plausibility. Some of the examples used in the experiments include such bland statements as "You have a great need for people to like you," "You have a tendency to be critical of yourself," and "At times you have serious doubts as to whether you have made the right decision."

Frank's interpretation very likely triggered the Barnum effect, or some variation of it; so too would a number of different interpretations, each one picking out different, and perhaps incompatible, cause and effect stories. His client's enthusiastic acceptance of the interpretation was not because it fit the facts and explained them; rather, it introduced a degree of intelligibility where before there was none; and it gave his client a sense of control over her otherwise confusing feelings and behaviors. This, Frank notes, is one of the factors common to all forms of healing, from the most ancient forms of shamanism to the most technologically advanced medical interventions to the most sophisticated of the talking cures: all of them supply patients with a rationale, conceptual scheme, or myth that explains, or *seems* to explain, their puzzling symptoms, fit to the facts and explanatory power notwithstanding.

Still more support for the idea that insights and interpretations in the talking cures may be little more than elaborate placebos can be found in a branch of social psychology that focuses on the vagaries of causal self-attributions and causal inferences. When people raise after-the-fact cause-seeking questions, such as "Why did I do that?," "Why did I make that choice?," or "Why did I react that way?"—the very sorts of questions that bedevil therapy sessions—the answers they produce typically fall prey to confabulation and rationalization. In tackling these questions, they might think that they are directing a careful introspective gaze to an inner landscape of desires and motives, and in so doing securing a clearer picture of what makes them who they are; or they might think that they are making discoveries about the hitherto unobserved causes of their behaviors, and thereby filling in some of the blanks in the enormous causal chain that links up past to present. What is more likely to be happening, however, is that they are pressing into service readily available generalizations about selves and their causal make-up that, derived from the social and cultural milieu, have surprisingly tenuous connections to the real causal story, and even more tenuous evidentiary credentials.[28–30] "When trying to decide why they performed a certain action, people call upon reasons that are available in memory and representative of (or similar to) the response, and use their culturally-learned and idiosyncratic theories about 'why I performed behavior X'. Similarly, if access to internal states is sometimes limited, people may call upon the explanatory system to infer how they feel. These conscious inferences are influenced by theories about oneself and about what feelings seem like plausible reactions to a stimulus."[31] More often than they like to admit, people are strangers to themselves.

The concept of self-alienation has deep roots in many of the world's philosophies, religions, and literary traditions. It can be traced back at least as far as the schools of skepticism that flourished in ancient Greece and Rome (e.g., Sextus Empiricus), ancient India (e.g., Nagarjuna) and ancient China (e.g., Zhuangzi), medieval Persia (e.g., Al Ghazali), and early modern philosophy. The Dutch-Jewish philosopher Spinoza, for instance, was one of the first to explicitly link the idea of self-alienation to the idea of causal self-opacity, thereby calling into question Descartes' claim that people enjoy a privileged access to their inner goings-on: "All men are born ignorant of the causes of things. . . . Men believe that they are free precisely because they are conscious of their volitions and desires; yet concerning the causes that have determined them to desire and will they have not the faintest idea, because they are ignorant of them" [32]

The evidence from social-psychological experiments on causal attribution and causal inference suggests that people have no privileged introspective access and that the introspective mechanisms that they *claim* to be using when trying to work out questions, such as "Why did I do that?," are inaccurate and in many cases just plain confabulated. The real causal action occurs at a level far below anything that can be consciously experienced, in what has been hypothesized to be a subpersonal *cognitive unconscious* that bears none of the familiar marks of first-person conscious experience. Appealing to introspective self-observation to explain their behaviors and decisions, people tell more than they in fact know: more significantly, in the words of Nisbett and Wilson, they "tell more than they *can* know."[28]

Not only do causal self-attributions populate large portions of common sense psychological discourse, they are also prevalent in the talking cures, where, like archaeologists, clients are engaged (or they *believe* they are engaged) in exploring the archaic and less than fully conscious causes of their behaviors and feelings. The poverty of introspection and causal inference is even more pronounced here than in other contexts; so too is the risk of causal confabulation. If the social-psychological experimental research can be feasibly extrapolated to the clinical context, then it would seem that the exploratory work that clients believe they are engaged in is really an exercise in learning to deploy new *a priori* causal theories and psychological narratives, rather than an exercise in genuine self-exploration. And it would seem that the hard-won insights that clients think they have acquired about themselves in therapy are really one-size-fits-all causal generalizations that typically adhere to the general psychological orientations defended by their therapists. (Many factors drive this theoretical adherence, including the intense pressures felt by clients to relieve the cognitive dissonance of the therapeutic encounter, their desire to win the approval of their therapists, and the high levels of cognitive suggestibility to which they are subject.)

Not only is accurate insight into oneself hard to acquire, and constantly beset with hard-to-detect and harder-to-uproot cognitive biases, such as attribution errors and Barnum effects, there is also evidence to suggest that it just doesn't pay. One strand of experimental research in social psychology on positive illusions and creative self-deception seems to show that positively biased illusions about the self, and creative forms of self-deception, play a more significant role in mental health, and in the maintenance of caring interpersonal relationships and a sense of well-being, than accurate self-perceptions and insights.[33] Among these illusions are unrealistically positive self-evaluations, exaggerated perceptions of personal control, and unrealistic optimism about the future. Illusions such as these are like cognitive filters that typically select and organize information that is relevant to the self in a direction that is self-serving and self-enhancing. Filtering effects include the distortion of negative information, the enhancement of positive information, and the disambiguation of ambiguous information. "[The] capacity to develop and maintain positive illusions may be thought of as a valuable human resource to be nurtured and promoted, rather than an error-prone processing system to be corrected. In any case, these illusions help make each individual's world a warmer and more active and beneficent place in which to live."[34]

Versions of this idea have been defended before. More than a century ago, for example, Nietzsche argued that the will to ignorance—which for him includes the full panoply of illusions, ignorance, deceptions, blind spots, over-simplifications, and falsifications—is one of the most basic and adaptive conditions of human life. The commitment to truth, to seeing things (and oneself) as they really are, is destructive of the blind momentum of life. "It is not enough that you understand in what ignorance humans as well as animals live; you must also have and acquire the will to ignorance. You need to grasp that without this kind of ignorance life itself would be impossible, that it is a condition under which alone the living thing can preserve itself and prosper: a great, firm dome of ignorance must encompass you."[35]

The plays of Henrik Ibsen and Eugene O'Neill, which illustrate these Nietzschean themes with searing intensity, depict ordinary people confronting extraordinary existential circumstances and negotiating them only with the help of comforting illusions, self-deceptive strategies, and "life lies." Stripped of these defenses, most people cannot function normally or achieve a barely tolerable level of self-contentment; sometimes, sudden confrontations with reality and sudden acquisitions of insight are followed by debilitating despair, and even tragedy. For Ibsen and O'Neill, the goal of trying to see things as they really are is psychologically and existentially dangerous. "Take away the life-lie from the average person," writes Ibsen, "and you take his happiness along with it."[36] "To hell with the truth!" says Larry Slade, one of the hard-drinking regulars at Harry Hope's bar, in O'Neill's play *The Iceman Cometh*. "The lie of a pipe dream is what gives life to the whole misbegotten mad lot of us, drunk or sober."[37] There may be some kernel of truth in this sage barroom advice, but the problem is that it also serves as a convenient strategy for avoiding the vicissitudes of life, and of learning and growing from the experience of suffering.[38]

———————

Given the full range of these forces of ignorance—the placebo effects, cognitive blind spots, cognitive biases, and self-attributive errors that bedevil insight—what are we to make of the talking cure's claims to insight and self-knowledge? Are psychotherapists who boast of helping clients to achieve insight deceiving or misleading their clients if they do not caution them that placebo effects may be at play?[2] If some of the therapeutic changes in the talking cures are functions of placebos that rally the mind's native healing powers in much the same way that placebo pills rally the body's native healing powers, then what do the talking cures really have to offer to the search for self-knowledge?

There are no easy and short answers here. But one way to at least begin to make sense of these questions is to look for clues in the long history of the talking cures. Some of the oldest forms of psychotherapy were inextricably linked with the ancient tradition of practical philosophy, proponents of which included the Epicureans, Stoics, cynics, and skeptics. The primary means of treatment involved nothing more elaborate than dialogue.[39–41] The main idea then, as now, was as simple as it was profound: self-examination and reflective self-evaluation that are conducive to well-being and to living well (in a social, political, moral, and aesthetic sense) are not solitary pursuits that involve turning away from society or retreating into the privacy of one's own thoughts; it is only talking with others that unlocks the soul and opens it up to ways of self-knowing and to caring for self that would otherwise be unavailable. This sort of dialogue—the original curing by talking—was unique. Not any type of dialogue could secure these ends, since some dialogues were harnessed to the wrong ends, and some were harnessed to the wrong interlocutors. (Some were also heavily embellished with meditation techniques, memory and attention-training exercises, "spiritual exercises," and powerful rhetorical devices such as irony, metaphor, and analogy.[42] Even Socrates, a master dialectician and conversationalist, observed that "the cure of the soul has to be effected by the use of certain charms, and these charms are fair words" exchanged between healer and patient.)[43] Despite large variations in how they were thought about and practiced, and who took part in them, dialogues directed to the goal of self-knowledge had a number of distinctive core features, which were built upon and refined across subsequent generations of healers and practical philosophers. Some of these features, or their vestiges, make their appearance in the talking cures as we know them today. However, the drive to medicalize the healing arts, and with it the fascination with technique, medical models of effectiveness, and the construction, defense, and testing of large-scale psychological theories, has issued in a displacement and ultimately a weakening of the role of dialogue. The result is that clients in the talking cures are typically regarded less as interlocutors on an equal footing with their healers, than as the placeholders where theoretical constructs are refined and validated, techniques applied, and diagnostic categories substantiated.[44] (Political, legal, and economic interests have also played an important role in the displacement of the role of dialogue.) The restrictive model of dialogue with which the talking cures now operate inadvertently encourages placebo effects, and with it, heightened suggestibility and epistemic vulnerability in clients.

What then are some of these core features? Then, as now, dialogues aimed at reflective self-evaluation take the form of back and forth exchanges between self and other. The fundamental practical questions that motivate these dialogues—"Who am I?," "What matters most to me?," and "Are these the desires, beliefs, feelings, and traits that I want to constitute my identity?"—are directed from self to other as a *call*; that is, they are a kind of appeal, or a kind of address, or even a summons, very often raised with a sense of urgency. Sometimes these appeals hit their mark; many times they miss or go unheard altogether. In the right material and social circumstances, however, and with the right interlocutors (e.g., people who have some degree of practical wisdom, who know and respect the value of the questions), they have the power to elicit responses that are oriented to the truth. The questions, in other words, do not involve the self pursuing an inquiry by itself and for itself.[1]

Both speakers, moreover, have to encounter each other frankly, without the interferences of prejudice, self-centered concern, competitiveness, or hidden motive. They have to be willing to let the other's differences in perspective and beliefs—what is sometimes today called the otherness of the other—be fully manifest. This ensures that the dialogue is emotionally and morally engaging, to the point where it evokes in both speakers a range of other-directed moral emotions and morally responsive

attitudes (such as care, compassion, sympathy, respect, shame, and desire). These are typically not found in dialogues where one speaker has adopted an objective or observational stance to the other, or, as in the case of classical Freudian psychoanalysis, the stance of a neutral screen, or, as in the case of many talking cures, the position of the object of transference. Upon hearing the question, "Who am I?," the other is called to listen, challenge, reason, and to bear witness to the self's struggles to know itself and to remove some of the darkness that separates it from itself. And the other is called to do this without hiding behind theory, technique, and managerial stances.[1]

Finally, the back-and-forth dialogic process is open ended, serving to remind the speakers that reality, including the reality of the self that is the target of the question, "Who am I?," is always richer than their knowledge of it. There is no point at which the speakers can declare the inquiry terminated. Nor can they know in advance where the dialogue will take them; nor can they know the outcome, or how their original starting points, including their original self-understandings, will be changed by it.

Dialogues that satisfy these conditions are not an automatic antidote to placebo insights in the talking cures. Nor are they an antidote to the many other forces of ignorance that typically plague our efforts to reflectively evaluate and know ourselves. But they provide a firm footing—perhaps as firm as is possible, given our finite and fallible state—to keep our reflective inquiries oriented in the right general direction, especially when they are focused on identifying and understanding the forces—including the placebo effects and cognitive biases—that typically deflect and deform our efforts to know ourselves.

Conflicts of interest

The author declares no conflicts of interest.

References

1. Jopling, D.A. 2000. *Self-Knowledge and the Self*. Routledge, New York.
2. Jopling, D.A. 2008. *Talking Cures and Placebo Effects*. Oxford University Press. New York and Oxford.
3. Harrington, A., Ed. 1997. *The Placebo Effect: An Interdisciplinary Exploration*. Harvard University Press. Cambridge, MA.
4. Guess H.A., A. Kleinman, J.W. Kusek & L. Engel, Eds. 2002. *The Science of the Placebo: Towards an Interdisciplinary Research Agenda*. BMJ. London.

5. Benedetti, F. 2009. *Placebo Effects: Understanding the Mechanisms in Health and Disease.* Oxford University Press. Oxford.

6. Benedetti, F. 2011. *The Patient's Brain: The Neuroscience Behind the Doctor-Patient Relationship.* Oxford University Press. Oxford.

7. Kirsch, I. 2010. *The Emperor's New Drugs: Exploding the Antidepressant Myth.* Basic Books. New York.

8. Humphrey, N. 2002. Great expectations: The evolutionary psychology of faith healing and the placebo effect. In *The Mind Made Flesh.* Oxford University Press. New York.

9. Brody, H. 1997. The doctor as therapeutic agent: A placebo effect research agenda. In *The Placebo Effect: An Interdisciplinary Exploration.* A. Harrington, Ed.: 77–92. Harvard University Press. Cambridge, MA.

10. Grünbaum, A. 1986. The placebo concept in medicine and psychiatry. *Psychol. Med.* **16:** 19–38.

11. Kirsch, I. 1997. Specifying nonspecifics: Psychological mechanisms of placebo effects. In *The Placebo Effect: An Interdisciplinary Exploration.* A. Harrington, Ed.: 166–186. Harvard University Press. Cambridge, MA.

12. Kirsch I., Ed. 1999. *How Expectancies Shape Experience.* American Psychological Association. Washington, D.C.

13. Ader, R.A. 1997. The role of conditioning in pharmacotherapy. In *The Placebo Effect: An Interdisciplinary Exploration.* A. Harrington, Ed.: 138–165. Harvard University Press. Cambridge, MA.

14. Ader, R. & N. Cohen. 1982. Behaviorally conditioned immunosuppression and murine systemic lupus erythematosus. *Science* **8:** 379–394.

15. Moerman, D.E. 2002. *Meaning, Medicine and the "Placebo Effect."* Cambridge University Press. Cambridge.

16. Miller, F.G., L. Colloca & T. Kaptchuk. 2009. The placebo effect: Illness and interpersonal healing. *Perspect. Biol. Med.* **52** (4): 518.

17. Frank J.D. & J.B. Frank. 1991. *Persuasion and Healing* (3rd Ed.). Johns Hopkins University Press. Baltimore.

18. Bok, S. 1974. The ethics of giving placebos. *Sci. Am.* **231:** 17–23.

19. Bok, S. 2002. Ethical issues in the use of placebos in medical practice and clinical trials. In *The Science of the Placebo: Towards an Interdisciplinary Research Agenda.* H.A. Guess, A. Kleinman, J.W. Kusek & L. Engel, Eds.: 53–74. BMJ. London.

20. Kaptchuk, T., E. Friedlander, J.M. Kelley, *et al.* 2011. Placebos without deception: a randomized controlled trial in irritable bowel syndrome. *PloS ONE* (5) 12. Bibcode: http://adsabs.harvard.edu/abs/2010PLoSO...515591K.

21. Park, L.C. & L. Covi. 1965. Nonblind placebo trial: an exploration of neurotic outpatients' response to placebo when its inert content is disclosed. *Arch. Gen. Psychiatry* **12:** 336–345.

22. Forer, B.R. 1949. The fallacy of personal validation: A classroom demonstration of gullibility. *J. Abnormal Soc. Psych.* **44** (1): 118–123.

23. Ulrich, R., T. Stachnik & R. Stainton, 1963. Student acceptance of generalized personality interpretations. *Psych. Reports* **13:** 831–834.

24. Dmitruk, V.M., R.W. Collins & D.L. Clinger. 1973. The Barnum effect and acceptance of negative personal evaluation. *J. Consulting Clin. Psych.* **41:** 192–194.

25. Snyder, C., R. Shenkel & C. Lowery. 1977. Acceptance of personality interpretations: the 'Barnum effect' and beyond. *J. Consulting Clin. Psych.* **45:** 104–114.

26. Sundberg, N.D. 1966. The acceptability of 'fake' versus bona fide personality test interpretations. *J. Abnormal Soc. Psych.* **50:** 145–147.

27. Dickson, D.H. & I.W. Kelly. 1985. The Barnum effect in personality assessment: A review of the literature. *Psych. Reports* **57:** 367–382.

28. Nisbett, R.E. & T.D. Wilson. 1977. Telling more than we can know: Verbal reports on mental processes. *Psych. Rev.* **84:** 231–259.

29. Nisbett, R.E. & L. Ross. 1980. *Human Inference: Strategies and Shortcomings of Social Judgement.* Prentice Hall. Englewood Cliffs, NJ.

30. Wilson, T.D. 1985. Strangers to ourselves: The origins and accuracy of beliefs about one's own mental states. In *Attribution: Basic Issues and Applications.* J.H. Harvey & G. Weary, Eds.: 9–36. Academic Press. Orlando, FL.

31. Wilson, T.D. 2004. *Strangers to Ourselves.* Belknap Press. Cambridge, MA. p.17.

32. Spinoza, B. 1677/1992. *The Ethics; Treatise on the Emendation of the Intellect; and Selected Letters.* S Shirley, Trans. & Ed. Hackett. Indianapolis, IN. p.57

33. Taylor, S. 1989. *Positive Illusions: Creative Self-Deception and the Healthy Mind.* Basic Books. New York.

34. Taylor, S. & J. Brown. 1988. Illusion and well-being: A social-psychological perspective on mental health. *Psychol. Bull.* **103:** 193–210. p.205

35. Nietzsche, F. 1968. *The Will to Power.* W. Kaufmann & R.J. Hollingdale, Trans. Vintage Press. New York. #609.

36. Ibsen, H. 1884/1997. *The Wild Duck.* M. Meyer, Trans. Norton. New York.

37. O'Neill, E. 1939/1946. *The Iceman Cometh.* Vintage Books. New York. pp. 9–10.

38. Jopling, D.A. 1996. 'Take away the life-lie': Positive illusions and creative self-deception. *Phil. Psych.* **9:** 525–544.

39. Lain Entralgo, P. 1970. *The Therapy of the Word in Classical Antiquity.* L.J. Rather & J.M. Sharp, Trans. Yale University Press. New Haven.

40. Gill, C. 1985. Ancient psychotherapy. *J. History Ideas* **46:** 307–325.

41. Nussbaum, M. 1994. *The Therapy of Desire: Theory and Practice in Hellenistic Ethics.* Princeton University Press. Princeton.

42. Hadot, P. 1995. Spiritual exercises. In *Philosophy as a Way of Life.* M. Chase, Trans. Blackwell. New York.

43. Plato, 1961. *Charmides.* B. Jowett, Trans. In *The Complete Dialogues of Plato.* E. Hamilton & H. Cairns, Eds. Princeton University Press. Princeton.

44. Jopling, D. 2001. Placebo insight: the rationality of insight-oriented psychotherapy. *J. Clin. Psychol.* **57** (1): 19–36.

Ann. N.Y. Acad. Sci. ISSN 0077-8923

Understanding, justifying, and finding oneself

Frances M. Kamm

Harvard University, Cambridge, Massachusetts

Address for correspondence: Frances M. Kamm, Ph.D. Department of Philosophy, Emerson Hall 209a, Harvard University, 25 Quincy Street, Cambridge, MA

This essay tries to explain some ways in which we can come to know about ourselves, in particular about what we think. It also tries to distinguish what we are and think from what we ought to be and think.

Deciding versus discovering

To begin,[a] it is important to distinguish two different senses of coming to know what we think. The first sense is that of "making up your mind" about an issue: for instance, this is generally what someone wants you to do when they ask, "What do you think now about the invasion of Iraq?" This requires you to consider the facts and values in favor of and against the invasion and come to a conclusion about its merits. It does not usually involve your trying to introspect (or to use some more sophisticated way of gaining knowledge about your mental states) in order to find out what settled beliefs you already have about the Iraq War.[b] The same can be true if you are asked about a moral issue, for instance, what you think about the morality of capital punishment.

These questions are also asking you to come to a conclusion about what you believe is *true* about the invasion and about capital punishment. They ask you to form a true opinion not about yourself but about a form of action undertaken by others. This does not mean that what you think will be true (your opinion might be wrong), but you are being asked to attempt to get at a truth about something other than yourself. This is so, even though the question asks about what you think.

This essay is primarily concerned not with how we come to know what we think in the sense of making up our mind, but with the acquisition of self-knowledge in the sense of discovering things about ourself that hold true independently of our now making up our mind.

Explaining oneself

Inference and the method of hypothetical cases

It is said by some psychologists (such as Timothy Wilson[c]) that we often do not understand why we do or believe certain things because it is our "adaptive unconscious" that is in control. Yet when asked why we have done or believe certain things, we nevertheless often confidently give answers that are, in fact, incorrect explanations. Wilson refers to these as "confabulations." For example, suppose there is a person who has been hypnotized to open a window at a certain time and does so. He may claim he did so because the room got hot even though there was no change in room temperature. Such events suggest that, at least sometimes, we have no privileged access to ourselves. That is, we do not know ourselves better than we know others and, in fact, others may know why we do or believe things better than we do.

---

[a]This essay was written in conjunction with (but after) the panel discussion entitled "Who Am I? Beyond 'I Think, Therefore I Am'" at the New York Academy of Sciences (NYAS), May 24, 2011. As this essay is short, none of the topics are dealt with thoroughly.
[b]The distinction between making up one's mind and discovering one's mind was emphasized by Richard Moran in his *Authority and Estrangement: An Essay on Self-Knowledge* (Princeton University Press, 2001).

[c]In his *Strangers to Ourselves* (Harvard University Press, 2005). All quotes from Wilson are from that book. Wilson was a fellow member of the NYAS panel.

doi: 10.1111/j.1749-6632.2011.06187.x

As a philosopher, I might be expected to disagree with this claim. However, I am inclined to agree that in many cases with which I have dealt, it is hard for someone to know why he believes something and yet he may often offer an incorrect explanation of his beliefs, and others may know better than he does why he believes certain things.

Consider the so-called trolley problem.[d] In one case that exhibits the problem, an out-of-control trolley is headed toward killing five immovable people on a track. If and only if a bystander presses a switch near to him will the trolley be directed away from the five onto another track. Unfortunately, there is a different immovable individual on that other track who, it is foreseen, will be killed by the redirected trolley (redirect case). Many people intuitively judge that it is permissible to turn the trolley, thus saving five and killing one. However, there is another variation of the trolley case in which the trolley headed toward the five can only be stopped if a bystander pushes a very heavy person from where the heavy person stands on a bridge over the track. The heavy person's falling in front of the trolley would stop it but kill him (bridge case). The same people who think it is permissible to divert the trolley in the first case usually intuitively judge that it is impermissible to push the man from the bridge. This is so even though in both cases five people will be saved and one will die.

While people have these responses consciously and with conviction, they do not consciously reason their way to them. That is why these responses are called intuitive judgments. Often people may not know how to explain why they respond as they do. Some have proposed that the reason many people respond differently to the two trolley cases is that the first case involves pressing a switch that leads to someone's death, whereas in the second case one must be "up close and personal" in pushing the person to his death.[e] (Those who have proposed this see it as a "debunking" explanation, in that the mere

fact that one kills someone up close and personally could not actually make a moral difference between the cases, even if people react as though it does.) The question is whether this simple explanation of why people respond differently to the two cases is a "confabulation" or, as I would put it, a wrong conjecture. I am tempted to distinguish between a confabulation and a wrong conjecture because it might be thought that a confabulation should refer only to an explanation about his own responses that a person makes up quickly and of which he feels confident. Since not all wrong conjectures (even about one's own responses) are like this, not all wrong conjectures would be confabulations.[f]

I believe that we can test our conjectures about why people make certain conscious intuitive moral judgments by using what I call the method of hypothetical cases.[g] Just as the two previous trolley cases did not occur in reality but were hypothetical cases, we may create other hypothetical variants on the basic trolley case and they can help us decide whether people are responding to the factor pointed to in the conjecture. For example, using this method allows us to mentally remove the factor of up close and personal pushing, creating another case that holds everything else constant as it was in the bridge case.

---

[d]First presented in one of its versions in Philippa Foot's "The Problem of Abortion and the Doctrine of Double Effect," reprinted in her *Virtues and Vices and Other Essays* (U. of California Press, 1978). I discuss the problem in my *Morality, Mortality*, Vol. 2 (Oxford University Press, 1996) and in my *Intricate Ethics* (Oxford University Press, 2007), among other places.

[e]This was suggested by the philosopher/psychologist Joshua Greene. See, for example, Joshua D. Greene,

et al., "An fMRI Investigation of Emotional Engagement in Moral Judgment." 2001. *Science*. **293**: 2105–2108. I have discussed Greene's views on moral judgment in my "Neuroscience and Moral Reasoning: A Note on Recent Research." 2009. *PPA*. **37**: 330–345.

[f]On the other hand, in considering some of my proposals for explaining my own different responses to different trolley cases, the psychologist Daniel Kahnemann compared me to a person who confabulates. (See his remarks in Chapter 3 in *Conversations on Ethics* by Alex Voorhoeve (Oxford University Press, 2009.) This was so even though it should have been clear that my conjectures are the result of considering many variants on trolley cases and rejecting different possible explanations of responses to them. Thus my ultimate conjectures about what underlies my responses to cases were not immediate responses or held with complete confidence; yet he thought of them as confabulations. It is for this reason that he may also conclude that Prof. Greene's proposal is a confabulation, if it turns out to be a false explanation of responses (at least if Greene intuitively also has these responses). I am not sure if Prof. Wilson would assent to such a broad notion of *confabulation*.

[g]I make heavy use of this method in my work as do many other contemporary philosophers.

So suppose a bystander needs only to press a switch that will activate a machine that will push the heavy person off the bridge. Will people who judged it impermissible to push the person off the bridge now think it permissible to press the switch? If not, then it is not being "up close and personal" per se that accounts for the differing views about the redirect and bridge cases. The conjecture would be shown to be wrong. (It would also help to test the conjecture to imagine another hypothetical case that also involves up close and personal pushing someone into a threat but was judged permissible, due to our varying some other factor in the bridge case.[h])

Scientists use experiments in which they can change one variable at a time, holding everything else constant, in order to see if that variable is crucial to an explanation of a phenomenon. The method of hypothetical cases is the use of thought experiments, which often seem bizarre because we can imagine a factor being present or absent, holding constant all other factors, though this could not happen in reality. But just as artificially controlled conditions in a lab can lead to results that are applicable to real life, the results of artificial thought experiments might help us explain intuitive responses in "messier" cases closer to real life.

Using the method of hypothetical cases to explain one's own intuitive judgments about cases does not involve unaided introspective knowledge. It is more like inferring what drives one's responses by a process of testing and eliminating conjectures. Wilson himself says that we can have inferential knowledge of what is going on in our adaptive unconscious (that underlies our conscious awareness of a judgment). He says: "Many human judgments, emotions, thoughts, and behaviors are produced by the adaptive unconscious. Because people do not have conscious access to the adaptive unconscious, their conscious selves confabulate reasons why they responded the way we did…In other words, to the extent that people's responses are caused by the adaptive unconscious, they do not have privileged access to the causes and must infer them."[i]

Daniel Kahnemann has said that when a philosopher offers explanations of his intuitive judgments he is like the hypotized person who offers a confab-

ulation (i.e., "the room got hotter") to explain his opening a window.[j] But when philosophers consider a wide range of cases in order to find out what factor may account for their judgments, they are trying to avoid the problem raised by the case of the hypotized person. The hypnotized person's explanation could be determined to be a confabulation by the method of hypothetical cases, for if we kept all factors constant except that we made the room colder we know that the person would still feel compelled to open the window, thus showing that his own explanation was wrong. By testing their conjectures on multiple cases, philosophers seek to identify an explanation that cannot be eliminated in this way.[k]

Self and others

The fact that we may acquire knowledge about ourselves through inference suggests that we may also understand others better than they understand themselves, and others may understand us better than we understand ourselves. This is because any given person may not have the ability to isolate a factor underlying his views that is only discoverable through consideration of many judgments about different cases. Someone else who has the ability may infer the factor that is leading another person to make judgments better than that other person could. Furthermore, if one does have the ability to come to understand what is underlying one's own judgments, then one may be able to understand others' similar judgments better than they can. So, if I were able to understand my responses to the trolley problem and your responses were like mine, I might have a true conjecture about what underlies your responses, while you do not.

Complex explanations

Suppose one uses the method of hypothetical cases. The factor that one ultimately uncovers that seems to account for intuitive judgments may be complex or at least unexpected; it could be very hard to consciously formulate the factor and it might be a factor that does not ordinarily play a part in conscious thought. Does this mean that it could not really

---

[h]I tried to do this in constructing what I call the lazy susan case. See *Morality, Mortality,* Vol. 2 and *Intricate Ethics.*
[i]Wilson, p. 104.

[j]As I noted in footnote *f.*
[k]The fact that one is conscious of intuitive judgments before becoming conscious of the (supposed) explanation for them does not mean that the explanation cannot point to factors that caused the judgment. The factors while unconscious could have caused the judgment.

causally underlie people's judgments? I have argued that our ethics may be "intricate," and that complex factors may account for our responses without our being capable of consciously formulating the factors or principles containing them.[l] Sometimes support is drawn for this view from the theory of innate grammar in that complex unconscious principles seem to guide our understanding and production of language.[m] I now find support in what Wilson says about "implicit learning" by the adaptive unconscious. He says about a demonstration of implicit learning: "The participants' task was to watch a computer screen that was divided into four quadrants. On each trial, the letter X appeared in one of the four quadrants, and the participant pressed one of four buttons to indicate which one. Unbeknownst to the participant, the presentations of the Xs were divided into blocks of 12 that followed a complex rule...Although the exact rules were complicated, participants appeared to learn them. As time went by their performance steadily improved...None of the participants, however, could verbalize what the rules were or even that they had learned anything. They learned the complex rules nonconsciously."[n] In this case, the formula that explained the placement of Xs in the grid was never made conscious. I have suggested that the method of hypothetical cases could help us make conscious the principle underlying certain moral judgments.

Beyond explanation to justification

Moral philosophers aim to go beyond finding out what factors one is responding to in cases. Moral philosophy is *normative*: it is concerned with the factors to which one should respond and, in general, with what one should think and do rather than with what one (or even everyone) actually thinks and does. So, if one uncovers factors or principles that explain one's responses, one has to reflect on whether those factors or principles also justify one's responses. That is, do they really represent or are they connected with reasons, considerations that

have moral significance. (One part of Kahnemann's sense that true moral judgments could not be the result of complex factors uncovered via the method of hypothetical cases is his sense that such complex factors or principles are unlikely to be inherently morally significant reasons, even if they do underlie our judgments. I suspect that he thinks this because he favors some form of utilitarianism [i.e., maximizing overall good understood as well being], and he cannot see the moral merit in various kinds of constraints on maximizing the good that prohibit bringing about the good in one way but not another.)[o]

Suppose the factors or principles uncovered do have moral significance. Indeed, suppose that a factor that caused different responses to different cases provides a sufficient reason for responding differently to the cases. Then it justifies the differential responses. Furthermore, given that one responds to a sufficient reason, even though an intuitive judgment was not reached by consciously considering reasons, it can be considered a reasonable (or rational) intuitive judgment. It is not merely a feeling that one tries to "rationalize" (in the sense of providing a confabulation for it after the fact.)[p]

If factors or principles sufficiently justify responses they cause, they can become the basis for requirements on everyone's conduct, should they face situations in reality like those presented in hypothetical cases, and standards against which to measure the correctness of anyone's intuitive moral judgments. One way of putting this is that taking account

---

[l]Though I have also noted that heuristics—approximations to a complex principle—might be causally operative, I here wish to consider whether the complex principle might itself be causally operative. See *Intricate Ethics*, Chapter 14, among other places.

[m]I referred to this example in my *Creation and Abortion* (Oxford University Press, 1992), Introduction.

[n]Wilson, p.28.

[o]See his remarks in Chapter 3 in *Conversations on Ethics*. For example, he says: "So I find it hard to believe that the two cases [of pushing the fat man in front of the trolley and of diverting the trolley onto the man on the side track] differ in morally relevant ways." I have discussed earlier work by Kahnemann related to moral theory in my "Moral Intuitions, Cognitive Psychology, and the Harming/Not Aiding Distinction," reprinted as Chapter 14 in my *Intricate Ethics*.

[p]This is contrary to the view of psychologist Jonathan Haidt. See his "The Emotional Dog and Its Rational Tail: A Social Intuitionist Approach to Moral Judgments," *Psychological Review*, 108, 4:814–34. I also discuss Haidt in my "Should you Save This Child? Gibbard on Intuitions, Contractualism, and the Strains of Commitment," which is my response to Allan Gibbard's Tanner Lectures (published with them) in his *Reconciling Our Aims* (Oxford University Press, 2008).

of the factors or principles is objectively correct and provides universalizable standards (i.e., they apply to everyone). If this is the case, self-knowledge that shows particularities about oneself that others do not share need not be relevant to whether one should judge or act in the way others should judge and act. Consider an analogy from another area. Suppose an art critic judges one work of art to be better than another. He is not just saying that he, in virtue of his particular history and characteristics, responds more favorably to one work than another. He is claiming to make a universalizable judgment. This is a judgment that everyone who is concerned with artistic merit should make, regardless of the particular personal characteristics that might distinguish him from the art critic and that might lead him to favor one work over another on grounds other than artistic merit (e.g., it reminds him of his parent).

The fact of normativity opens up the possibility that how one ought to judge or behave can differ from how one is revealed to actually judge and behave. Objective and universalizable truths about morality (and other things) open up the possibility that one could know what one should or should not do, or how one should judge, independently of knowing much about one's distinctive personal psychology. This possibility is one ground on which to be skeptical of the importance of self-knowledge, for finding out about oneself leaves one with the normative question of whether to endorse or reject what one finds in oneself. For example, if one finds that one has a strong desire to harm people, one may wish to be different and try to change, or at least to not give vent to the desire. People often wonder whether many things true of them are due to nature or nurture, but regardless of the origin of traits, the question remains of evaluating them either positively or negatively and deciding what to do about them. The fact that something is due to nature rather than to nurture does not mean it should be endorsed.

However, it should be noted that it might be argued[a] that one's true self (knowledge of which should be in question) is the part of oneself with

which one identifies, giving it an authoritative standing in relation to one's thoughts, desires and actions. So, it has been said, a drug addict may crave drugs and all the while judge that the craving is one he does not want to have because it is bad to have. These are not just two equal and conflicting "parts" of the self pulling in opposite directions. The person could, for example, identify with the negative judgment of his craving and ultimately want to get rid of it. This gives the judging aspect authority. The question is whether this means that the part of oneself that craves the drug is any less one's true self for being rejected. In any case, notice that knowing where one ultimately stands on the issue of craving for drugs—pro or con—is (often) a matter of making up one's mind rather than merely discovering where one already stands. This brings us back to the very first distinction we discussed in Part 1, between making up one's mind and discovering it.

There is another reason for being skeptical about the importance of a person acquiring knowledge of himself. Discovering things about oneself and even deciding what about oneself to endorse or reject may be less important than just quite unreflectively being a good self. And if one is already a good self—doing and thinking correctly—then one will presumably consider whether acquiring knowledge about oneself is the right thing to do, by contrast with doing other things; for example, acquiring knowledge about how to cure cancer. Acquiring self-knowledge may be the right thing to do only if it is a means to making oneself or some other aspect of reality better. Indeed, the self knowledge that people usually seek involves "finding oneself" in the sense of finding what one can do in life that is both worthwhile and authentic (true to oneself).[r] Notice also that acquiring knowledge about oneself is to be contrasted with acquiring knowledge about self-knowledge. The latter is an inquiry into people's acquisition of knowledge of themselves, not the acquisition of knowledge of oneself in particular. Thus, inquiring into the acquisition of self-knowledge could be important even when acquiring self-knowledge is not itself important in particular cases.

---

[a] Perhaps with support from the views of Harry Frankfurt in "Freedom of the Will and the Concept of a Person," *Journal of Philosophy* **68**(1): 5–20, and Gary Watson in "Free Agency," *Mind*, Vol. 96, no. 382, April 1987.

---

[r] It may be that certain fairly mechanical techniques (such as repetition meditation) can help with this task.

Ann. N.Y. Acad. Sci. ISSN 0077-8923

Corrigendum for Ann. N. Y. Acad. Sci. 642: 148–166

Philpott, M.P., G.E. Westgate & T. Kealey. 1991. An *in Vitro* Model for the Study of Human Hair Growth. *Ann. N.Y. Acad. Sci.* **642:** 148–166.
doi: 10.1111/j.1749-6632.1991.tb24386.x

The above article is based on an article published earlier in *Journal of Cell Science* (Philpott, M.P., M.R. Green & T. Kealey. 1990. Human hair growth *in vitro. J. Cell Sci.* **97:** 463–471. PMID: 1705941) and arises from an invited conference presentation on the subject. Apologies are given to the publishers, editors, and readership of *Journal of Cell Science.*

doi: 10.1111/j.1749-6632.2011.06231.x

Ann. N.Y. Acad. Sci. ISSN 0077-8923

Corrigendum for Ann. N. Y. Acad. Sci. 1173 S1: E20–E30

Hinoi, E., *et al.* 2009. An Osteoblast-dependent Mechanism Contributes to the Leptin Regulation of Insulin Secretion. *Ann. N.Y. Acad. Sci.* **1173 S1:** E20–E30.
doi: 10.1111/j.1749-6632.2009.05061.x

The authors have noted that this conference proceedings report did not credit the original source of the majority of the text and figure content to the following publication: Hinoi, E., *et al.* 2008. The sympathetic tone mediates leptin's inhibition of insulin secretion by modulating osteocalcin bioactivity. *J. Cell Biol.* **183:** 1235–1242.
doi:10.1083/jcb.200809113

Apologies are given to the publishers, editors, and readership of *Journal of Cell Biology*.

Ann. N.Y. Acad. Sci. ISSN 0077-8923

Erratum for Ann. N. Y. Acad. Sci. 1229: 99–102

Kim, H. 2011. Inhibitory mechanism of lycopene on cytokine expression in experimental pancreatitis. *Ann. N.Y. Acad. Sci.* **1229:** 99–102.
doi: 10.1111/j.1749-6632.2011.06107.x

In the above article, there are two changes in the reference list.

Reference 34 should read as follows:
Kim, H. 2008. Cerulein pancreatitis: oxidative stress, inflammation, and apoptosis. *Gut Liver* **2:** 74–80.

Reference 52, the old Ref. 34, should be added to read as follows:
Okumura, N., A. Sakakibara & T. Hayakawa. 1982. Pancreatic endocrine function in experimental pancreatolithiasis in dogs. *Am. J. Gastroenterol.* **77:** 392–396.

doi: 10.1111/j.1749-6632.2011.06233.x
Ann. N.Y. Acad. Sci. 1234 (2011) 175 © 2011 New York Academy of Sciences.